THE ANATOMY OF
THE CAR

One hundred years of development from the Benz Tricycle to the 1988 Porsche

THE ANATOMY OF
THE CAR

One hundred years of development from the Benz Tricycle to the 1988 Porsche

JEFF DANIELS

Longmeadow Press

CONTENTS

Designed by Derek Avery
ISBN 0-681-40475-2
Printed in Italy
0 9 8 7 6 5 4 3 2 1

INTRODUCTION

About a hundred years ago – the exact date is a matter of disputed national pride – the first motor cars were built for sale. Earlier pioneers may have built 'one-off' self-propelled vehicles for their own satisfaction but it was not until the 1880s that car designers became more interested in systematic production and car factories, car showrooms, test tracks, motor shows and all that goes with the modern process of designing, making and selling cars started to develop.

Naturally enough, those pioneer cars bore little relation to their modern counterparts. Nobody cared about the finer points of performance, economy, comfort or convenience when it was still a minor miracle that a car went at all. Yet the 19th Century cars were the starting point for all that has happened since and in essence they embodied every aspect of what has come to be known as vehicle engineering. They had engines to provide the power, transmissions to take the power to the wheels, and some kind of suspension to locate the wheels and provide a modicum of comfort. They had steering, brakes, and a body of sorts and that added up to the basic anatomy of the car which has since been developed to an amazing degree.

This book looks at the development of those parts of the changing anatomy of the car. The pattern of development was never even, for example the engine was brought to its present efficiency through a whole series of changes in layout, helped by inventions like the distributor and the discoveries of modern metallurgy and fuel technology, whereas the transmission has been fundamentally changed only once, with the introduction of synchromesh.

Like the pattern, so the pace of development has been far from even although the picture is clearer. The hundred-year history of the motor car can be split into three equal parts, but there were many more worthwhile developments in the middle period than in the pioneer days and many more still in the most recent years. Remember that to go back to 1952 is to retrace a third of motor car history and the cars of 1952 were for the most part extremely crude compared with their 1988 counterparts. In particular, the techniques of mass-production have been improved since then and most of what we know about good suspension design for safe and superior handling and roadholding has been developed in recent years.

That is why this book will pass quite briefly over the pioneer days, and look much more closely at the cars of the last 50 years or so. It is not that veteran cars should not be regarded with interest and reverence; simply that until the 1920s at least, the anatomy of the car did not take shape in any coherent way. The anatomy of the modern car was arrived at by trial and error: engineers tried idea after idea and if the first 50 years taught the motor industry anything, it was how not to do things. As little by little the errors were discarded so what was left grew almost inescapably into the classic car of 1935 to 1970, unitary-bodied, rear-driven through a live axle, crossply tyred . . . but to go into such detail is to jump too far ahead.

The development of the car's anatomy is illustrated by examining certain key cars through the years. For the most part they are well-known makes as the best and most significant cars usually find some way to make their mark. Thus the book looks in more or less detail at each car's engine, transmission, suspension, steering, brakes, body design and other systems starting with the primitive but effective Benz Tricycle and ending up with the high-tech wizardry of the latest Porsche. It also examines all the engineering links which bind the one development to another.

The 1987 Pontiac Fiero was an exciting car, but production ended in the following year.

DEFINING THE ANATOMY

Modern cars are extremely complex, and their anatomy needs to be studied methodically. The initial breakdown is clear enough, all cars have engines, transmissions, steering, brakes, wheels and tyres, a body and other systems. The question is, what are the significant features within each of those main categories?

Engine

Generally, cars have always been powered by the four-stroke internal combustion engine demonstrated by Nikolaus Otto in 1876. There have been other types of power unit over the years, but none has come close to taking over from the Otto-cycle engine. There have been electric vehicles and steam-powered ones and more recently the need to reduce exhaust emissions has renewed interest in alternative power units, but the four-stroke engine continues to reign supreme. Even those engines which look different in principle, like the automotive diesel and the rotary Wankel unit, still use a four-stroke cycle with phases closely related to those of the Otto cycle. At one time the two-stroke engine was quite a popular alternative, but high fuel consumption and terrible exhaust emissions soon stopped the two-stroke's career as a power unit for cars.

The Otto cycle consists of four parts which engineers, with their love of simple language, often refer to as 'suck, squeeze, bang, push'. More accurately, the engine consists of a piston in a cylinder and the complete cycle is run through as the piston moves up and down twice. Starting with the piston at the top of the cylinder, its downward movement sucks in a mixture of air and fuel. Eventually the piston reaches the bottom of its stroke and starts up again, but by this time the valve through which the mixture entered is closed, so the mixture

The basic principles of the four-stroke engine. Induction stroke. The inlet valve is open and the rotation of the crankshaft is moving the piston down the cylinder, sucking in a mixture of fuel and air. Compression stroke. Both valves are shut and the rotating crankshaft is raising the piston, compressing the fuel/air mixture above it, into the combustion area. Power stroke. Both valves are shut, and a spark jumping across the electrodes of the spark plug has fired the mixture. This burns extremely rapidly, expanding just as the piston begins its downward movement. Its energy rams the piston to the bottom of the cylinder, driving the crankshaft round half a turn. Exhaust stroke. Spent gases leave the combustion chamber through the open exhaust valve, helped by the pressure created by the rising piston. When this reaches the top of the cylinder at the end of this stroke, the exhaust valve will close, the inlet valve will open and the cycle will begin again with another induction stroke.

itself becomes compressed. As the piston again reaches the top, compressing the mixture to its maximum, a spark is fired causing it to burn very quickly and expand. In its expansion, it pushes the piston down again and the work it does is taken out through the crankshaft to drive the vehicle. It then only remains for the piston to move up once more, this time with the exhaust valve of the cylinder open in order to drive out the burned and useless exhaust gases and end up where it started.

That is the basic Otto cycle and it raises a number of engineering questions which everybody, even the most pioneering of designers like Benz and Daimler, had to answer. It is those answers which are the flesh on the bones of an engineering anatomy where the engine itself is concerned.

In the first place, there has to be a cylinder and a piston, and some means of connecting the piston with the crankshaft which takes the power out of the engine and also controls the piston's movement. This basic layout has never changed and was not new even when Otto first built the engine, since steam engines had already been around for over 100 years and had brought such essential mechanical details to high efficiency. However, the car-driving Otto engine was improved as many further advances were made in the design of piston, cylinder and crankshaft.

One of the most interesting things about the early development of engines is the way multi-cylinder arrangements were built up. In the first place, most four-stroke engines have more than one cylinder for the obvious reason that with only one power stroke for every two revolutions of the crankshaft, a single-cylinder engine tends to bounce up and down on its mountings. Even two cylinders are much better, but four have become the modern norm and several cars used had engines with up to 16 cylinders.

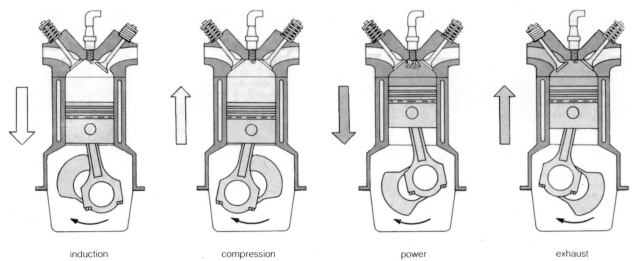

induction   compression   power   exhaust

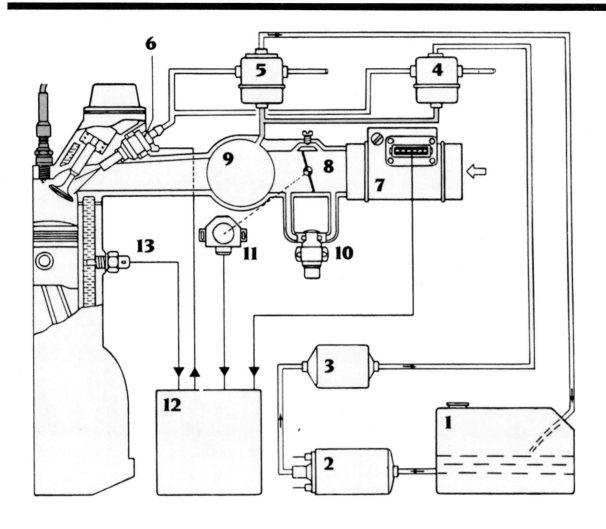

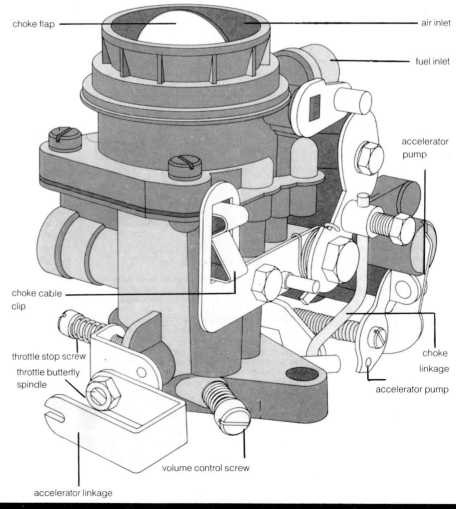

Below: a fixed-jet carburetter. This has a fixed venturi in the barrel which allows the correct fuel/air mixture to be supplied under all engine-load conditions.

Above: a fuel injection system shown in diagrammatic form.
1. Fuel tank
2. Fuel pump
3. Fuel filter
4. Pressure dampener
5. Pressure regulator
6. Injection valve(s)
7. LH air sensor
8. Throttle valve housing
9. Intake air distributor
10. Auxiliary air valve
11. Throttle valve switch
12. LH control unit
13. Temperature sensor

choke flap

air inlet

fuel inlet

accelerator pump

choke cable clip

throttle stop screw

throttle butterfly spindle

choke linkage

accelerator pump

volume control screw

accelerator linkage

Next on the inspection list comes the operation of the valves. Even the most basic specification had to include the presence of an inlet valve to admit the fuel/air mixture and an exhaust valve to release the burned exhaust gases. The actual shape of the valves and their manner of operation is a fascinating study in itself, bearing in mind the fact that valve operation takes place at half the engine speed because each valve opens just once for every two revolutions of the crankshaft. What is surprising perhaps is that the mushroom-shaped poppet valve used by the pioneer car designers has survived all the changes and shrugged off all the challenges.

The next most basic aspect of engine design is the way in which the air/fuel mixture is prepared. If an engine is to operate at all efficiently, it must be provided with enough air to burn all the fuel, yet not so much that it 'puts the fire out'. A weak mixture with too much air for the amount of fuel delivered is wasteful because the engine must pump all its air from the inlet through to exhaust and the energy used for pumping is 'subtracted' from what is available to drive the crankshaft. The development first of the carburetter, and much later of fuel injection, is another fascinating area of study.

Next there is the tricky matter of setting light to the highly inflammable mixture in the cylinder. For maximum engine efficiency a spark must be applied in exactly the right place at exactly the right time and it took many years of patient development to come close to that ideal. Looking at the ignition arrangements adopted by the pioneers, one is inclined to wonder how it was that their engines ever worked at all and certainly one appreciates why they were so inefficient by any modern measure.

Finally, there were also important developments to those functions which are a little less fundamental but which remain essential to the efficient working of the modern engine. There must, for example, be some means of keeping the cylinder head and the top of the cylinder cool while just inside a fire burns at a temperature sufficient to melt metal. There must be some way of delivering the fuel from the tank to the carburettor. There must certainly be a system for ensuring the engine is properly lubricated to stop its moving parts from rubbing one against the other. Modern cars would be unthinkable without some means of starting the engine at the twist of a key. In short, simply within the engine, there are dozens of details each of which has occupied design engineers since the earliest days of the motor car. Nor has development come to a stop, since today's designers are still hard at work trying to apply the calculating power and speed of electronic response to wring still further efficiency out of what has already become a power unit that would astonish the pioneers of 100 years ago.

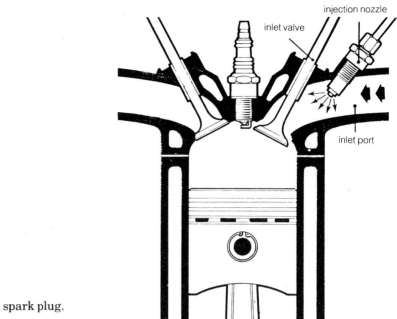

injection nozzle

inlet valve

inlet port

Below: a spark plug.

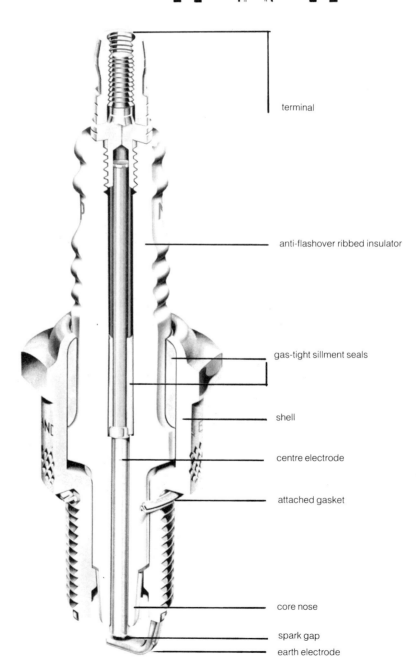

terminal

anti-flashover ribbed insulator

gas-tight sillment seals

shell

centre electrode

attached gasket

core nose

spark gap

earth electrode

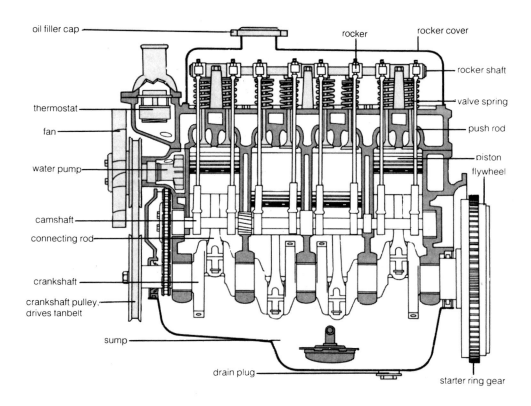

oil filler cap
rocker
rocker cover
rocker shaft
valve spring
thermostat
fan
push rod
piston
water pump
flywheel
camshaft
connecting rod
crankshaft
crankshaft pulley, drives fanbelt
sump
drain plug
starter ring gear

Above: section of a four-cylinder engine.

Left: the 2.9 litre engine of the 1988 Jaguar XJ6.

The lubrication system of a modern four-cylinder engine (the Citroen BX power unit).
1. Oil filter
2. Oil sump
3. Suction filter
4. Oil pump
5. Filter cartridge
6. Oil pressure switch
7. Gallery supplying crankshaft bearings
8. Supply for camshaft

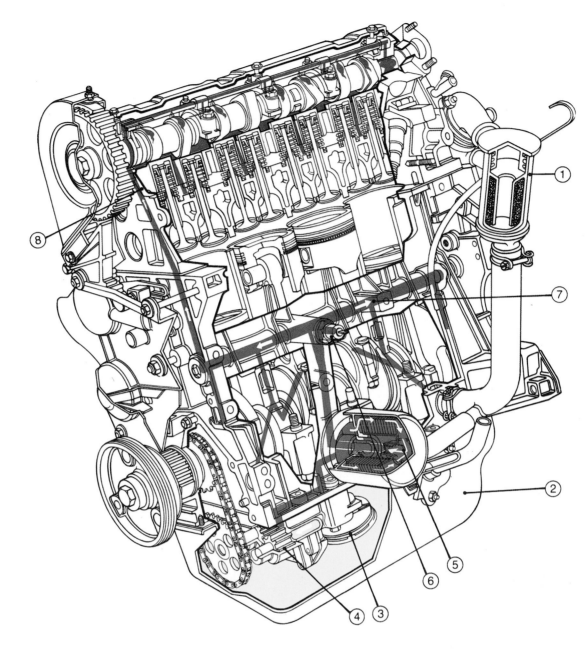

Right: the cooling system of a typical four-cylinder engine, showing the passenger compartment heater feed.

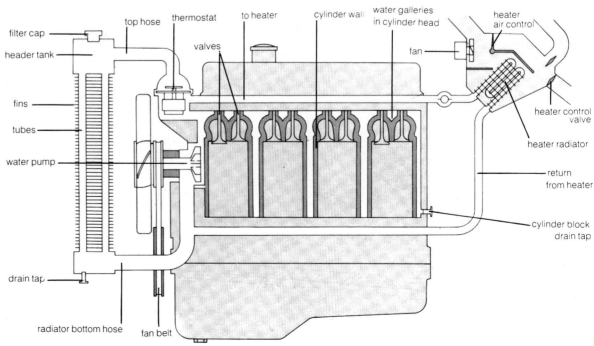

Transmission

The transmission is a little-appreciated aspect of car engineering. It has three essential tasks. The first is to carry the power from the engine to the driven wheels; the second is to provide the driver with some way of controlling the drive; the third is to overcome the unavoidable short-coming of the Otto cycle engine, that it delivers its pulling power over a very narrow range of speed. Interestingly, the practical form of the transmission had been settled more or less by the turn of the last century and since then developments have concentrated on these areas: attempts to find something altogether better and detail improvements to make transmissions easier to control.

Normally, the power taken from the engine crankshaft is first applied to a clutch, the means by which the driver may disconnect the engine from the driven wheels. It then passes to a gearbox, which makes it possible for the engine to run at a suitable speed whatever the speed of the car. Finally, the power passes along suitable shafts, or other forms of linkage, until it reaches the point at which it is delivered to the wheels. At this point, all modern transmissions use some form of differential gearing which enables the power to reach two, if not all four wheels, without affecting the car's ability to turn corners. A 'solid' axle driven at its centre tries to run in a straight line: it is the function of the differential gear to allow the inside wheel in a corner to run slower than the outside one while still taking power from the transmission.

The earliest car pioneers were little concerned with the niceties of control and were generally extremely happy if they could deliver power reliably to the wheels, though in this ambition they were certainly helped by the fact that steam-engine engineers had solved many of the problems of gear design. On the other hand steam engines are much better than Otto-cycle engines at delivery pulling power (torque) at very low speeds and so the steam-engineers had never given any thought to multi-speed gear-boxes. Here the car pioneers found themselves almost on their own and they adopted some very strange solutions. Even after the modern form of manual gearbox had been invented by Panhard, it remained tricky to operate for another thirty years, until synchromesh was invented.

Even Panhard, the man who first applied the layshaft gearbox to the motor car, admitted that it was 'brutal, even though it worked'. For nearly a century engineers have been looking for something better, but the only alternative to be accepted thus far has been the automatic transmission with its torque-converter fluid drive (taking the place of the clutch) and the epicyclic gearbox (taking the place of the layshaft gearbox). We shall be looking at the rise of the automatic alongside the eradication of the manual clutch and gearbox and the rest of the transmission.

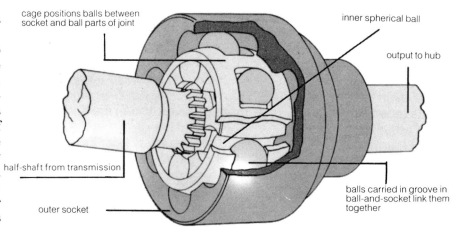

cage positions balls between socket and ball parts of joint

inner spherical ball

output to hub

half-shaft from transmission

balls carried in groove in ball-and-socket link them together

outer socket

Above: the Birfield constant velocity joint, which transmits power through steel balls linking a ball-and-socket joint

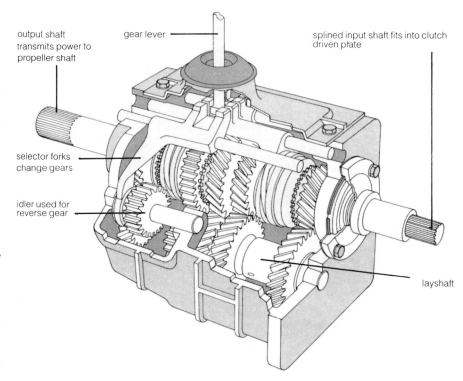

output shaft transmits power to propeller shaft

gear lever

splined input shaft fits into clutch driven plate

selector forks change gears

idler used for reverse gear

layshaft

Above: the gear selector mechanism comprises a series of rods and forks connected to the gear lever. An interlocking arrangement means that only one collar can be engaged at a time.

Suspension

For a long time, the suspension was the Cinderella of motor car engineering. It was appreciated that some kind of springing was essential if the car's occupants were to be protected from the shocks caused by uneven road surfaces, though if the pioneer designers had enjoyed access to modern tyres, they might have tried to do away with springs altogether! For many years it was hardly appreciated how the suspension influenced not only ride comfort, but also a car's stability and the way it went round corners. Those early cars which handled well did so mainly by accident, or because of the designer's intuitive feeling for what was right, rather than through the application of real knowledge or principle.

The development of suspension lagged many years behind that of the engine or transmission and when good suspension systems were finally developed, they in turn placed new demands on the transmission. It took designers some time to realise that the traditional semi-elliptic 'cart' spring could be replaced by something much better, and to appreciate the merits of independent front and rear suspension. In many ways it is a story which is still being written, but the suspension of each of the cars examined in this book is carefully looked at.

Wheels and tyres

Any discussion of the suspension naturally includes a look at wheels. The motor car wheel of today bears little relation to its forebear of a hundred years ago except that it is still round. Otherwise it tends to be smaller, wider, and certainly made of different materials; and the steady progress of these changes is of great significance.

Likewise, tyres have changed out of all recognition although here it is possible to identify three distinct leaps in technology. First came the pneumatic tyre itself, replacing the solid tyres of the earliest cars. Then, in the 1929s, there came the low-pressure 'balloon' tyre which improved both comfort and roadholding. Finally there was the radial-ply revolution wrought by Michelin in the 1950s, bringing with it not only new standards of road behaviour, but also much longer life for the tyre.

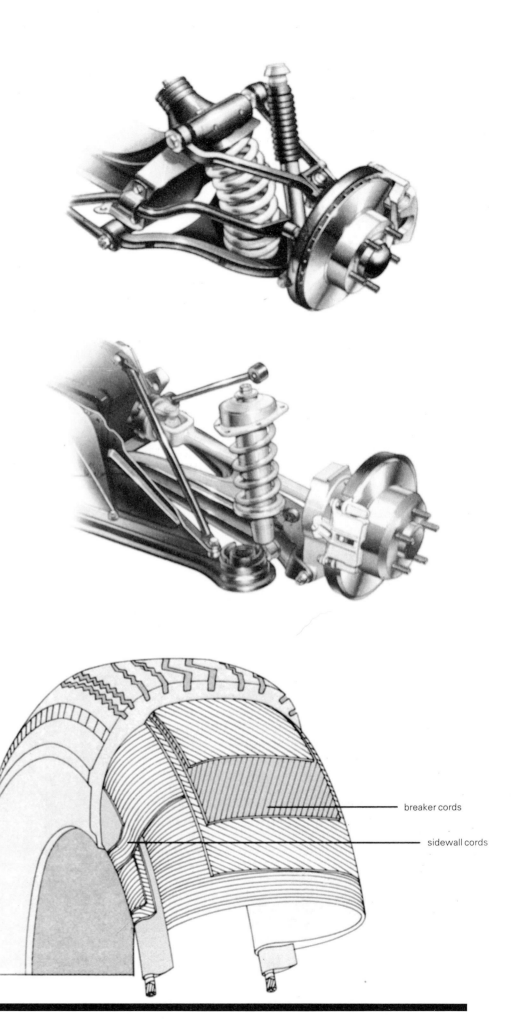

Top: a typical front suspension layout.

Centre: rear suspension.

Right: in a radial tyre the sidewalls are reinforced by cords at right angles to the wheel, and there are additional layers of breaker cords beneath the tread sidewall cords at a right angle to tyre crown

breaker cords

sidewall cords

Right: a ventilated disc brake.

Brakes

Even more than most aspects of design, the brakes of the earliest cars were crude in the extreme. That was natural enough; when the main concern is to make something that goes at all, one is not over-concerned about stopping it. Also, there was very little in the way of technology to inherit from the ancient carriage trade because carriages never went fast enough to need highly effective brakes. Nor did the metal-to-metal brakes of railway engines have much to offer the early car designer.

The story of brake development is, therefore, one which starts right from the beginning – unlike that of some other parts of the car's anatomy. It is a story of steady progress for the most part, from the transmission brakes of the early days, through drum brakes of increasing effectiveness first on the rear wheels and then on all four, to the latter-day features of disc brakes, vacuum serve assistance and asbestos-free lining material.

Right: braking system.
1. Rear suspension sphere
2. Front caliper
3. Rear caliper
4. Brake side valves
5. High pressure from pressure regulator
6. Pistons
7. Disc
8. Return circuit to reservoir

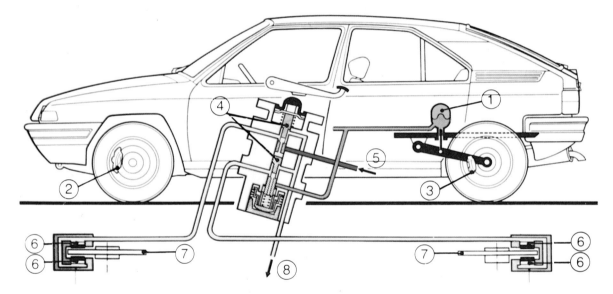

Opposite above: left front suspension of a modern automobile.
1. Needle-roller bearing
2. Suspension turret
3. Elastic couplings
4. Bump stop
5. Coil spring
6. Rebound stop
7. Spring tray
8. Damper body
9. Pivot
10. Suspension arm

Opposite lower: body construction of a 'conventional' front-engine, rear-wheel drive car.

Steering

Like the suspension with which it is so closely bound, steering was too little appreciated by the early car designers. To begin with that was understandable because the performance of the first cars was hardly enough to pose serious problems. Later on it was a different matter and the most powerful cars of the 1920s were often highly dangerous unless driven with both skill and restraint. Consequently, the industry had to study the way in which the link was made from the steering column to the front wheels and how the wheels themselves were constrained to move in ways which did not cause control problems. Later on, there came the power-assisted steering systems which are now commonplace on cars with engines of more than about 2-litre capacity.

The four-wheel steering systems introduced by Honda and Mazda in the second half of the 1980s certainly made for easier parking, but the claims of broader advantages were not confirmed by many experienced test drivers.

Car bodies

The body is a vast area of study, calling for a book in itself if it is to be treated in real depth. However, working through the lists of cars it is worth looking at the way in which the early bodies, little more than devices to give passengers somewhere to sit clear of the machinery, evolved into fully enclosed shapes with a high degree of structural efficiency.

The early designers borrowed techniques directly and extensively from the horse-drawn carriage trade. But the real breakthrough in body construction came with the elimination of the separate chassis and the adoption of the 'unitary' design in which the body shell itself bore the stresses set up through the transmission, the engine mounts and the suspension. This enabled cars to be made at once both lighter and more aerodynamically efficient. Conversely, the overall shape of the vehicle can change regardless of the method of body construction employed and examples of this are also included together with a look at the

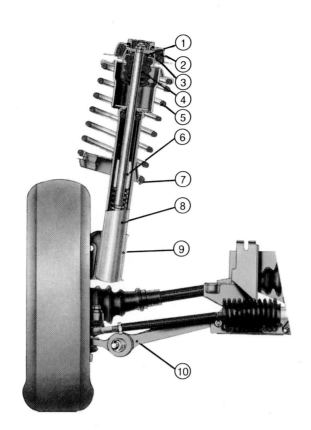

evolution of the sports car and at the origins of the present-day mode for hatchbacks. The first stirrings of what may yet become a major struggle between sheet steel, the traditional material for the manufacture of unitary-construction car bodies, and synthetic plastic materials is also described.

Car systems

One aspect of car design to which the pioneers paid no attention whatsoever was that of auxiliary systems. The reason already begins to look familiar. Why on earth bother with such frills as instruments for the driver, lights for driving in the dark, wipers for keeping the windscreen clean or a heater for the sake of comfort, when the principal concern is to persuade your machine to go at all?

A valiant rearguard action was fought against cars having proper self-contained electrical systems with generator and battery, but even the critics of electricity admitted the need for lamps. On the other hand, it is only in the last 30 years or so that cars have had heaters as a matter of course.

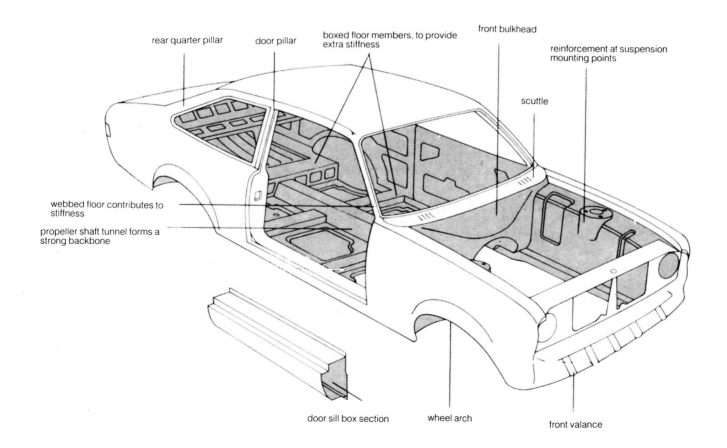

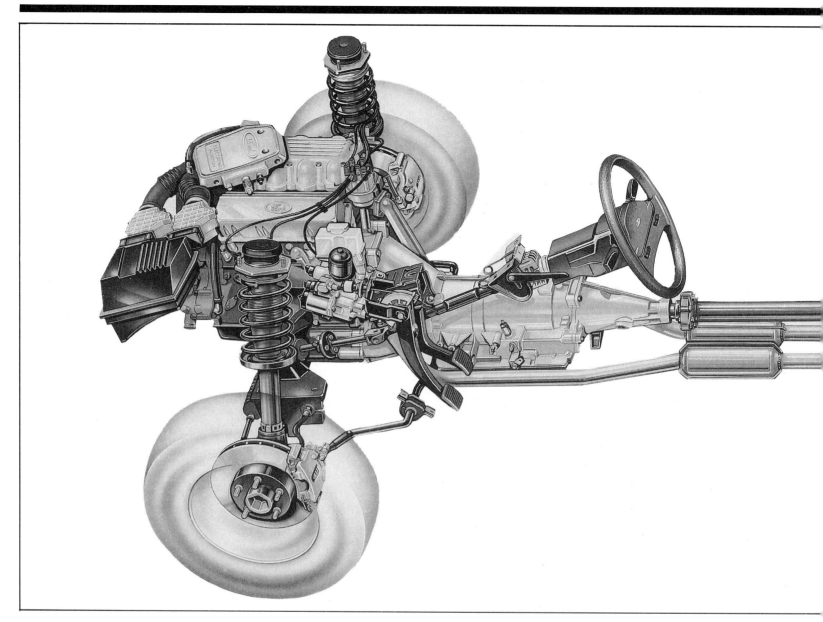

Above: the 2.8 drive line of a modern automobile. As in all cars, its main purpose is to carry the power from the engine to the driven wheels in a controllable manner.

Left and right: Components of the drive line.

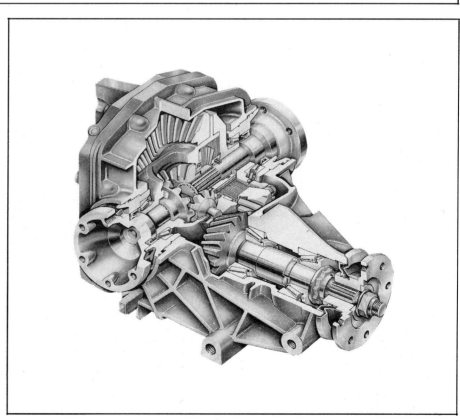

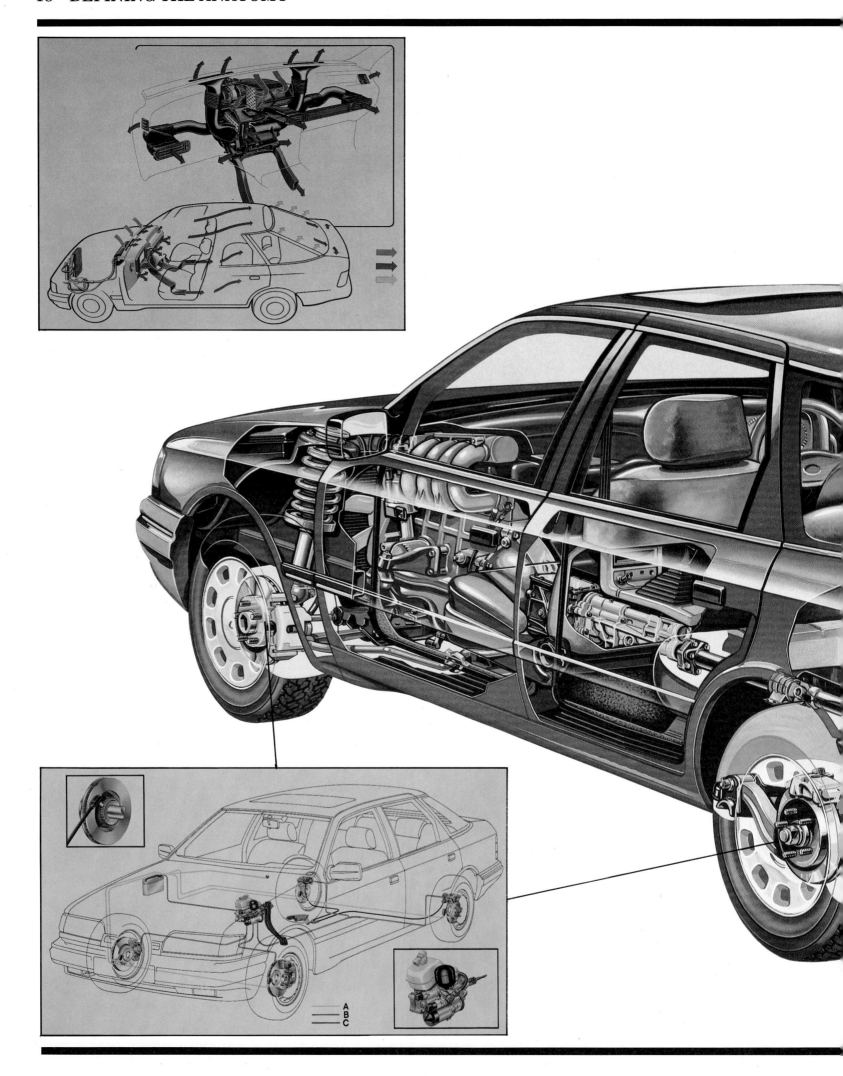

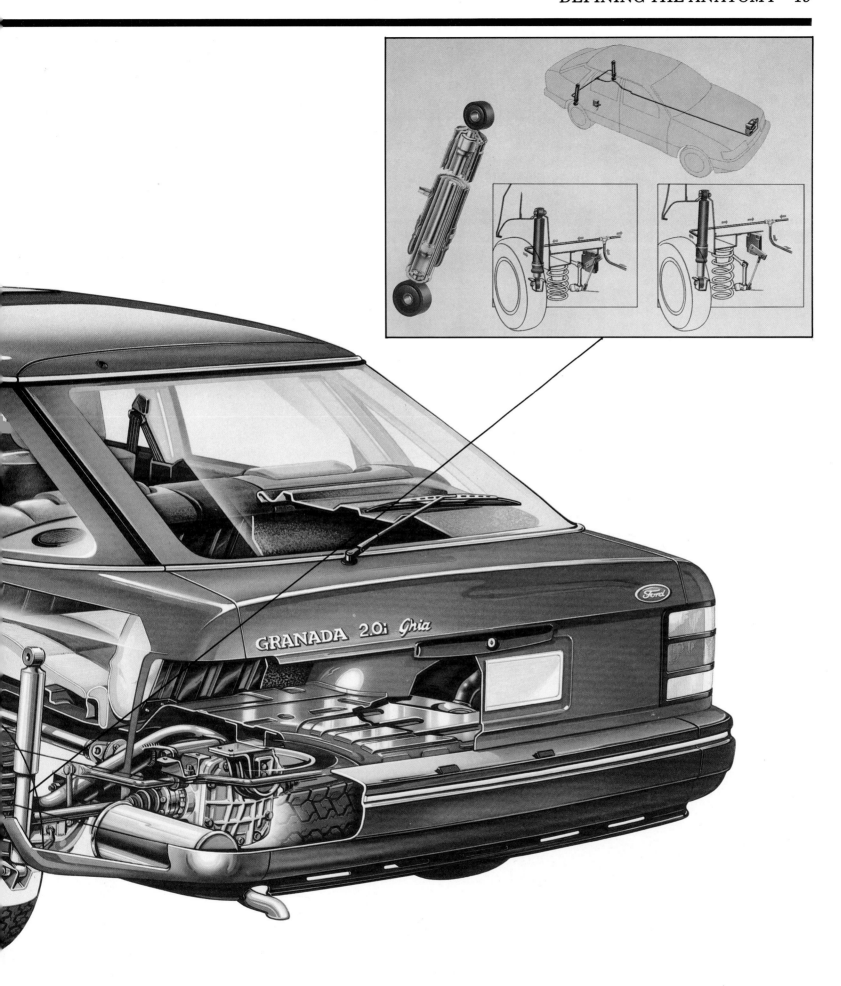

1885 BENZ TRICYCLE

Whether or not one regards Karl Benz as the first man to build a practical motor car, he was without doubt the first man to sell cars on an organised basis. Starting in 1885 with his flimsy-looking tricycle, examples of which still exist both in the Daimler-Benz museum in Stüttgart and in the London Science Museum, he built up sales even to the extent of having a French concessionaire in Paris. Benz's great rival in the years before 1900 was Daimler, but it seems that he was more of an engines man, while Benz took an interest in the entire vehicle. Eventually of course the two names fused into the great Daimler-Benz organisation which today produces Mercedes cars and trucks.

It is rather a pity, considering Benz' approach to vehicle design as a whole, that by the early 1900s most of his ideas had been discarded and that the mainstream of design had gone off in another direction. Even so, he was the first; and his first car deserves careful consideration to see what kind of solutions the pioneer designers adopted.

Benz' engine was a single-cylinder four-stroke mounted so that the centre-line of the cylinder was parallel with the centre-line of the car as a whole. The crankshaft was at the rear and installed vertically so that the flywheel (which needed to be massive if the single cylinder was to run at all smoothly) rotated horizontally beneath the engine. It is interesting to note that even in the 1880s, the pioneer engineers mostly felt the four-stroke engine was a better bet; Benz was an engine manufacturer before he turned to cars and had spent some time working on two-strokes in the belief that Otto's patents had an ironclad grasp on the four-stroke principle.

The first real problem faced by Benz was that Otto had run his demonstration engine on gas, thus avoiding the need for anything so complicated as a carburettor. Benz realised that to be a practical proposition his car would have to run on liquid fuel and he chose a mixture of petrol and naptha. In order to obtain his fuel/air mixture, he resorted to a 'surface carburettor' in which the incoming air flowed over a porous surface kept constantly wet with fuel. The resulting mixture would have been very weak indeed had the speed and power output of the engine not been extremely limited. As in most of the pioneer engines, the stroke of the crankshaft was much greater than the bore of the cylinder but in modern terms the capacity of the engine was 1.6 litres. Despite this, the power output was less than 1 horsepower, not least because the engine's maximum speed was only 250rpm. Yet the Benz engine had its advanced features, for example its use of mechanically-operated inlet and exhaust valves. The inlet was a slide-valve, no doubt borrowed from steam engine practice, while the exhaust valve was of the poppet type with which we have become so familiar. The Benz engine was also advanced in using electric ignition, using a battery to supply a trembler coil which in turn fired a spark gap in the combustion chamber more or less at the right time. The engine was water-cooled, with a simple jacket round the cylinder head and a crude but seemingly effective tubed radiator.

Benz used an ingenious transmission which overcame several problems though at the expense of introducing others. He was of course faced with the need to provide a clutch, and to allow for the movement of his car's driven axle relative to the engine. He did this by driving a cross-shaft from bevel gears at the upper end of the engine crankshaft. In turn, a pulley on this shaft drove a leather belt which ran forward and could be shifted on to either of a pair of pulleys on a second shaft. One pulley was free to rotate on the shaft and thus provide a neutral gear; the other drove the shaft through a differential gear. Another example of Benz' advanced thinking. Sprockets at each end of this shaft drove the rear wheels via chains. Shifting the primary drive belt from one pulley to the other acted as the clutch while the flexibility of the chains maintained the drive even if the rear axle changed position.

The Benz suspension was as primitive as one might have expected. The rear axle was mounted on two double-elliptic springs. In other words, two of the more latterly familiar semi-elliptic 'cart' springs with one inverted above the other. They not only sprung the axle; they were its only form of location, but fortunately the Benz proceeded at snail-pace. As for the single front wheel, that was provided with no springing at all beyond that provided by the flexing of the frame. It is interesting to note, however, that the two seats were spring-mounted, in line with the best coach-building practice of the day.

Another primitive device avoided by Benz was the platinum-tube igniter. This consisted quite simply of a tube of the precious metal which penetrated the wall of the combustion chamber and was heated by an external petrol burner. Thus there was always a red-hot point within the chamber, and whenever the fuel/air mixture was sufficiently compressed against it, burning took place. It had the virtue of simplicity, but as a means of ensuring that combustion happened at the best possible moment it left a great deal to be desired.

The Benz tricycle layout was widely echoed by other early cars, the reason for its adoption always being the same: that it avoided the apparently fearsome problem of developing a

proper steering mechanism. Yet it was also obvious that the tricycle could not seat several people in comfort and stability. Benz himself designed later tricycles with more elaborate frames and with a single rearward-facing seat perched over the front wheel, but before long he too had accepted the need for a proper front axle leaving room for a front seat perched high between the wheels. As speeds slowly increased, with the adoption of slightly more efficient two-cylinder engines, the extra stability of the four-wheel layout soon became obvious.

One thing Benz never abandoned was his transmission layout and his original engine installation at the rear. This was elegantly boxed-in and although less obvious in his later designs, it always occupied the same place. His company became one of the most successful early car manufacturers and actually delivered its 2,000th vehicle before the 19th century was out. But the drawbacks of leather drive belts which wore when they were dry and slipped when they were wet, plus the difficulty of providing more than two speeds, and the high

build and limited space which resulted from the rear engine installation meant that the Benz became less and less popular. In the very early 1900s, the company saw a disastrous fall in sales as other, more technically advanced cars mounted their challenge. In a sense, Benz also provided an early warning of the dangers to come for all companies which pin too much faith in a single idea and fail to move with the times. It was a fate which nearly befell both Ford and Volkswagen amongst others.

It was the transmission more than anything else which ultimately cost Benz his sales. Elsewhere, there were others working away at producing a more effective layout of both trans-mission and chassis and for a time, the centre of motor car development moved from Germany to France. In the mid-1890s a vehicle which set a general pattern, faithfully followed by the majority of the world's cars for the next seventy years, was being developed in Paris.

The first Benz used delicately spoked wheels which clearly owed a debt to the bicycle industry, though later Benz models turned to

Benz Tricyle
Country of origin: West Germany
Date: 1885
Engine: one-cylinder; four-stroke; 'surface carburettor'; water cooled
Gears: rear driven via pulley and chain system
Capacity: 577cc
Maximum Speed: 10mph (16km/h)
Chassis: rear axle mounted on two double-elliptic springs
Tyres: wood-spoked wheels
Steering: originally tiller to front driving wheel
Brakes: block system

wood-spoked wheels in order to carry their greater weight. By any modern standard the rear wheels are huge and must have contributed something to ride comfort with their ability to smooth over potholes rather than dropping into them. That was just as well, since the tyres were of necessity solid – a few more years were to elapse before Dunlop began making the first pneumatic ones.

Finally, Benz eased his way round the worst of the steering problems by making his first car a tricycle with a single front wheel. This enabled him to ignore the complication of devising a linkage to steer both front wheels individually, and to avoid the evils of steering by rotating the whole front axle about its centre-line as was done in most horse-drawn vehicles. Instead, Benz was able to provide his driver with a simple tiller directly linked to the shaft of the front wheel. For braking, Benz elected to use a block which pressed against one of the pulley wheels of his car's transmission. This was a much simpler method than extending any kind of braking system to the wheels themselves and was amply effective at the speeds of which the car was capable.

That simply leaves the question of the Benz body itself. There was not a lot of it, just a bench seat and toeboard bolted to convenient points on a tubular steel chassis which also served to hold together the various mechanical components. The chassis was an extremely simple U-shape closed half-way along its length by a single cross member which formed the mounting point for the head end of the single cylinder. There was no more to it than that; but from such simple beginnings there grew the motor car as we know it today.

When looking at the Benz, it is worth bearing in mind the standards set by some of its rival designs. There were plenty of engines in the closing years of the last century with inlet valves which were not mechanically operated but simply spring-loaded. Air was drawn past them by the suction of the piston moving downwards: an almost perfect recipe for restricting engine power output. There was of course no way in which the exhaust valve could be made automatic in a standardized way, so each and every engineer had to invent his own way of opening it mechanically; almost everyone chose to do it by driving a camshaft from the crankshaft at half-speed and thus it has continued.

1895 PANHARD-LEVASSOR

Here indeed was a car which contrasted vividly with the Benz pattern and which ultimately proved to have much greater potential for development. Panhard and Levassor ran an engineering works in Paris and when they came to design a car they drew on the engineering they knew best – that of industrial machinery. Among other things, this gave them two powerful weapons, the cone friction clutch and the sliding-gear speed change mechanism used in such machines as thread-cutting lathes. The cone shape of the clutch meant it could join the engine to the transmission without needing enormous springs to impose a clamping load, while the use of spur gears on two shafts meant that different gear ratios could be achieved by sliding one set of gears into and out of contact with the fixed gears on the other shaft.

Panhard-Levassor's first attempt at car design was a strange-looking back-to-back prototype in which the passengers sat over the mid-mounted engine, but this was not successful. It was then that the partners redesigned their layout and placed the engine at the front under a bonnet, driving aft through their cone clutch to their spur-gear box. In the earliest cars the gears operated in the open air which must have made any mangled shifts of ratio even more embarrassing. However, by 1895 they were enclosed quite literally in a box.

At a stroke, the Panhard-Levassor transformed the motoring scene even though it may not have been immediately apparent. The early appeal of the rear-engined layout, with the weight of the engine over the rear wheels for good traction and the driven wheels conveniently close, was one which continued to win engineering adherents until very recently. However, the Panhard-Levassor made its point: with the engine at the front the weight was spread more evenly on all four wheels, improving the stability of the car at higher speeds. Levassor set out to prove this with winning performances in some of the first classic road races. A front-mounted engine also means that the transmission can be spread out in a way which makes it easy to install the in-line clutch and gearbox. Also, at least potentially, passengers can be seated at a lower level and in a better protected body because there is no need to leave clearance above the rear-mounted engine.

The car's engine was typical of the period, an in-line twin and therefore far better balanced than any single-cylinder unit could be. It was of modest size by any standards, with a cylinder bore of 80mm and crankshaft stroke of 120mm giving a swept volume of just 1206cc. Power output was reckoned to be 4bhp, sufficient to show the advance inefficiency already achieved

by comparison with the pioneer Benz engine, and enough to confer a claimed maximum speed of nearly 20mph (32km/h). Already, horse-power was available in multiples rather than fractions but that did not mean that the Panhard-Levassor represented an advance upon the Benz in every respect. For example, the engine depended on automatic inlet valves and hot-tube ignition but it did use a primitive form of jet carburettor, the fuel being sucked through a delivery tube by the reduced pressure of the air rushing past into the engine inlet.

Undoubtedly, the transmission was the real strong point of the Panhard-Levassor. A double-cone clutch was needed to pass even the modest torque of the engine through the primitive lining materials of the day but at least it provided a positive coupling and decoupling of the engine to the gearbox. The gearbox itself was of the sliding-pinion type already described and different versions were available offering either three or four forward speeds. Further aft the car retained the old-style chain drive to the rear wheels from pinions on a cross-shaft. Three years later Renault would invent the modern propellor shaft with universal joints to accommodate plunge and a sliding spline to allow for small changes in length caused by the movement of the final drive on the rear springs.

Another key feature of the Panhard-Levassor

was made possible by its 'in-line' layout. Its chassis consisted essentially of two parallel rails, joined by cross-members, with the engine and most of the transmission carried between them. The rails not only provided convenient mounting points for the springs – still of the multi-leaf variety, naturally – but also a solid footing for two pairs of seats with the beginnings of a body around them. If nothing else, that front engine formed some kind of barrier against the elements when the car was moving.

This, therefore, was a highly significant car despite its wood-spoked wheels, the tiller steering and terrible front axle arrangement which, it is thought, was mainly responsible for the 1896 race crash in which Levassor was very badly injured. The vehicle had solid tyres and Levassor, after seeing Michelin spend almost four days repairing punctures in one pioneer road race, was of the strong opinion that pneumatic tyres would never be any use for cars. The outward shape may be antique, but the Panhard-Levassor was truly the shape of cars to come.

Nor did the company rest on its laurels as Benz tended to. By 1896 it was offering cars with some of the first in-line four-cylinder engines, and the first steering-wheels as distinct from tillers. As Panhard, the company remained well-known until after the Second World War, when it was absorbed by Citroën.

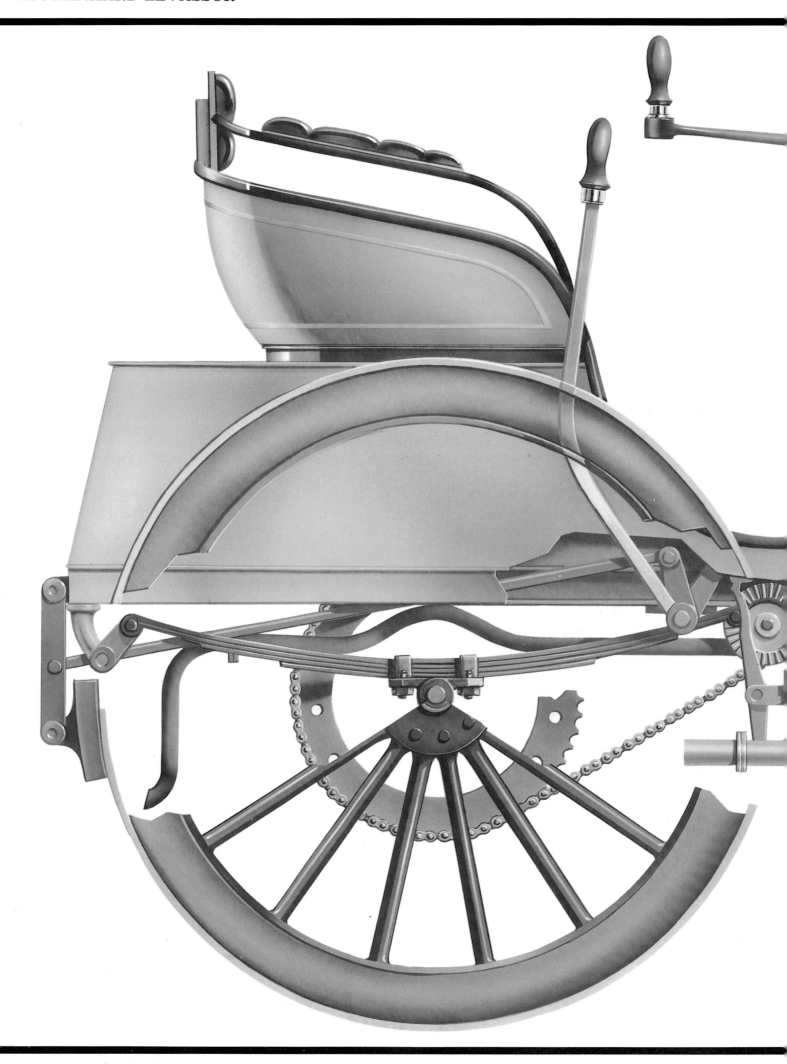

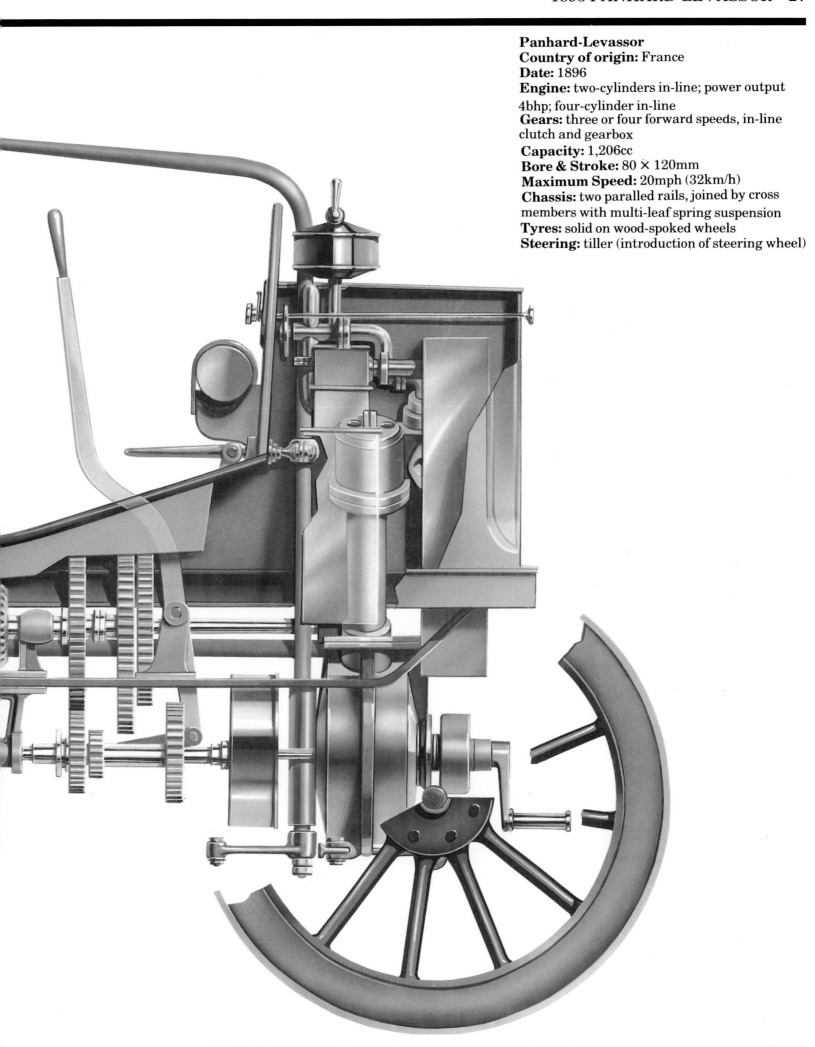

Panhard-Levassor
Country of origin: France
Date: 1896
Engine: two-cylinders in-line; power output
4bhp; four-cylinder in-line
Gears: three or four forward speeds, in-line
clutch and gearbox
Capacity: 1,206cc
Bore & Stroke: 80 × 120mm
Maximum Speed: 20mph (32km/h)
Chassis: two paralled rails, joined by cross
members with multi-leaf spring suspension
Tyres: solid on wood-spoked wheels
Steering: tiller (introduction of steering wheel)

1907 Rolls-Royce Silver Ghost

The Ghost is not, as some people still think, the original Rolls-Royce but it is the first significant one. Less than ten years after the Panhard-Levassor had set the pattern of overall car layout the Silver Ghost was produced and remained on the market almost until the 1960s. In some ways its appearance was deceptive as the Silver Ghost was not fundamentally different from the French car of the earlier decade. It looks more familiar mainly because it is longer overall and in its bonnet, and that in turn makes it look lower. But it retains the chassis built up on two great lengthwise beams and its transmission is of the Panhard type as refined by Renault: the cone clutch, the four-speed sliding-pinion gearbox, the propellor shaft to the rear differential.

The Silver Ghost had a six-cylinder engine, like several of its counterparts including its great rival, Napier, who introduced the first of all. The great virtue of the in-line six-cylinder engine, it was quickly realised, was that it offered near-perfect balance: the forces caused by all the firing strokes and the motion of the pistons cancelled each other out in a way that was not possible even with a four-cylinder engine. Such smoothness came very close to perfection in an engine put together with the skill and care brought to it by Rolls-Royce.

Equally, there were problems associated with the in-line 'six'. The foundrymen of the time had difficulties in producing so long a block, complete with all necessary cooling and lubrication passages. Engineers therefore built up their power units with single cylinders, or pairs of them at most. Rolls-Royce solved the problem by making their six-cylinder as two blocks of three, which was considered daring. Unusually, by the standards of the time, the engine bore and stroke were the same, making it 'square' to give a capacity of just over 7-litres. Running with a compression ratio of 3.2-to-1, the Rolls-Royce produced 48bhp when running

at 1,200rpm. That may not sound much (any respectable 1980s engine produces over 50bhp per litre of capacity) but the Silver Ghost's torque figure would look much more impressive and was developed at such a low speed as to endow the car with colossal 'flexibility' – the ability to run and pull smoothly at low speed in high gear. The Silver Ghost exploited its ability in one famous 1907 run in which it was taken from the south coast of England all the way to Scotland in top gear only.

The Rolls-Royce engine combined features which even today we would consider quite advanced with others that are undeniably primitive. Its mounting showed better understanding of engineering principles than was seen in most rivals since the front mountings were flexible. Most other cars bolted their engines solidly to the chassis with the result that then the chassis flexed, it placed extra stress on the cylinder block with sometimes disastrous results. Rolls-Royce made their own elegant progressive twin-jet carburettor which worked extremely well. The crankshaft was a magnificent design, pressure-lubricated and running in seven main bearings (one at each end and one between each pair of cylinders, in line with 1980s practice). At the other extreme, the cylinder head was not detachable – the gaskets of the time were not good enough to promise reliability despite the low compression ratios they had to withstand – and the engine used side-valves operated by a low-set camshaft. There were two sparking plugs per cylinder, one fired by magneto and the other by trembler coil: belt and braces, in fact.

In other design areas there was little that was new about the Silver Ghost. Its axles were suspended on multi-leaf springs, though the rear axle arrangement is unusual in using three such springs, the third one mounted across the car with the aft ends of the other two attached to it. The idea may have been to seek some extra softness, but the scheme was soon dropped from the later production Rolls-Royces. Where the steering was concerned, swivelling front axles and tillers had already departed the scene and the Silver Ghost had a steering wheel and worm gearbox to link with the front wheels. There were drum brakes for the rear wheels only; ultra-conservative Rolls-Royce held out against front wheel brakes longer than most car manu-facturers. The wheels themselves were wood-spoked but wore pneumatic tyres, already well established despite Levassor's earlier condemnation!

Perhaps the most noticeable feature of the Silver Ghost by comparison with earlier cars is that it provided the driver with information. There was no such thing as an instrument

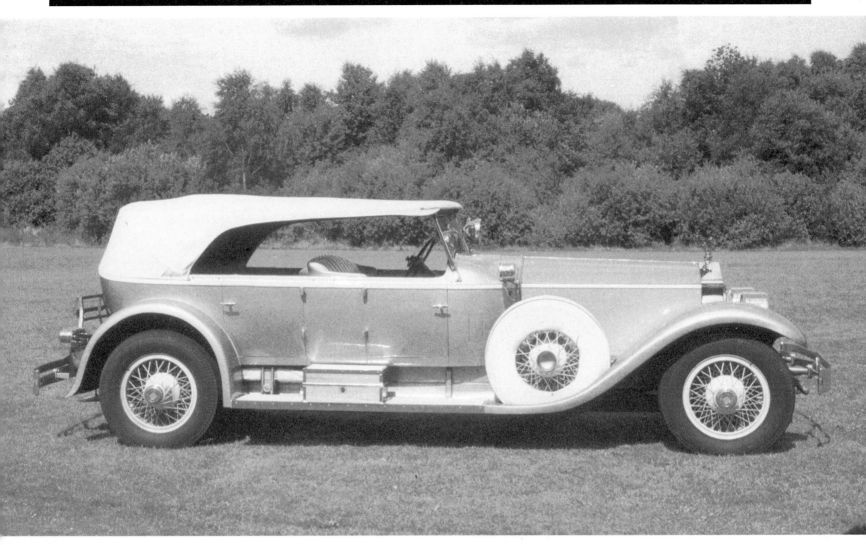

panel, but scattered around the bulkhead one finds a speedometer (already compulsory in many motoring countries by 1907), an oil pressure gauge and a fuel pressure gauge. This last instrument was a necessity because early fuel systems had no fuel pump but pressurised the airspace above the fuel in the tank. When the pressure as shown on the gauge fell, the driver was expected to pump the tank up again. Quite apart from the provision of information, the Silver Ghost also underlines the degree of mechanical understanding, not to say dexterity, demanded of the Edwardian driver. There were for example controls for adjusting the ignition timing and the richness of the carburettor mixture while on the move, both controls being slides on quadrants within the steering wheel. Both of these controls survived for many years: the ignition adjuster until the evolution of the distributor, and the mixture control until carburettors had become much more efficient.

The Rolls-Royce body was merely super-structure, however heavy, on top of the chassis which carried all the stresses. Evidently, weather protection had not yet seriously entered the minds of car designers nor indeed had the need for any special provision for stowing luggage. Magnificent though it looked and silently though it ran, the Silver Ghost was not in itself evidence of any real advance in the anatomy of the car, apart from the adoption of

multi-cylinder engines and higher compression ratios which led to greater efficiency and better power output.

It should not be assumed from looking at the Rolls-Royce that other significant engineering changes were not being studied and exploited. Even before the Silver Ghost emerged, engines had been run with overhead valves and even overhead camshafts. Such developments were if anything ahead of their time, for the poor quality of fuel in the years before the First World War meant that engine compression ratios had to be extremely low in order to avoid the problem of detonation or "knocking" which can quickly lead to mechanical disaster. Given a low compression ratio, the designer has much less interest in achieving the most efficient combustion chamber shape, through the use of overhead valves. The problems of the engine "top end" were also eased by the extremely low speeds at which most of the early engines ran. One of the lifting factors here was the use of cast-iron pistons, whose weight placed a great strain on the connecting-rods and the crankshaft. Not until aluminium pistons came into general use during the 1920s did engine speeds begin to rise significantly. It is worth noting that in 1964 Rolls-Royce "cheated" by equipping the surviving Silver Ghost – still owned by the company – with aluminium pistons in place of the cast-iron originals!

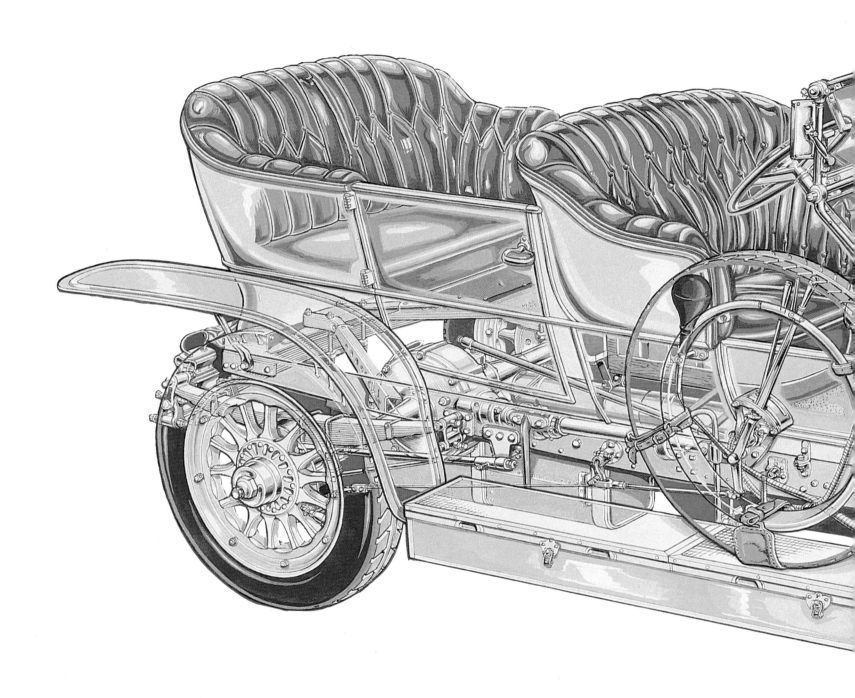

Rolls-Royce Silver Ghost
Country of origin: Great Britain
Date: 1907
Engine: six cylinders in line; 48bhp at
1,200rpm; twin-jet carburettor
Gears: four-speed
Capacity: 7,036cc
Maximum Speed: 63mph (101km/h)
Chassis: suspension by multi-leaf springs
Brakes: wood-spoke wheels with pneumatic tyres

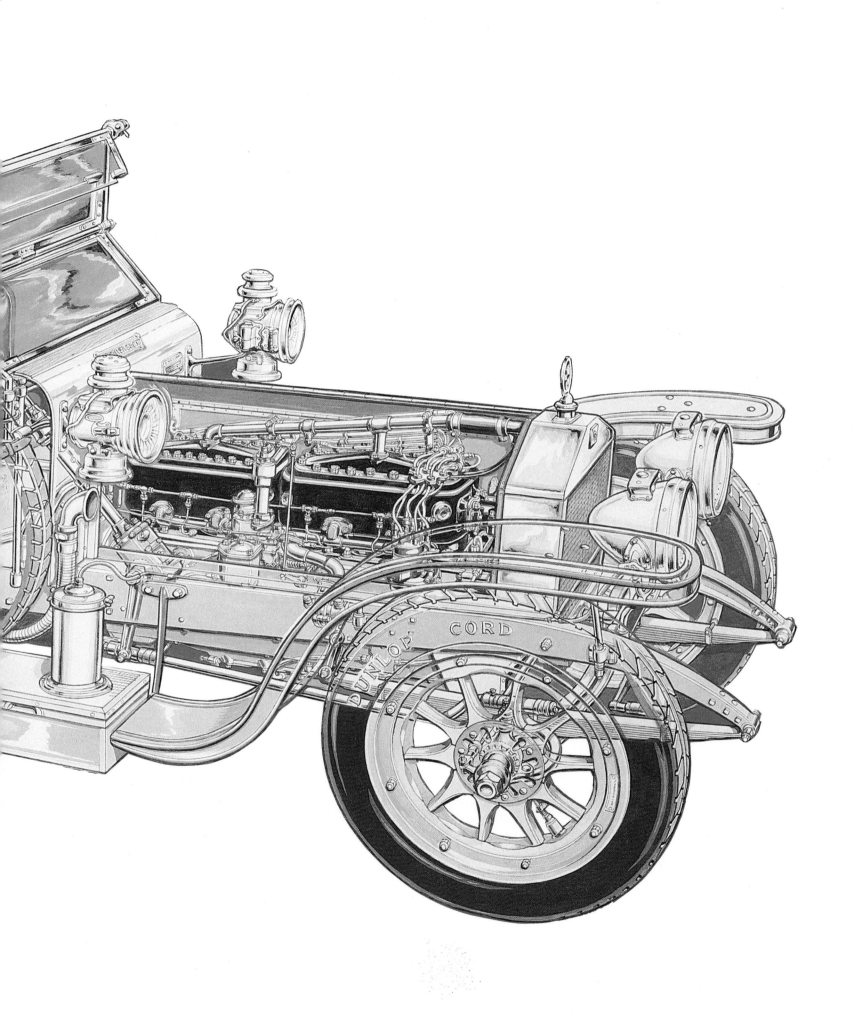

1908 FORD MODEL T

If the Silver Ghost was the epitome of careful workmanship whatever the cost, then the Ford Model T was certainly its antithesis. The Model T was by no means Henry Ford's first car: as its name implies, Ford had worked through more than half of the alphabet in a few years before settling on his historic formula. Much has been written about the Model T, the car which sold 15 million examples before being phased out of production in 1927, and most of it has assumed that the car's success was due to Ford's decision to put it into mass-production on a moving-chain conveyor system.

That is, obviously, a large part of the story but it ignores the merits of the vehicle itself. Ford designed the Model T for mass production, involving him in decisions which had never before been taken in the history of motoring. He also conceived exactly the car to match America's motoring needs and there is much that is worth studying in its anatomy.

Essentially, the Model T was another car in the mainstream of development which started with the Panhard-Levassor. It had a twin-rail chassis, a forward engine, in-line gearbox and propeller shaft drive to the rear differential. Yet within this entirely conventional outline, the details were filled in so as to suit the car closely to America's motoring needs of the time. The engine would be easy to dismiss as a crude lump of cast-iron: a side-valve four-cylinder unit of 2.9-litre capacity producing about 20bhp but, like the Rolls-Royce, offering an abundance of torque at very low speed. It should not be so lightly dismissed, however, because its apparent crudity hid three very real virtues. In the first place, the engine like the rest of the car was skilfully designed for mass-production. Ford's genius lay partly in being able to ensure an

absence of bottlenecks in his production process, and there was no point in his Highland Park factory being able to make hundreds of cars a day unless the engine plant was able to supply the same number of power units. Thus the Model T engine was designed with very few parts and was easily assembled. This automatically ensured its second virtue: it was cheap to make and that contributed greatly to the ultimate success of the car as a whole. Finally, the engine also made use of what were then some of the most advanced ironfounding techniques available.

The Model T transmission was absolutely unusual. Instead of using the sliding-pinion gearbox, Ford adopted epicyclic gearing, an arrangement in which "planet" gears rotate around a central "sun" gear with the whole assembly contained in an outer annular ring gear. By braking or locking together the various parts of this assembly, Ford was able to offer two forward speeds, a reverse, and a neutral gear without the driver having to worry about operating a conventional clutch. By this means he made driving much easier for millions of customers who might otherwise have worried about driving demanding too high a degree of skill. In a sense, the Ford transmission was a dead-end, although the epicyclic principle reappeared twenty or so years later in the first realistic moves towards true automatic transmission.

There was more to the Model T than a flexible engine and a cunning transmission. Ford sought simplicity but also good ground clearance in his chassis and suspension design. His concern for ground clearance was well-founded because America's farmers had nothing but dirt roads or open country on which to drive. His solution was

to perch his chassis high, attaching the Model T's two axles by means of transverse leaf springs. The springs were mounted upside-down in then-conventional engineering terms, with the ends attached to the axles and the central points clamped to the chassis cross-members. The result was that no part of the structure, other than the lower lip of the final drive casing, needed to protrude below the centre-line of the wheels. Since the wheels themselves were large wood-spoked affairs, shod with the narrow high-pressure pneumatic tyres of the day, the Model T could straddle a foot-high rock with ease. The car had the further advantage that it was light – the 1,200 pounds (544kg) of the basic model was in its own way a remarkable figure – because Ford chose to use high-strength alloy steel in vital parts of the chassis. This too helped its ability to cope with rough and muddy tracks.

The Ford's remaining advantage, although it was common to all early cars with their stress-carrying chassis, was that the bodywork was easily adapted for all manner of purposes. In the case of the Model T this factor was exploited to the point where it became not only the most popular car in the world, but the most popular light truck too. Henry's genius soon realised the existence of a benign spiral; sell the cars cheaper, more people will buy them, and by making more of them you can sell them cheaper still. By the early 1920s the basic Model T was selling in the USA for the dollar equivalent of £60. Nor should we forget that in 1914, with his commercial success growing rapidly, Ford cut the factory's working day from 9 to 8 hours and raised the standard day's pay from $2.34 to $5.

By most standards, even in 1908, the Ford Model T was crude; but it was tough and it was cheap, and well adapted to this chosen market place. It did little to advance the anatomy of the car as such, in fact by remaining in production for 19 years it may well have held back purely technical progress. In some of its aspects, such as its transmission, it was almost a technical blind-alley. Its real significance in the wider world of motor car design was that it made other designers think more carefully about the needs of large-scale production: the need, above all, to avoid undue complexity and to ensure the interchangeability of parts. Eventually and inevitably, the Model T was overtaken by technical progress. Its demise was nearly that of Ford as between May and November 1927 the Detroit factories produced nothing while they were re-tooled for the introduction of a new Model A.

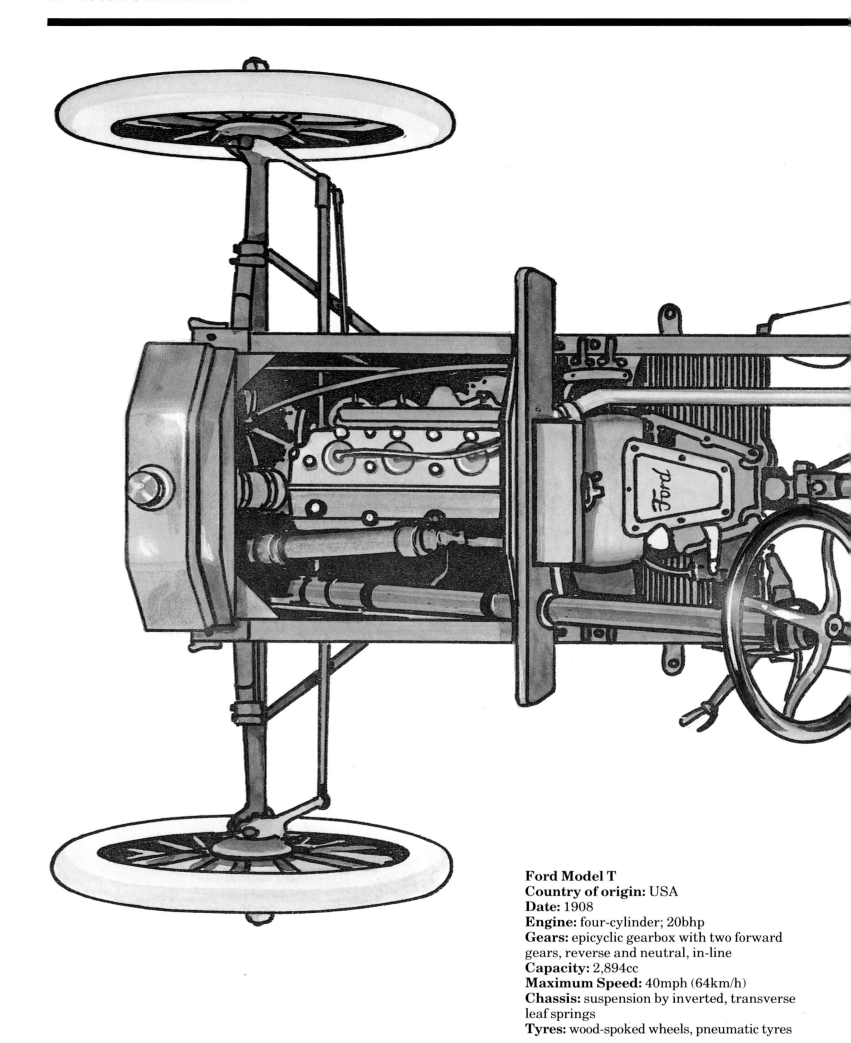

Ford Model T
Country of origin: USA
Date: 1908
Engine: four-cylinder; 20bhp
Gears: epicyclic gearbox with two forward gears, reverse and neutral, in-line
Capacity: 2,894cc
Maximum Speed: 40mph (64km/h)
Chassis: suspension by inverted, transverse leaf springs
Tyres: wood-spoked wheels, pneumatic tyres

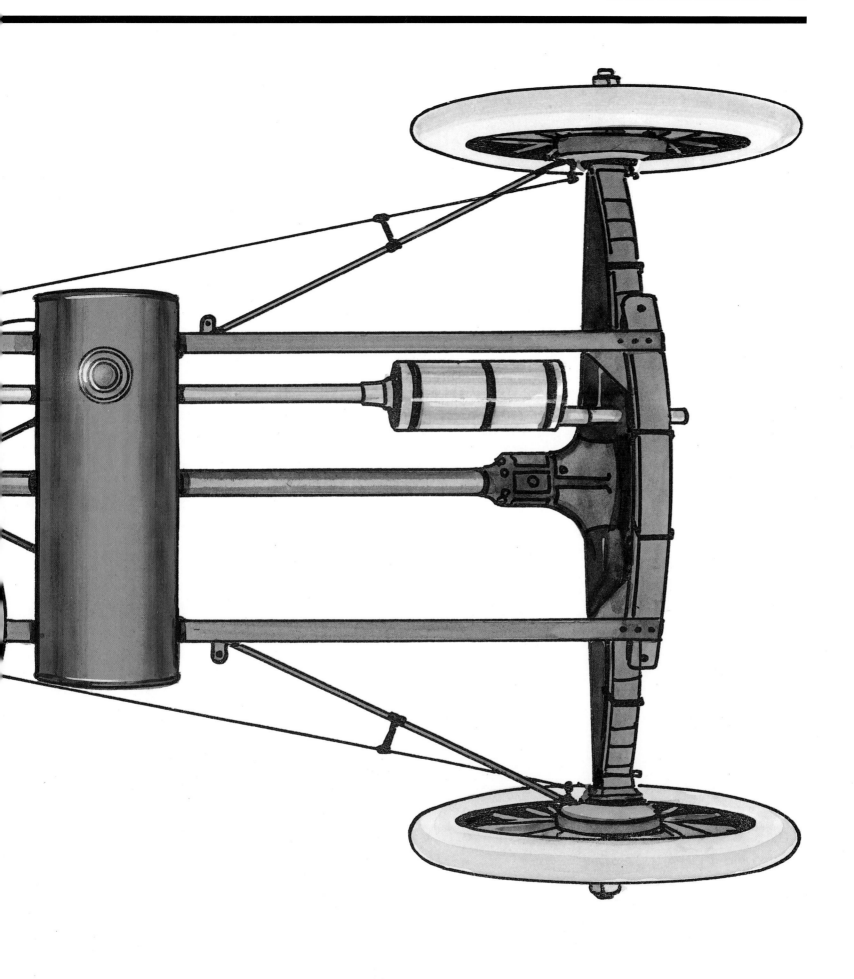

BUGATTI MODEL 13

Just as the Ford Model T was the antithesis of the Rolls-Royce Silver Ghost, so the Bugatti contradicted everything the Ford stood for. Ettore Bugatti was an Italian who worked all his life in France and was devoted to the manufacture of fine motor cars in small quantities. In this, Bugatti ran exactly parallel with Rolls-Royce; but while the British company chose always to be deliberately conservative in its engineering, Bugatti's attitude was that true excellence could only be achieved by adopting the latest and most advanced techniques. But like many a true genius he had blind spots: he was reputed to scorn careful brake design because 'his cars were made to go, not stop', while he refused to accept twin overhead camshafts for his engines for 20 years and retained a profound distrust of independent front suspension. All that, however, was still in the future when the Type 13 appeared.

The Type 13 was Bugatti's first design of note to carry his own name although previously he had designed good cars for Peugeot. It was typical of what was to become his outlook, for it was deliberately made small, light and agile. In this it had to tread a careful path between the 'proper' cars of its day, which were becoming increasingly big and heavy, and the mass of flimsy and uncomfortable cyclecars which came about as a reaction to the direction in which such cars were being developed. Bugatti was convinced that the right way to make an efficient vehicle was to make everything just strong enough to do its job. He was as much concerned with beauty as with engineering efficiency, and believed like many others of his calling that 'what looks right, is right'. In a real sense, therefore, Bugatti's influence on the anatomy of the car was to make it lighter and more delicate as is illustrated in the Type 13. It did not greatly differ in its layout from that of the Panhard-Levassor, Silver Ghost or Model T for it retained a girder-type chassis and the classic in-line engine and transmission to drive the rear wheels. The difference was that everything appeared to have been scaled down and better adapted to its purpose. That can be seen for instance in the way the lower edges of the body blend flush with the chassis rails to give a lower, cleaner look: a mark of Bugattis for years to come.

Bugatti influenced two particular areas of car design, both of them evident in the Type 13. The first was engine design for efficiency, while the second was chassis design for good stability and handling. The Type 13 engine is an in-line four-cylinder unit just like that of the Ford Model T, but there most resemblance ends. The Bugatti engine, originally of only 1.3-litres – less than half that of the Ford, produced more power. Its secret lay in several things, but most obviously in Bugatti's ability to remove weight while leaving what mattered for strength. By reducing the weight of all his engine's moving parts Bugatti was able to run it at quite remarkable speeds of 14,000rpm and more. In this way he increased the unit's volumetric efficiency and so was able to exploit the better breathing (the ability to get larger quantities of fuel/air mixture into the cylinders, and exhaust gases out), afforded by overhead-camshaft valve operation. Later in its career, after the First World War, the Type 13 was revised and given four valves per cylinder – two inlet, two exhaust. In this, it anticipated a trend which is only just growing among today's higher-performance engines.

Looking at a picture of the Type 13 it is not immediately obvious that the car is of the type which handles well. It is easy enough to say that it has good static balance, high roll stiffness, high roll centres at both ends and a near-level roll axis to give something close to neutral handling but Bugatti could not have explained it like that. Yet in the way he designed the neat little leaf springs and their attachments, not to mention the geometry he chose for his steering layout, he brought to the Type 13 a response and ease of control which, together with excellent ratio of power to weight, enabled the car to run in races hounding competitors with engines many times its own size. Part of the car's neatness comes from having quarter-elliptic leaf springs at the rear, with the 'fat' part of the

spring set into the rear of the chassis rail while the end of the longest blade locates one end of the axle. This results in excellent axle location and allows the chassis and body to be built lower.

Bugatti's interest in stream-lining also produced some less desirable effects. Look, for instance, at the brakes: despite using expanding shoes inside cast-iron drums these were fitted to the rear wheels only. This meant there was nothing to interfere with the purity of the steering, but stopping the car from any speed without turning sideways was a major problem.

Notice also Bugatti's return to light, efficient, spoked wheels. Again, he must have felt the need to make the wheels as light as possible without being able to explain why. Today we know that the ratio of sprung to unsprung weight – the latter being all those parts of the car which do not have springs between themselves and the road – is vital in determining ride quality and roadholding. Yet at the time Bugatti was carefully fitting his lighter wheels, some motor sport enthusiasts were still fitting lead weights to their cars' axles in the belief that it would improve roadholding! Bugatti was also one of the first to appreciate the potential of light-alloy wheels.

Bugatti's contribution to the anatomy of the car lay in intuitive genius and pointed more methodical workers along the right road. Today we are all interested in saving weight, in better handling and superior overall efficiency but Bugatti was the pioneer.

The Bugatti Model 57 was introduced in 1934 and was the last important sedan to be introduced before Ettore Bugatti's death in 1947.

1919 CHEVROLET FB-4

The enthusiast might wonder why the Chevrolet FB-4 is included in a fairly short list of the world's most significant cars. The simple answer is that it became the car which eventually unseated the Ford Model T from its proud position as the world's best-selling car. By that time, in 1927, it was no longer known as the FB-4 but was still the four-cylinder Chevrolet. It was also suited to the new American motorists' needs; in the years after the First World War, as the roads had been improved, and many richer consumers began to spurn the crudity of Ford's 'Tin Lizzie'. Chevrolet set a style which remained, for in most years right up to the present, it has remained America's biggest-selling marque.

After many years of financial manoeuvrings and difficulties Chevrolet finally became part of the huge General Motors combine. The result of this merger was that Chevrolet, who in earlier years had primarily made cars with six-cylinder engines and with the earliest V8s, returned to a more basic product with an overhead-valve four-cylinder engine. These four-cylinder cars were offered with a range of engine sizes – the FB-4 being a 3.6-litre – and were considered by many enthusiasts more attractive than the Model T.

The success of this four-cylinder car is easy to understand but from the innovative point of view one has to say that the FB-4 did not greatly advance the development of the anatomy of the car. In fact, very few new cars of the era did advance the fundamental design and the radical departures from convention were often signal failures. Either they were simply before their time, or they charged off with developments in totally impractical directions. Not so the Chevrolet: here once again we have the two-railed chassis and the conventional arrangement of engine and transmission.

Compared with the Model T, however, the Chevrolet has something to offer. For example it has an inherently more efficient engine since the overhead valve layout makes for a more efficient combustion chamber. Add that to the larger engine of the FB-4 and the result is a superior performance, something that was beginning to matter in the American world of 1919. The performance gap was further widened by Chevrolet's use of a conventional three-speed sliding-pinion gearbox which enabled the engine's output to be more fully exploited: and such was the painstaking development of the Detroit engineers that clutch operation was already becoming less of a nightmare for novice drivers.

When it came to handling, the Chevrolet sat lower than the Ford: not a lot lower as there were still plenty of bad roads around but sufficiently enough to lower the centre of gravity. The more conventional leaf-spring suspension behaved better in high-speed driving than Ford's transverse-spring arrangement. On the other hand the brakes (at least to begin with) were still on the back wheels only and the wheels remained wooden-spoked.

It was perhaps at this point that styling began to make its first impact on the American car-buying public, and the FB-4 had a great significance here. Since its overhead-valve engine was much taller than Ford's squat side-valve, the bonnet had to be higher and this allowed the one to be carried attractively aft with the bonnet blending into the car's natural waistline. The effect was much more modern than the Ford's very obvious scuttle rising from a low-set bonnet. In other ways, the Chevrolet remained a car of tradition with, for instance, no

special provision for luggage space.

In 1919 the Americans had already overtaken Europe in the provision of better equipment. One of Chevrolet's companion companies in General Motors was Cadillac and they had introduced electric starter motors and full electric lighting as early as 1916. It was not long before other major conveniences, such as mechanical windscreen wipers were also introduced. In its way this was just as significant a development in the car's anatomy as the major European innovations which were about to emerge. Where, after all, would modern motoring be without the starter motor? The Americans, and especially General Motors, were determined to make further large contributions to the efficiency of the motor car and the well-being of its driver. Through the 1920s, the major

American companies for the most part eschewed technical revolutions like independent suspension and unitary body construction, but their research into fuel quality and combustion gave us the modern coil ignition system, perfected for General Motors by Charles Kettering. Their search for better all-round performance also quickly led to the widespread use of the V8 engine, although after the launch of the FB-4 and its companion models, Chevrolet built nothing but four-cylinder cars until 1929. The companion search for better comfort led to the invention of the low-pressure 'balloon' tyre by Firestone in 1923. In that sense, the Chevrolet and is companion cars were indeed changing the shape of motoring; but the more visible and obvious changes were left to adventurous European pioneers.

1922 AUSTIN SEVEN

The Austin Seven was launched as a 'proper' car in the middle of a cycle-car craze, and it achieved its results, like the Bugatti Type 13, by making everything as small and light as possible. It may well have been, in its own way, just as much a work of genius as the Bugatti and it certainly sold in infinitely greater numbers than all the Bugatti Types ever made; but the purpose of its lightness and miniaturisation was to get it down to a price not to build it up to a standard.

It was, nevertheless, a highly significant car for several reasons. The first was that it got the Austin Motor Company out of trouble at a time when it was being overrun in sales terms by Morris. A second was that it caught the public imagination and affection to the extent that an attempt to exploit the appeal of the 'little Seven' for a completely different car very nearly worked. But the most significant thing of all about the Austin Seven was that it put the motor car within reach of a large part of the British public for the first time.

By comparison with the Austin models that had gone before, the thoroughly conventional Twenty and Twelve, the original Seven was tiny. In what were to become the best traditions of the motor industry, Herbert Austin himself designed and built the prototype with the aid of

a small, hand-picked team in strict secrecy and in remarkably short time. The result of his labours was less than nine feet (2.7m) long and weighed well under half a ton (500kg). Critics called it a 'hip-bath on wheels' but that was less than fair; the Seven was a miniaturised version of an ordinary car. Had Austin actually made a hip-bath on wheels, implying the use of the body as a stressed member, the Seven might have been even lighter and certainly much more significant.

The Seven engine was not only small, but crude. It was a four-cylinder side-valve unit of only 696cc, producing a derisory amount of power though a mere 30 years before, Benz would have been amazed by it. Its most notable engineering feature was the use of a spindly little crankshaft with no internal support whatever, simply the main bearings at each end where it passed through the crankcase. The theme of simplicity and low cost also led Austin to adopt crude 'splash' lubrication rather than a pressure feed. The engine drove the rear wheels through a tiny three-speed crash gearbox and a modern-looking plate clutch: by the early 1920s some valuable basic research work by Herbert Frood (the founder of the Ferodo company), had resulted in much more efficient lining materials for clutches and brakes alike.

The Seven chassis was one of its weakest features, literally and metaphorically. It was little more than a vee of inverted pressed steel channel, its apex towards the front of the car. The front axle was mounted on a transverse leaf spring whose centre picked up on this apex; at the rear, two quarter-elliptic springs emerged from the ends of the chassis members to locate the driven axle. There was actually little enough wrong with the back end of the Seven except for a dire lack of spring travel which could lead to a dreadful ride for any passenger shoe-horned into the tiny back seat; but the front end was the first thing to receive major attention from anyone. As time went on there were many enthusiasts who wanted to make the Seven into a competition car. However, the Seven was very prone to 'front wheel wobble' which meant that when one of the wheels passed over a bump, the whole steering system would vibrate violently until the driver slowed down, often almost to a stop. The explanation of this phenomenon was hardly appreciated at the time but actually it was due to the natural vibration frequency of the front axle on its springs, complicated in the case of the Seven by the willing vibration of the chassis itself, and this supply of energy from the rotating front wheels to keep the motion going. As wheels and tyres became heavier, and front drum brakes popular, so more and more cars

suffered from this fault until the arrival of independent front suspension put a stop to it.

If nothing else, the Seven was in advance of its time in providing front-wheel brakes from the very beginning; the Silver Ghost only adopted them three years later. For a long time designers resisted adding brakes to the steered wheels, rightly suspecting that problems would result, but eventually the need for better stopping meant that the move to four-wheel brakes had to come.

The more it is assessed by modern technical historians, the less convincing the Austin Seven becomes, especially if it is reckoned as no more than the sum of its parts. Its engine was tiny and primitive, its suspension crude and its chassis lacking in strength. Its attraction at the time lay mainly in its price which on the car's introduction was £225 but was quickly cut to £165 as the orders rolled in. However, despite its drawbacks the Austin Seven was safer, more comfortable and more fun to drive than contemporary cycle cars or motor cycle combinations, and as an exercise in motor car anatomy it had many interesting conclusions. It showed that a deliberate scaling-down process, making a standard car smaller component by component, could be made to work. In the years that followed, it was a theme taken up by other major manufacturers, often with a great deal of success.

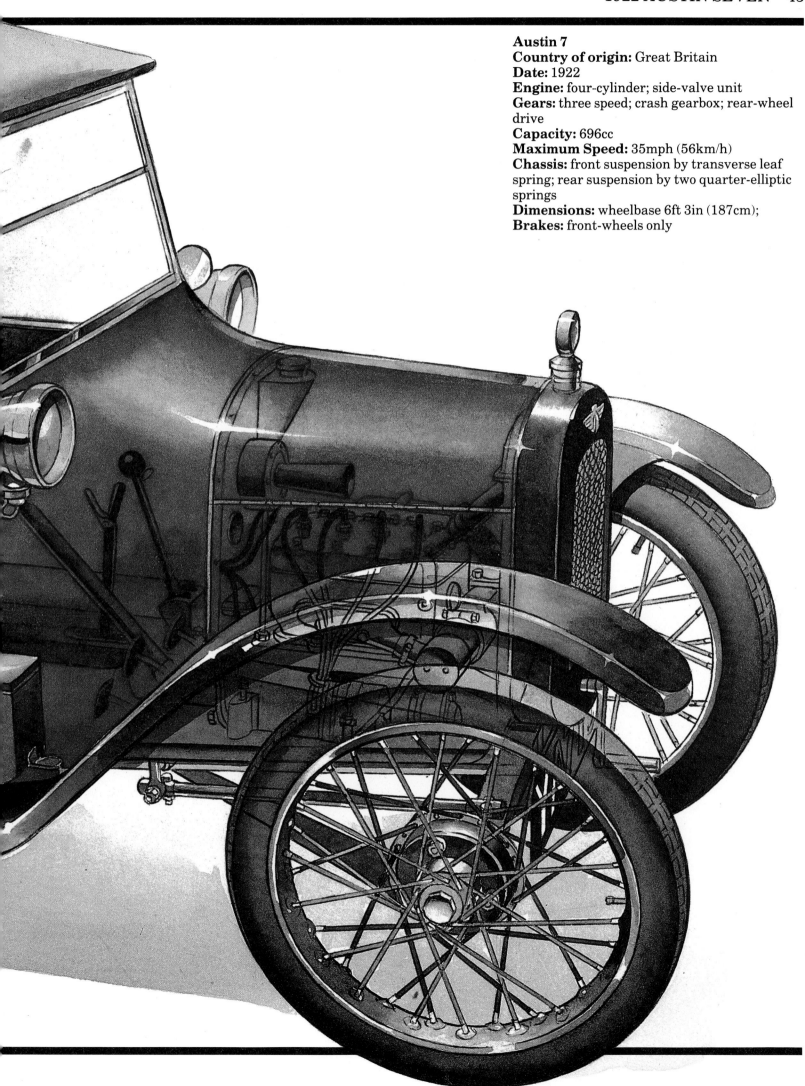

Austin 7
Country of origin: Great Britain
Date: 1922
Engine: four-cylinder; side-valve unit
Gears: three speed; crash gearbox; rear-wheel drive
Capacity: 696cc
Maximum Speed: 35mph (56km/h)
Chassis: front suspension by transverse leaf spring; rear suspension by two quarter-elliptic springs
Dimensions: wheelbase 6ft 3in (187cm);
Brakes: front-wheels only

1923 LANCIA LAMBDA

The period after the First World War was one in which the motor car began to be developed in various ways. There were teams like Ford's who discovered how to make the car cheaper through mass-production and standardisation, others like General Motors who combined this technique with steady progress towards making the car more comfortable, easier to drive and live with and others again like Austin who found out how to extend the appeal of the car (especially in countries lacking America's burgeoning wealth) by making it smaller, lighter and cheaper to run as well as less expensive to buy. Yet there had also to be a fourth strand of development: the engineer who would achieve the real technical breakthrough and take the motor car to new heights of efficiency. One such man was Vincenzo Lancia.

Thus far, we have not looked at the contribution the Italians made to the development of the car. It might well be said that the Germans invented it, the French made it into a practical proposition and the Americans ultimately turned it into a mass-produced, everyday means of transport. However, the Italians also contributed towards its development and many engineers based in cities like Turin and Milan brought to the motor car an inventiveness that was to everyone's eventual benefit.

Lancia came from Turin and had worked for Fiat before starting in the motor car business on his own account. By the early 1920s he already had a string of successes in his name, but he was unhappy with what he saw as the sterile nature of so much vehicle engineering. The result of his

unhappiness was the Lambda. Today it is hard to appreciate the shock which the car must have had on its motoring world. For 25 years virtually every car, large and small, pedestrian or powerful, had been built to the pattern of the Panhard-Levassor as refined by Renault. The motorist looked for certain differences between cars, but he knew that under all there would be a chassis and a front axle. The Lambda had neither.

The essence of the Lambda lay in two things. First, instead of having a chassis, a frame or ladder through which the stresses of power transmission and suspension operation were passed and on which the body was mounted, the car used the body frame itself to contain all the loads. Previously, the body of the car had only served to provide the occupants with seats and shelter. Second, instead of having the front wheels mounted and pivoted at each end of an axle beam, it had one front wheel hung on a mechanism from each side of its nose and able to work without reference to its companion.

There are many stories about the way in which Lancia arrived at the Lambda concept. One is that the 'monocoque' body was based on a ship's hull. Another is that the independent front suspension was born out of a front spring breakage on one of his earlier cars, resulting in an accident which nearly killed his mother and causing him to seek a safer arrangement. The truth is probably that all kinds of minor inspirations plus his own great engineering vision led Lancia in the right direction.

One would not have guessed it was the right direction from the car's initial reception. How could a car *not* have a chassis frame to hold everything together? How could one trust a car in which the front wheels were not safely bound together by an axle? Yet the logic of Lancia's ideas soon penetrated even if it was a long time before another major manufacturer dared to follow along the same path. The Lambda body consisted of floor panels on either side of the transmission tunnel and deep side frames, all bound together by cross-frames at the front bulkhead, aft of the front seat and at the rear. The result was that the whole of the lower body acted as a highly efficient girder framework which resisted loads, especially those which tried to twist the car front to rear, more efficiently than most conventional chassis frames. It also meant that the whole car could be built lower, because the body no longer had to leave room for a separate chassis underneath, and that it could be made lighter by most of the weight of what would have been a separate body (in the Lambda the roof and its pillars were still unstressed; that development would come ten years later).

These were significant gains to be balanced against the one clear loss resulting from monocoque construction, the intrusion of the transmission tunnel into the cabin space because the body was no longer high enough to sit over the top of it. Eventually, Lancia also found the answer to this in the form of front-wheel drive, but not for many years to come. Building the car low meant better handling and roadholding, while reducing the weight enabled it to offer good performance in relation to its engine size. The Lambda was not a small car; its wheelbase measured over 10 feet (3.05m) and its overall length was nearly 15 feet (4.6m). Its engine was a modest four-cylinder of 2.1-litres, producing just 49bhp, yet it was capable of more than 70mph (113km/h), the kind of speed normally the province of outright sports models.

If the Lambda body was a masterpiece then so was its front suspension. In a remarkable piece of engineeering analysis, Lancia sat down one night and sketched most of the independent suspension layouts that have since been tried, with one important exception – the layout introduced nearly 30 years later as the MacPherson strut. It is interesting that, having sketched several variations on the double-wishbone layout including some with inboard springs which must look very familiar to modern racing-car designers, Lancia elected to use a sliding-pillar arrangement in which the wheel hubs moved vertically between tubes attached to the front of the car via a rigid framework. He thus made sure the wheels remained parallel to each other at all times – a piece of far-sightedness which also made the design of a good steering layout that much easier.

Lancia faced one special problem as a result of the front suspension layout he adopted, and that concerns the damping of wheel movement. It had never been widely realised that wheel movement needed to be not only sprung, but damped – with springs alone, the wheels would continue to bounce up and down (or rather would allow the body to do so) for a long time. Luckily for the motoring pioneers, the traditional multi-leaf spring provided damping of its own, through the friction which occurred between the spring leaves. Sundry inventors had offered the motor industry ways of increasing the damping, the front-runner of the day being the Hartford friction damper, but Lancia needed something altogether more effective because he was going to use coil springs which gave no inherent damping whatever. In a move typical of the man, he solved the problem by a telescopic hydraulic damper, integral with his suspension tube but otherwise similar in principle to the damper units that became commonplace fifteen years later, when others had followed his lead into independent front suspension.

Even the Lambda could hardly break new ground in every aspect of the car's anatomy. Its engine layout became another Lancia speciality, a space-saving narrow-vee layout with just enough of an angle between the banks to enable the cylinder block to be made much shorter and stiffer. The engine drove through a multi-plate clutch (with engines of any power, a single plate was still rarely enough to cope) and a three-speed gearbox to the rear differential. The car did have four-wheel brakes, the wheels themselves being wire-spoked for lightness.

The Lambda was expensive. Like Bugatti, Lancia built up to a standard rather than down to a price. Even so, his Turin factory delivered 13,000 Lambdas in seven years of production and even if the world's motor car designers did not rush to follow suit, they knew from then on that there were better ways of doing things.

Lancia Lambda
Country of origin: Italy
Date: 1923
Engine: 13-degree V-4; single ohc; single carburettor; 49bhp at 3,250rpm
Gears: three-speed manual, four-speed from 1925
Capacity: 2,120cc
Bore & Stroke: 75 × 120mm
Maximum Speed: 71mph (114km/h)
Chassis: pressed steel integral with body; front suspension independent by enclosed vertical coil springs on sliding pillars and hydraulic dampers; rear suspension by underslung semi-elliptic springs; friction dampers
Brakes: four-wheel drum brakes

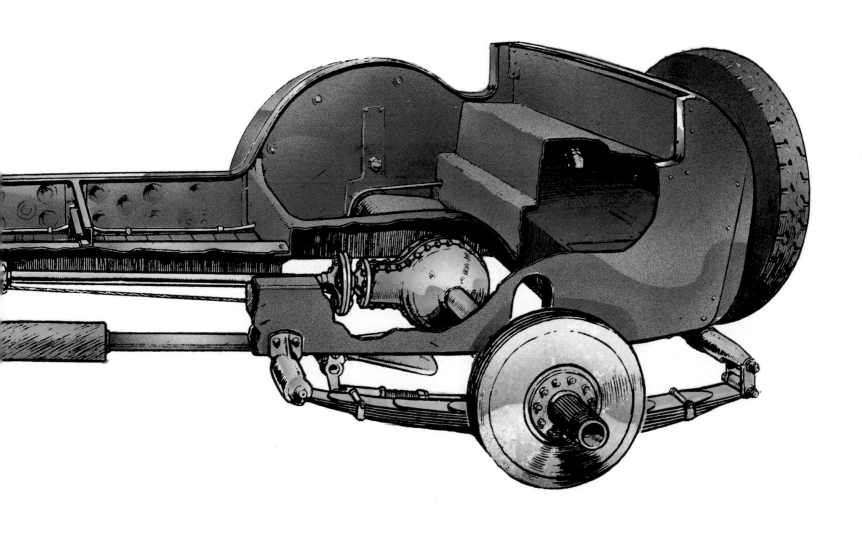

1927 BENTLEY 3-LITRE

In many ways it is an anticlimax to return from the engineering heights of the Lancia Lambda and contemplate instead a car which has all the subtlety of a bludgeon. It was Ettore Bugatti, stung by Bentley's effrontery in winning the Le Mans 24 Hours race four times running (from 1927 to 1930) who called the car 'the fastest lorry in the world'.

If the Bentley is significant, it is for two reasons. In the first place it represents a kind of pinnacle of achievement; in this study, only two other cars with the traditional type of chassis frame and unstressed body are represented and the Bentley took this form of construction about as far as it could usefully go. Secondly, the exploits of the Bentley sports car in competition gave rise to something like patriotic fervour in the Britain of the Depression years and encouraged the development of a generation of light sports two-seaters which were, in their way, miniature versions of their hero. The classic MG was to the Bentley as the Austin Seven was to the full-sized luxury four-seater.

The Bentley 3-litre, as Bugatti observed, was about as strong as it could be made without being absolutely grotesque. Its chassis side members looked as though they came from the Forth Bridge; its multi-leaf springs were huge and so were its finned drum brakes. Even unladen, with open four-seater sports bodywork, the Bentley came uncomfortably close to weighing two tons (2032kg).

Yet the Bentley should never be written off as a dinosaur. Its engine was a fascinating mixture of the old and the new. The 3-litre unit was a four-cylinder with fixed cylinder heads like so many of the pioneer cars of 20 years before. But the Bentley also used an overhead camshaft, neatly if noisily driven by a bevel-geared shaft from the front of the crankshaft and operated four valves per cylinder via rocker shafts. The engine dimensions were old-fashioned enough: a huge crankshaft stroke of 149mm compared with a cylinder bore of only 80mm to make the unit look almost alarmingly tall and thin in cross-section. On the other hand, Bentley was a pioneer user of aluminium rather than cast-iron pistons, so that piston inertia worried him less than rival designers. The engine's output from its 3-litre capacity was about 80bhp, showing what could be achieved with good four-valve breathing even in a long-stroked, slow-running power unit, while the torque was mightily impressive.

The Bentley is also the first car described here to use the ingenious and highly successful SU carburettor, in which the fuel flow is controlled by a needle-valve opened and closed by the movement of a piston that responds to the air pressure inside the engine's inlet manifold. This clever idea was the answer to a lot of engine designers' problems and was enthusiastically embraced especially by British engineers in the Midlands where the SU company was based; once the SU patents had run out, a lot of competitors also began exploiting the principle. SU itself is now part of British Leyland and remains a major force in the world of carburettors. The SU carburettor was important, in the context of the 1920s because of its fine control of the fuel/air mixture. This was good enough to allow the driver's manual mixture control to be dispensed with, other than to provide a richer mixture for cold starting – what is now thought of as the choke control.

In other respects, Bentley remained a traditionalist. He retained combined magneto

and coil ignition, like the Rolls-Royce, and used only friction-type dampers for his cars' ultra-stiff suspension. Where the transmission was concerned, he had little choice but to use the normal type of four-speed manual gearbox, with suitably close-set sporting ratios. His cars are however notable, among those listed here, for being the first to be equipped with the new-fangled 'balloon' tyres of a size which even today we would recognise as familiar. Typically, the Bentley sports car was equipped with 6-inch (15.2cm) wide tyres on 15-inch (38.1cm) wheels: by no means large for a sports car of the 1980s, but a long way from the narrow, high-pressure types of only a few years earlier.

Bentley did not stop with the 3-litre, of course. He sought in particular to increase the power at his disposal by every means possible. He built bigger engines (of 6-litre and finally, 8-litre capacity) but most of all he resorted to supercharging, to create the 'blower Bentley' of the early 1930s. The idea of supercharging, actually forcing the air into the cylinders rather than leaving it to be sucked in, was not new, having been tried in America as early as 1907. But Bentley was able to exploit the Roots supercharger, a notably elegant and efficient device, to achieve power outputs that kept his sports cars competitive despite their huge weight. Had he developed chassis as well as he did engines, his company might have avoided its 1931 takeover by Rolls-Royce.

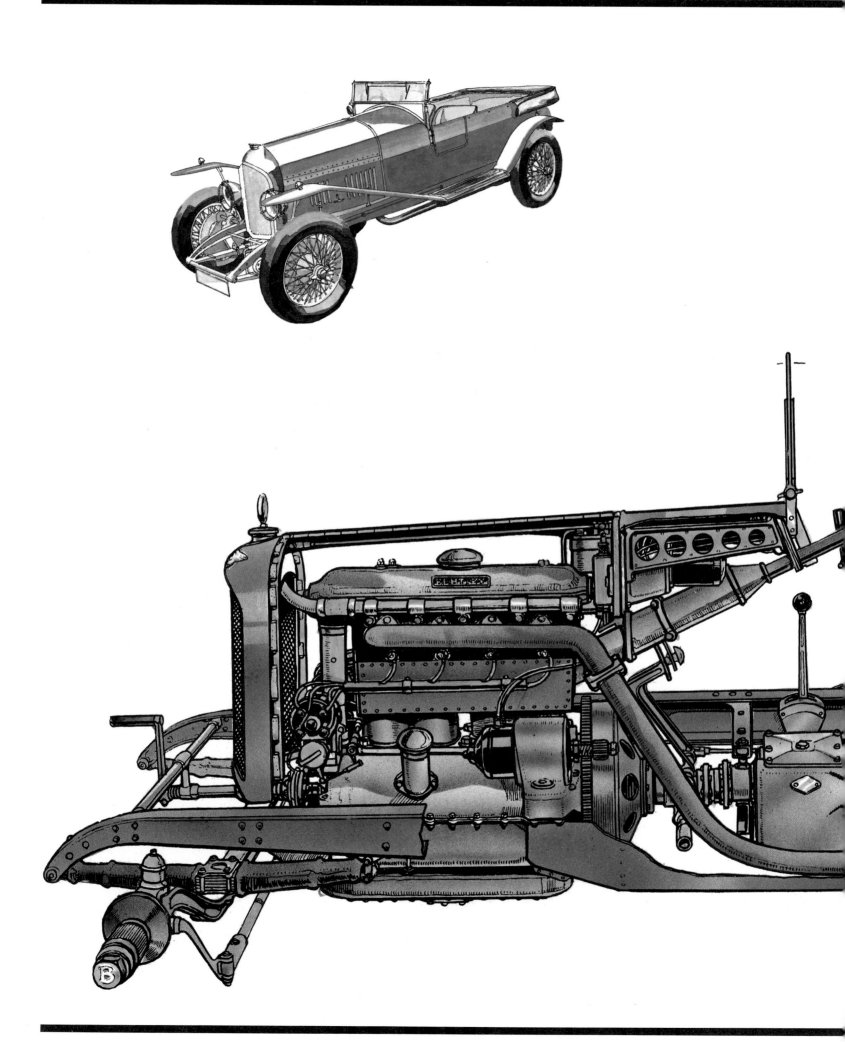

Bentley 3-litre
Country of origin: Great Britain
Date: 1927
Engine: straight-four; single ohc; four valves
per cylinder; single or twin carburettors; 65bhp
at 3,500rpm on introduction, rising to 85bhp
from 1925
Gears: separate four-speed manual
Capacity: 2,996cc
Bore & Stroke: 80 × 149mm
Maximum Speed: 90mph (144km/h)
Chassis: pressed steel side members; semi-
elliptic springs front and rear; friction dampers
Dimension: wheelbase *Red Label* – 117½in
(298cm); *Blue Label* – 117½in (298cm) or
130½ (331cm); *Green Label* – 108in (274cm);
track 56in (142cm)
Brakes: two-wheel drum brakes, four-wheel
drums from mid-1923

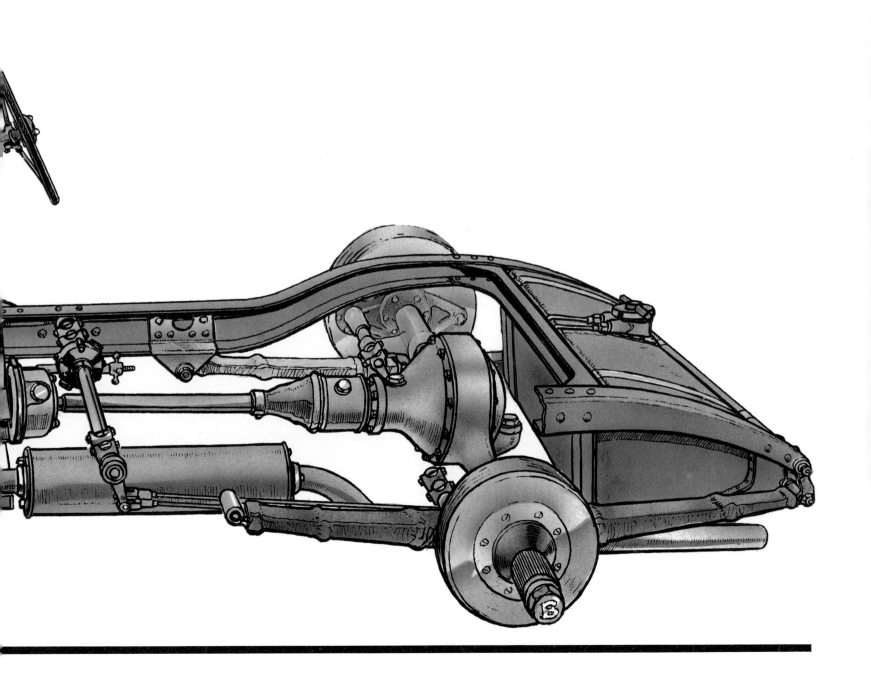

1928 MG M-TYPE

A whole host of sporting two-seaters, many of them British and highly respected, span the years from about 1924 to the outbreak of the Second World War. Many of them are recognised classics, eagerly sought after by collectors, yet none of them strikes the same note as the MG.

One says *the* MG because the immediate vision is of a tiny but elegant open two-seater with a huge steering wheel, a happy young man behind it and a happy young woman beside him. The odd fact is that 'the' MG in question – which is beyond doubt the M-type Midget and its immediate successors – was hardly the first MG. Morris Garages of Oxford had, since 1923, been building slightly more sporting versions of the standard Morris cars; sporting, but by no means small and not especially elegant either.

The M-type came about at least partly because of the Austin Seven. Morris Motors, Austin's principal British rival, eventually realised that it needed a small car of its own to compete with the Seven, which had done so well to carve out a new market for itself. In a bid to upstage the Seven, Morris launched its Eight, complete with what was for those days an advanced small engine, of 847cc and with an overhead camshaft. Since it was already becoming a tradition that MG built a sports version of each Morris model, a prototype was made ready in which that small two-seater body was mounted on a slightly adapted Morris Eight chassis. This was the first MG Midget.

That is the outline of the story, but what is the significance of the Midget in terms of development of the motor car's anatomy? The Midget emphasised particularly another form of adaptation: that of the saloon into a sports car. Of course, Morris Garages had been doing as much for some time, and so had the many coachbuilders (including the forerunners of today's Jaguar) who had been busily adapting the Austin Seven into a more sporting form. But the MG Midget was different. It was a regular model – Austin never offered a Seven Sport for general sale – and it was pitched exactly right to catch the public imagination. The purpose-built, quality two-seaters were also expensive: the Midget, adapted from and using most of the components (other than the body) of a mass-produced small saloon, was in an altogether lower price category and accessible to many drivers who might otherwise merely have dreamed of sports cars. In that respect, the Midget was to the sports car what the Austin Seven had earlier been to motoring in general

It has to be said also that the Morris Eight chassis was better suited to sporting conversion than the Austin Seven. It had a ladder-type chassis which gave much better front-end stiffness and altogether more secure handling.

The side rails provided convenient mounting points in later Midget versions for the new Armstrong lever-arm hydraulic dampers to which MG would remain faithful for many years. The springs remained semi-elliptic leaves and produced a typically stiff ride with some control problems on bumpy surfaces. By the late 1920s the final mental block about front-wheel brakes had been overcome and the Midget used 8-inch (20cm) drums on all four wheels. By this time, too, brake operation was by cable – still vulnerable to stretching, but better than the rod linkages formerly employed in most cars. Some of the more adventurous car manufacturers (including Duensenberg and Chrysler in the USA and Triumph in Britain), already offered hydraulic brake operation by this time.

The Midget's engine was advanced in some respects, especially in its use of an overhead camshaft. The camshaft was driven rather ingeniously by a bevel-gear shaft (shapes of the Bentley itself!) at the front of the engine, forming as it did so the armature spindle of the dynamo. Less praiseworthy was the engine's crankshaft which ran in only two main bearings, like that of the Austin Seven, though again the Morris/MG crank was a good deal more robust than its rival's. The caraburettor, naturally, was an SU. Drive was taken through a single-plate clutch and a three-speed 'crash' gearbox to the rear axle.

It says something for the standards of sports car performance which was thought acceptable in those days that the Midget was originally offered with 20bhp under its bonnet – not much more than half the current output of a basic Austin Mini. On the other hand, that figure must be related to the size of the car, which by any current standard was tiny: a wheelbase of 6ft 6ins (1.98m), (much less than that of the Mini), with so little width that the occupants of the two seats more or less had to be good friends. In any case, once MG was given permission to tune the engine, the output was rapidly increased to 27bhp.

The MG Midget went on sale in 1928 at an advertised price of £175, which gives some idea of its appeal and its value for money. However, Britain's makers of small saloon cars were battling their prices down towards the magic £100 and in the end, they just about succeeded. As a piece of automotive anatomy its significance depends on the way it is viewed. Seen as a bare chassis, it would be difficult for any but an expert to tell it apart from the Morris Eight saloon: but the influence of that tiny sports body would be hard to underestimate. In its way, it created a whole new class of car and awoke many other designers and product planners to the possible adaptation of saloon cars into something more exciting and attractive even if less practical.

1934 CITROEN TRACTION AVANT

It is entirely appropriate that 1934 should mark the half-way point in the development of the motor car to the present day, because the year saw the announcement of one of the most technically significant cars of all, the Citroen 'Traction Avant' – literally, 'Front-drive'. The Citroen was by no means the first front-driven car; others had been tried even in the years before the First World War and Citroen himself admitted to having studied the front-driven Tracta sports cars built in the late 1920s by fellow-Frenchman Gregoire. The significance of the Citroen 7CV as it was officially named, was that it was the first car deliberately to exploit the advantages of front-wheel drive.

There was more to the Citroen than that, however. Like Lancia some years before, Andre Citroen was anxious to break out of the mould imposed by the still-standard system of car manufacture: the chassis frame and the superimposed but unstressed body. Certainly Citroen was aware of Lancia's cars but his ambitions lay in a rather different direction. The car he foresaw must be cheap enough to have wide public appeal – to sell in one year as

many as Lancia had sold in the last ten. Therefore, while he embraced the idea of the body as a fully stressed member, carrying loads imposed by the engine and the suspension, he needed to employ a different manufacturing system: one which had been suggested to him by the American engineer William Muller of the Budd company. This was the concept of 'unitary' construction in which the pressed-steel sheets which made up the body are welded together so that their own shape provides the necessary stiffness in bending and torsion, and it provided the basis upon which the Traction Avant was developed.

Had Andre Citroen had his way, these two sensational features would have been joined by a third. He was convinced that the motoring world needed saving from the chore of gearchanging and that he had found the answer in an ingenious automatic transmission devised by a fellow-Frenchman (though born in Brazil!), Sensaud de Lavaud. Sadly, it was not to be. The cost and complication of trying to make the transmission work, on top of the rest of the development necessary to bring the new car into

production, crippled Citroen's company financially and sent Andre to an early grave. That did not stop the Traction Avant from remaining in production for nearly 20 years, nor from being accepted as a classic, setting new standards for the performance and behaviour of mass-produced cars.

The principle behind front-wheel drive is a simple one – at least, the way Citroen explained it. It is more natural for a car to be pulled along by its front wheels than pushed along by its back ones, he explained: after all, horse-drawn vehicles are pulled, not pushed. It is beyond doubt true that cars with most of their weight on the front wheels tend to run straight, especially in sidewinds. It is also true that cars with driven front wheels feel extremely stable, though the technical reasons are more complicated: using the front wheels to transmit the driving power as well as to steer the car can lead to the kind of handling now known as 'understeer', the tendency for a car to run wide of the driver's intended line. This calls for the application of more steering lock than would be necessary in a 'neutral steer' car which went exactly where the front wheels pointed. Today, at least in Europe, the majority of cars on the road are front-driven and the implications for handling are widely appreciated: when the new Citroen was on the drawing board, such nuances were hardly even theory. Citroen, and his chief engineer Andre Lefebvre, knew they were right even if they did not really know why.

Citroen had to tackle the problem universal to all front-driven cars: how to take the drive to the front wheels while also steering them. In order to do this, he adopted independent front suspension. At the time, this was a daring enough concept in itself despite the pioneering of Lancia and others. He then used 'double wishbones to articulate the wheels in a way that could be followed by the drive shafts, without the shafts suffering severe changes of length. He solved the further problem of taking the drive 'around the corner' to wheels that were being steered, by making use of the then-recent invention of the constant-velocity joint. This overcomes the drawback of the much older Hooke-type universal joint in which the speed of the output shaft is not constant when it is driven at an angle. It would obviously not have suited the Citroen, or any other front-driven car, to find its front wheels running alternately faster and slower as it tried to round a corner!

In order to get the power to his front-drive shafts, Citroen mounted his engine aft of the front axle with the gearbox in front of it and a shaft bridging the differential. This allowed the front wheels to be set far forward, while the car's nose was made elegantly low and sloping. The penalty was the need for a long linkage to the gearbox, a problem solved partly by the Traction Avant's characteristic gear lever which sprouted from the centre of the dashboard rather than the floor.

The front end design had one further

complication which had to be overcome and that was where to put the springs. The traditional leaf spring was out of the question and coil springs would have been difficult to install without getting in the way of the drive shafts. Citroen therefore elected to use yet another solution never before tried in production, the torsion bar spring, running aft from the front lower wishbones into the main body structure.

Having solved the complexities of the front end, Citroen was at least free to enjoy the ease with which the car's rear suspension could be designed. He used a light 'dead' (unpowered) axle held by trailing arms and sprung again by torsion bars, but this time running across the rear of the body.

Then, of course, there was the body. Citroen's notion was that having used front-wheel drive to isolate all the main mechanical components and their stresses at one end of the car, he could use his unitary body to trail along behind with its rear end supported by the back wheels. Better still, because he had completely eliminated the transmission tunnel, he could sit his passengers lower down and yet in great comfort. In turn, he could then lower the roof to reduce the car's frontal area and its resistance to motion through the air. All this he succeeded in doing – and admirably. There was even proper space at the back of the smoothly styled body for a luggage locker above the rear suspension.

Compared with all this, the mere mechanical details of the Traction Avant verge on the unexciting. The engine was a new and competent overhead valve unit which proved to have plenty of 'stretch' for development into larger sizes and remained in production in its final form even longer than the car. The clutch – fitted forward of the engine, but aft of the differential – was a single dry-plate type and the gearbox (forgetting about that fatal automatic) was a three-speed pinion type with the newly-invented synchromesh on second and top gears. It seems almost superfluous to point out that the Traction Avant was also the first mass-produced car to use Lockheed hydraulic brakes on all four wheels. This solution must have appealed to Citroen not least because it overcame the problem of threading any type of mechanical brake linkage through everything else attached to the front wheels. Finally, after a couple of years in production, the Traction Avant became one of the first mass-produced cars to be fitted with rack-and-pinion steering, by now an almost universal feature.

Obviously, the Citroen was a great success; those who drove it were amazed at its stability, its handling and roadholding and its excellent ride comfort. It was also produced in a number of more powerful versions, some with six-cylinder engines. It remained in production until the mid-1950s, when eventually it was replaced – as we shall see – by another car which was in its own way just as remarkable.

Citroën Traction Avant
Country of origin: France
Date: 1934
Engine: four-cylinder; overhead valve
Gears: three-speed synchromesh; front-wheel drive
Capacity: 1,628cc
Maximum Speed: 65mph (114km/h)
Chassis: unitary; front suspension independent with double wishbones, torsion bar; rear suspension with trailing arms and torsion bar
Brakes: Lockheed hydraulic on all four wheels

1935 MERCEDES 540K

The Citroen is engineering elegance, an example of daring new concepts to achieve as much as possible with as little commotion as possible, whereas the Mercedes typifies the attitude of much of the German industry in the 1930s: excellence and high performance at all costs, but steady step-by-step development of existing concepts.

Indeed, the Mercedes may be described by some as a dinosaur and is the last car on our list with an old-type chassis built up on two massive side members. However, the antiquated chassis of these last great pre-war Mercedes sports cars was elegantly clothed by coachbuilding specialists who had long ago learned the art of building low and hiding the worst of the machinery. Yet, under its skin, the 540K was a close descendant of the brutal-looking SSK Mercedes with its chassis rails carelessly exposed to show how they had been drilled for lightness. The SSK had taken brave men to victory in races like the Mile Miglia, indeed only Mercedes had ever wrested that prize from the Italians during peacetime. Mercedes, like Rolls-Royce, built with almost excessive care but developed with assiduity. The great Grand Prix cars of the 1930s were their mobile laboratories and the lessons learned were applied with care,

especially to the chassis and suspension design. This is the area where the 540K reveals ultra-conservatism as the Mercedes design team remained faithful to leaf springs, rigid axles and settings which they already knew gave reasonable stability and predictable handling, if limited roadholding. Mercedes knew how to engineer all-independent suspension and achieve quicker handling response and higher ultimate grip in the racing cars, but only at the expense of easy handling. The improvements to the road cars would come with time. Meanwhile it was always possible to improve the owner's prestige by adding more power and torque and this was something at which during the 1930s, Mercedes was supremely good.

The standard 'big' Mercedes engine of the day was a straight-8 cylinder, an engine which resulted in a hugely impressive length of bonnet and looked marvellous when that bonnet was lifted. It could also be miraculously smooth, especially when assembled to Mercedes' standards of accuracy and was beautifully balanced and carefully engineered to avoid that bugbear of long, straight engines – the tendency for the crankshaft and camshaft to twist along their length, upsetting both balance and valve timing. The Mercedes ploy was to take the drive

from the centre of the crankshaft, thus splitting the engine into two effective four-cylinder units, each one stiff in torsion. Valve operation, naturally, was by overhead camshaft. The Mercedes designation showed, as it does to this day, the engine size. Thus the 540K has a 5.4-litre engine, having succeeded the 5-litre 500K. The company was only prevented from announcing the 580K by the outbreak of the Second World War.

Such engines produced prodigious amounts of smooth, useful power. The 540 was good for 140bhp but we are actually talking about the 540K, in which the K stands for *Kompressor* (supercharger); this was the centrifugal 'elephant' type which increased the engine's output even more at higher speeds. The performance of such cars was impressive by any standards, even those of today, although one must remember not only the power output, but also the colossal weight of such beasts and their poor aerodynamic design. The 540K's acceleration and maximum speed would have been dragged down by such characteristics though it would certainly have been a king of the autobahn, cruising at 100mph (161km/h).

It is interesting that Mercedes have never made a V-12 engine for a car; the Messerschmidt 109 power unit was something else! In pre-war Germany there was a great deal of interest in the V12 and the V12 Maybach was reckoned by some to be the true 'German Rolls-Royce'. However, Mercedes remained faithful to the straight-eight until 1939, just as they now show no sign of moving beyond a V8 for their 1980s cars.

One might also muse on the huge strength of the Mercedes design organisation, especially in the 1930s. It could maintain the most up-to-date support for the Grand Prix racing team, produce 'ultimate' sports cars like the 540K alongside grandiose luxury saloons such as the 7-litre Grosser Mercedes, and still find time to investigate novel concepts like the rear-engined 190 which was intended to be the company's budget-priced (relatively) model. In a way, though, the Mercedes situation reflects the huge technical strength of the German motor industry during the 1930s. It was a strength which produced many fine motor cars and yet had surprisingly little long-term significance apart from the Volkswagen.

1938 FIAT 508

Despite the highly original shape of Citroen's Traction Avant, there was little sign during the 1930s that car manufacturers were willing to stray very far from the established saloon car shape and move towards the designs which became familiar in the second half of the century. Adventurous moves like the Chrysler Airflow met with public disapproval and put off the other. Thus the shape of the saloon car especially of the small European saloon, remained depressingly 'upright' and faithful to the traditional running boards, semi-separate wings and headlamps perched up in their own little housings. Yet there were pre-war cars which gave the styling traces a well-judged kick and got away with it, pointing the way to the better cars of the immediate post-war era. One such car was the Fiat 508C Balilla.

The 508 series had started life in 1932 as the new 'bottom end' of the Fiat range with a simple side-valve engine of just under 1-litre capacity. Like all good small cars it tended to grow, and by 1937 it metamorphosed into the 508C with a number of important changes. Among these was an engine re-design to enlarge the unit to 1,089cc and convert it to more efficient overhead valve operation, a four-speed gearbox with synchromesh on third and top, completely re-designed chassis which amounted to a stressed box-frame, independent front suspension and a completely new body which was daring in its aspect.

The traditional saloon body of the 1930s had a bonnet which narrowed itself towards the front of the engine, and from the base of which the wings rose to cover the front wheels; the wings themselves of course usually ran aft to mate with the running-boards. The headlamps were perched above the wings and the front end of the bonnet terminated at the radiator, or a shutter

immediately in front of it. In the late 1930s, Fiat's new range of small saloons changed all that. The 508C, the larger 1500 and the delightful little 500 'Topolino' had unashamedly decorative grilles whose lower ends pushed forward towards the front bumper. Here the grille was joined by the front wings, which swept back high on the bonnet sides. Gone was the valley between bonnet and wing. As a finishing touch, the headlamps were faired directly into the front wings instead of standing proud. The end result was that the Fiat 508C, launched in 1937, still looked modern in 1957 when most of its British contemporaries were distinctly outmoded. The shape was also good from an aerodynamic point of view, and helped the Balilla attain a high maximum speed in relation to its power.

The 508C had a very different chassis: the siderails and crossmembers had been replaced by a network of welded-up channels whose shape was carefully calculated to achieve maximum stiffness for minimum weight. The 508C represents an intermediate stage in structural development acceptable to manufacturers who appreciated the lessons of Lancia's and Citroen's cars but who sought to benefit from the results without upsetting their established production methods too much. In many factories there was a chassis department, a mechanical assembly department and a body department which built the body and dropped it onto the otherwise finished product. If the body and chassis departments should be amalgamated and the mechanical assembly department adopt completely different and in many cases more difficult techniques of installation, then the new techniques had to justify colossal spending. Eventually, as far as saloon cars were concerned, the Europeans gave up and moved wholesale into unitary body construction. The Americans held out a while longer but the advanced chassis techniques of the late 1930s were not lost forever since they led directly into some of the better sports cars of the 1960s.

But to return to the 508C Balilla, the prototype of the post-war European small car. It had of course a front-engine, which drove the rear wheels through a transmission which for all its detailed sophistication – the single dry-plate clutch, the synchromesh in the gearbox – owed a great deal to Panhard-Levassor and Renault. Engine design had settled down. For small cars, four cylinders were the norm and thoughts of expensive overhead camshafts, as in the little Morris which gave rise to the MG Midget, had been rejected in favour of pushrods and overhead valves. The typical 1-litre engine of the period produced about 30bhp at 5,000rpm and breathed through a single, now much improved

carburettor; the spark was provided by a coil-and-distributor system, for the magneto had already faded from the scene.

The 508C is a reminder that the 'beam' front axle was also on the way out and even before the Second World War any car with ambitions to be thought of as technically advanced, needed to have independent front suspension. Independent rear suspension had to wait a good deal longer. The 508C suspension is interesting because each upper member of its double wishbone arrangement acted as a lever-arm on a neatly combined coil spring and hydraulic damper enclosed in a steel-tube oil bath; the system survived in some Fiat models until the mid-1950s. Naturally, the rear suspension stuck to the good old multi-leaf 'cart' springs. Outside of racing cars, there was very little interest in any alternative until well after 1945, with the obvious exception of the Volkswagen.

In other ways too, the 508C shows that a pattern had been established which was not to be broken until the 1950s. There were hydraulically-operated drum-brakes on all wheels, worm and sector steering – Citroen's use of rack-and-pinion had done nothing to endear it to anyone else – and cross-ply tyres on the steel-disc wheels that had taken over because they were so cheap to make. This kind of attention to detail was to remain constant even as manufacturers rethought the shape of the small family car.

1939 VOLKSWAGEN

The German motor industry of the 1930s was technically strong and efficient, it made a wide variety of cars from the massive Grosser Mercedes down to well-built small models like those from DKW and Wanderer in the Audi combine. The one item that was missing was a car both cheap and practical enough to be universally available: a German car to rival the achievement of the Ford Model T in the USA or the Austin Seven in Britain. The decision was taken and the car designed. Furthermore it would not merely be cheap enough to bring motoring within the reach of every German citizen; it would also show sufficient technical achievement to be the envy of the world.

In 1934 this uncompromising requirement was thrown at Dr Ferdinand Porsche, from whose drawing-board had come the fearsome rear-engined Auto Union Grand Prix cars that fought with Mercedes. Porsche responded with a design of startling originality. As his racing cars testified, Porsche had long believed the best place for a car's engine was at the back. There are good and convincing reasons for this: assuming the back wheels are those which are driven, then the entire engine and transmission can be combined into a single light, efficient unit with no wasteful length or weight of propeller shaft. By placing this unit at the back rather than the front of the car, as Citroen had done, Porsche avoided all the complication and expense of mixing drive shafts with steering: constant-velocity joints and components of that kind. The weight of the engine was placed squarely over the driven wheels for good traction and, since the effective weight of a car tends to shift forward under braking, the car had good braking balance.

All this Porsche knew and had tried in his racing cars. However, for his People's Car – his 'Volkswagen' – he had also to design a new engine and a new saloon car structure. His engine design philosophy was twofold. Firstly, the unit must be simple and reliable; secondly, it must have a very long service life. He met the first need above all by making his engine air cooled: a startling innovation when the vast majority of motor car engines were water-cooled. Porsche was also original in choosing a flat-four layout for this engine – two pairs of cylinders directly opposing each other – when the in-line four was the universal choice for small-car propulsion. His reasoning was that the flat-four shape was more compact for back-end installation and also easier to cool with air blown across the cylinder heads by a large engine-driven fan. With an in-line engine, it would have been difficult to avoid the fourth cylinder running hotter than the first. It was an equally adventurous move to make as much of the engine as possible out of light alloy instead of cast-iron:

it added to the cost but by reducing weight, made the car more efficient and at least postponed the day when the disadvantages of rear engine mounting became apparent.

As for making the engine last a long time, Porsche hit upon a very simple expedient. He installed an extremely small carburettor which caused the engine to 'choke' if it was taken beyond a certain speed. Thus the Volkswagen in standard form could, as post-war road testers discovered, be driven 'flat-out all day'. The artificial restriction of maximum engine speed meant that the Volkswagen engine seemed inefficient in terms of power output per litre of capacity, especially after the war, though its light weight meant that its power-per-pound was more reasonable. There was another advantage in Porsche's design approach: the small choke meant the fuel/air mixture entered the cylinders at high speed even when the engine was running slowly, and this gave the car excellent flexibility and low-speed pulling power.

The Volkswagen's body consisted essentially of a strong 'pontoon' platform with the front suspension attached to one end and the main mechanical unit at the other. The characteristic Volkswagen body shape, which years later became universally known as the 'Beetle' was built up on this but played little part in the car's structural strength. The shape actually resulted from Porsche's interest in aerodynamics which led him to realise that reduced drag would enable the car to be driven along Germany's expanding network of autobahns at a very reasonable speed considering how little power it had: the 1937 prototypes, which were actually assembled by Mercedes, had engines of only 704cc, though this was quickly increased to 984cc before production began.

Another of Porsche's master-strokes was to make the suspension all-independent. This was much easier to achieve with a rear-engined design since the rear suspension had to be independent anyway and Porsche achieved front independent suspension by using a peculiar but effective double trailing-arm arrangement. Following the example of Citroen, he used a torsion-bar springing for all four wheels. However, it was his choice of the rear suspension system, the simple and cheap swing-axle system, which provided the Volkswagen with its biggest single drawback.

In this system, the car's rear wheels are located by the drive shafts themselves, being attached to hubs at the shaft outer ends, and located fore and aft by simple trailing arms. This is a simple and elegant system which appears to have much to recommend it, since it reduces the number of drive shaft joints which are needed and avoids the need to allow for any change in

shaft length with suspension movement. The drawback is that it leads to the rear wheels to assume angles which are very bad for the car's handling and stability. This is especially the case where the rear end rises 'on tiptoe' with both wheels tucked partly underneath on a very narrow track. The effect was made worse by the car's rearward weight bias and its shape, which made it easily disturbed by crosswinds.

Production of the Volkswagen Beetle failed to get properly under way before 1939 but during the late 1940s the huge Wolfsburg factory was completely rebuilt and began to produce the car in very large numbers. The reasons for its sales success are many, though they have less to do with the product itself than the skill with which it was marketed and supported in service. It is true that compared with many of the immediate post-war European small cars, the Beetle looked refreshingly new and interesting. Other 40s designs were strongly reminiscent of pre-war days, indeed, in 1946, the British motor industry simply put back into production the cars it had been making up to 1939. In Germany Volkswagen was helped by being the only major domestic producer of small, cheap cars since Ford and General Motors (Opel), who owned Germany's other main mass-production car factories, made no attempt to enter this lowest market sector.

The Beetle's independent suspension made it more comfortable than any leaf-sprung car and Dr Porsche had had the foresight to fit a powerful heater as standard. This heater re-cycled the generous quantities of warm air emerging from the engine cooling system and was a major attraction at a time when the heaters in most small cars were optional extras. Then again, there was the appeal of its 'unburstable' engine and outstanding reliability.

However, the Beetle did have drawbacks; it was slower than average, by no means outstandingly economical, and was not especially cheap in most of its markets – especially once the West German Mark became stronger. As time went on, more people realised too the serious problems which afflicted its stability and handling and criticised features such as its poor luggage space. Volkswagen progressively improved the car in detail to meet some of the criticisms, but until 1970 the company adhered rigidly to the basic formula: the rear mounted, air-cooled flat-four engine. It even built two larger cars with the same layout, but neither was a success. In the end, demand for the Beetle fell dramatically in its major export market, the USA, and the resulting loss of earnings was almost the end of Volkswagen, but fortunately the company came up with an outstandingly good and completely different replacement design.

Yet the popular Beetle legend would not altogether die and even in the 1980s the car is made in Volkswagen's Mexican factory. The car is an example of how an accident in history can turn an adventurous design with at least as many bad as good points, into a major success. Yet despite its success, most aspects of car design eventually moved in a completely opposite direction.

Above: Dr Ferdinand Porsche pictured here with his own 1939 Volkswagen

Volkswagen Beetle
Country of origin: West Germany
Date: 1939
Engine: four cylinders, horizontally opposed;
overhead valve; rear engine; air-cooled; 3,300rpm
Capacity: 1,131cc
Maximum Speed: 62mph (100km/h)
Chassis: front suspension independently by
double trailing-arm arrangement; rear
suspension independent by swing-axle system
Brakes: cable-operated drum brakes

1948 CITROEN 2CV

Shortly after Dr Porsche received his design brief for the Volkswagen Beetle another design team received its own set of instructions to set about preparing an all-new car. The result of those instructions was another extremely unusual vehicle, one which was almost as much of a sales success as the Beetle and in its own way even more prolific, for it continued in production in its original French factory through to the late 1980s. That car was Citroen's 2CV.

The seed of the 2CV was sown when Citroen was still reeling from its financial collapse, the death of its founder and a takeover by the Michelin Tyre company. The Michelin-appointed managing director, Monsieur Boulanger, saw an opportunity to produce a rugged, low-cost car which would appeal to the large French peasant farming community. With a touch of genius far removed from that of the Volkswagen's prime mover, he asked his designers to build him 'a powered platform, with four seats and an umbrella capable of carrying a basket of eggs across a ploughed field without breaking'.

The designers set to work and came up with a concept which bore a few uncanny resemblances to the Volkswagen. Citroen's new engine was also air-cooled and horizontally opposed, while the car also consisted of a self-supporting 'pontoon' floor to which the mechanical parts were attached, and upon which the body was erected.

There the resemblance ended, not least because its tiny engine of just 375cc capacity and 9bhp output, had only two cylinders and was installed at the front of the car. So small, light and low was the engine that the Citroen engineers had no need to place it aft of the front axle, as in the Traction Avant. Citroen designed the engine to be very strong indeed but should major repair work be necessary, the whole 'works' could easily be lifted out of the chassis by two men. The car's reliability was due to its rotating assembly – the crankshaft and connecting rods – being built up from machined components which were shrink-fitted by heating and cooling. There were no bolts: once the thing was together, it was together for good. There was no distributor, just a contact breaker on the crankshaft nose. The generator was also driven directly by the crankshaft. The original car had no starter motor either, only a starting handle – shades of the 1900s.

So low was the power and performance that the Citroen engineers did not even bother with constant-velocity joints for the drive shafts though these were introduced later, along with a starter motor and other creature comforts. The drive was taken through a three-speed gearbox, producing a maximum speed of 30mph (48km/h), but the 2CV achieved almost 60mpg (25km/l).

The greatest feature of the car, proved to be its suspension. The engineers took the basket of eggs challenge very seriously indeed and the result of their deliberations was a suspension system in which each wheel was jointed to a corner of the platform chassis by a single huge swinging arm; leading arms at the front, trailing at the back. The pair of arms on each side was joined by a single huge spring mounted lengthwise in a tube. There were no hydraulic dampers but rather a clever arrangement of weights attached to the swinging arms, sprung so as to oppose the basic motion: the so-called 'inertia dampers'. The amount of wheel travel was huge and the 2CV really did fulfil its ploughed-field specification. Also, although it rolled enough to look as though it was about to fall over, it proved to have tenacious roadholding and very safe handling.

The 2CV steering was by rack and pinion, and it was equipped with hydraulically operated brakes at the front and mechanical ones at the back. Citroen, then and now, insist on the

handbrake operating on the front rather than the rear wheels and on using narrow Michelin tyres on big steel-disc wheels. Most unusual looking of all, though, was the body which resembled a flimsy corrugated-tin shed with four small doors and a canvas roof which rolled back to accept awkwardly long loads. Utilitarian was the only word to describe the 2CV which was also equipped with plain steel-tube and canvas hammock-type seats. The whole object of the 2CV was to be as light, cheap, reliable and economical as possible, and in that object it admirably succeeded.

Citroen prepared 250 2CVs for a 1939 Paris Motor Show that never happened and all but one were destroyed before the Germans invaded. The survivor, hidden until the 1944 liberation, is now lovingly preserved. Unfortunately, the same care has not been accorded to many of the other 7 million-odd 2CVs built since its eventual 1948 launch, and most of them have been driven flat-out and generally mistreated just as Pierre Boulanger foresaw.

Like the Traction Avant before it, the 2CV proved above all that front wheel drive could be made to work well, in a variety of cars, and that was a valuable lesson in itself. It also showed the need to distinguish carefully between springing and damping of wheel movement, and indeed proved that safe handling can always be achieved by making sure each pair of wheels remains parallel no matter what the rest of the car may be doing. The 2CV has also proved that there exists a large market for any car which is cheap enough and offers enough benefits to excuse its crudity.

A recent Citroen managing director was of the opinion that the only way to replace the 2CV would be to return to Pierre Boulanger's original specification and start all over again with the benefit of modern methods and materials. It may be that Citroen engineers are doing just so at this moment.

Citroën 2CV
Country of origin: France
Date: 1953
Engine: two-cylinders horizontally opposed;
9bhp at 3,800rpm; 4.76hp; Solex carburettor
Gears: three-speed; front-wheel drive
Capacity: 375cc
Bore & Stroke: 62 × 62mm
Maximum Speed: 30mph (48km/h)
Chassis: suspension front and rear by
horizontal coil
Dimensions: wheelbase 7ft 9½in (237cm);
            track (front) 4ft 1⅝in (126cm);
            track (rear) 4ft 1⅝in (126cm)
Brakes: hydraulic on all wheels

1948 MORRIS MINOR

British motor industry picked up after the Second World War by restarting the production lines of its 1939 models. It was not a state of affairs that could last for ever, though some companies spun it out for a long time with the aid of styling 'facelifts'. Morris Motors realised that it needed a new small car and immediately the war was over Alec Issigonis, one of its senior engineers, was commissioned to produce one. The result of his efforts was the Morris Minor. The Minor, launched in 1948, became a classic in its own way like the Beetle and the Citroen 2CV, though for other and equally instructive reasons.

If the Beetle succeeded because it was simple and reliable, and the 2CV because it was tough and cheap, then the Minor survived on the production lines for over 20 years with more than a million examples because it was above all, easy and rewarding to drive. Issigonis was a keen driver himself with something of a record of competition success, and he was determined that within the limits imposed by designing in post-war Britain, he would produce a stable and enjoyable vehicle, which would be a pleasure to handle.

The limitations involved meant that the designer had to use the ancient and inefficient Morris side-valve four cylinder engine of 918cc, because there was neither the time nor the money to develop anything better. That engine had to drive through a conventional transmission system of the type favoured by Panhard

and Renault, to a live rear axle suspended on and located by the multi-leaf spring. Issigonis achievements can be characterised in two ways: he adopted a more efficient unitary body construction and by engineering the car's front suspension, he produced an improved kind of handling.

For several reasons Issigonis decided to make the Minor much wider than the cars it was supposed to replace. Firstly the extra width would mean that it was easier to make this new unitary body stiff in torsion (that is, able to resist twisting forces) if he made it wider; a large-diameter tube is more difficult to twist than a narrower one. The designer was sure the answer to achieving good steering and handling, especially with independent suspension, lay in keeping the body stiff to prevent movements other than those designed into the suspension system. Secondly, a wider body meant a wider wheel track and that in turn meant greater roll stiffness, that is resistance to body roll during cornering. That was admirable because the less the roll, the less the suspension movement and the chance of upsetting the handling. Finally, the wider body – combined with much more modern styling than anything previously seen from Britain's family car producers – meant a wide and comfortable cabin which would prove to be a strong selling point.

Alec Issigonis achieved his high-quality front suspension through careful combination of existing techniques and components. He chose to use double-wishbone suspension geometry, skilfully calculated to make sure the front wheels never did anything untoward. He sprung the wheels by lengthwise torsion bars, firmly anchored in his unitary body and in the lower suspension arms. The upper arms he made into the levers of the Armstrong hydraulic dampers. Finally, he fitted rack and pinion steering. Issigonis was certainly not shooting in the dark with any of these developments. In particular, Morris Motors had taken over the old British firm of Riley, whose pre-war cars – the respected 1½-litre and its sisters – had proved the worth of the torsion bar system and of rack and pinion steering. The genius of the Minor was to combine all these things in a small car that was good enough to outshine the drawback of its engine and rear suspension.

Certainly the Minor was rapturously received at its 1948 launch and everyone who drove it was enchanted by the precision of its steering and at that time, few British 'family' drivers had ever had the chance to experience the rack-and-pinion system. Its braking system was entirely conventional but again, the chassis design made the most of it.

The Minor had 14-inch (35.6cm) wheels,

which would be considered very large for a car of its size and power output today, but it is arguable whether smaller wheels would have improved the car very much: the main influence in favour of smaller wheels in the last thirty years has been the wish to gain more body space by making the wheel arches smaller – a process which Issigonis himself eventually took to its logical conclusion. Whatever its wheel size, the Minor's unitary construction made it lighter than most cars in its class, especially when the cabin space was taken into account and that lightness enabled it to achieve reasonable performance and good economy despite its engine.

One of the drawbacks of unitary construction showed up when Morris wanted to make the Minor into a convertible, a good commercial move because the version sold well. Substantial frames had to be added beneath the floor, to take the bending stresses no longer passing through the roof. Yet the conversion was a success, as was

the Minor's change of style into one of the better-loved small estate cars of the 1950s.

What are the anatomy lessons to be learnt from the Minor? Firstly, as was mentioned previously, one should not under-estimate sheer pleasure and ease of driving as factors in establishing the car as a favourite. In combination with or even instead of such things as beauty, reliability or economy, ease of driving can be an influential reason for the cars popularity. The Minor, which suffered its way through some of the least praiseworthy years of the British motor industry, was certainly not renowned for reliability. Secondly, that good results can be achieved by a determined and clear-sighted designer even when his freedom of action is limited by consideration of time or budget, as long as he is able to exploit one or two real technical advances and concentrate on certain areas of special significance, like the Minor's body construction and front suspension.

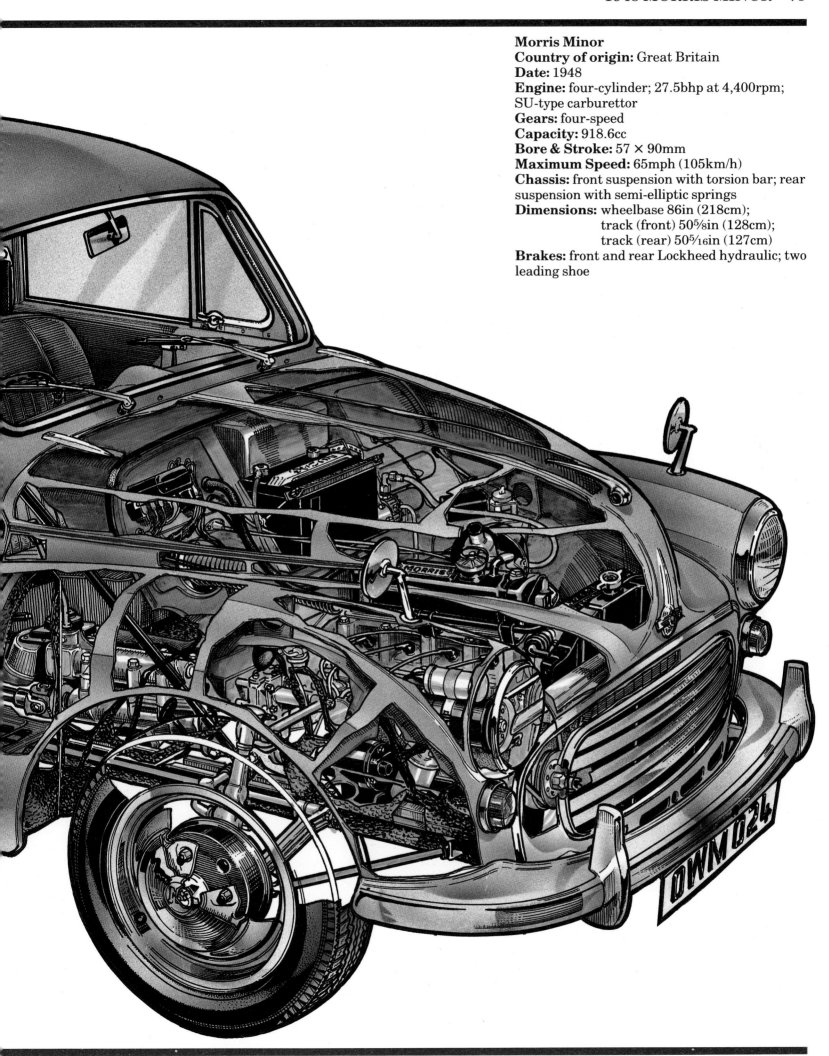

Morris Minor
Country of origin: Great Britain
Date: 1948
Engine: four-cylinder; 27.5bhp at 4,400rpm;
SU-type carburettor
Gears: four-speed
Capacity: 918.6cc
Bore & Stroke: 57 × 90mm
Maximum Speed: 65mph (105km/h)
Chassis: front suspension with torsion bar; rear
suspension with semi-elliptic springs
Dimensions: wheelbase 86in (218cm);
track (front) 50⅝in (128cm);
track (rear) 50⁵⁄₁₆in (127cm)
Brakes: front and rear Lockheed hydraulic; two
leading shoe

1955 CITROEN DS

The DS, like the other two Citroens already mentioned, was front-driven. Like them, it caused a major sensation when first shown in public, though for different reasons, for by 1955, people were used to Citroens being front-driven, indeed the Traction Avant was already twenty years old and an established classic. This time Citroen set out to achieve a tour de force and they succeeded probably more than any car manufacturer since by producing a car that surprised everyone both in technical content and appearance.

The impact of the Citroen DS lay in its form: it was not merely modern, but totally avant-garde

and quite deliberately so. The smooth, wide sweep of its nose meant that there was no visible radiator air intake, instead it was hidden underneath the bumper. Such oddities were all very well for the Volkswagen Beetle, which everybody knew was air-cooled and had its engine at the back, but what was Citroen up to? In fact, the design of the car diverted attention away from the startling truth that the futuristic DS had much the same transmission layout and 1930s vintage pushrod ohv engine as the old Traction Avant. Once again the engine was aft of the front axle, the gearbox was forward of it, and the two were joined by a shaft running bridge-like above the differential casing. This type of layout, seen either at the front or the back of a car, became known as the 'transaxle' because it combined gearbox and back axle into a single unit.

The DS body shape, swelling out from the extreme nose towards the front of the cabin and then tapering towards a slim-hipped rear with no properly defined boot – a distinctly peculiar feature to 1955 eyes – represented a real effort to come to terms with low-drag aerodynamics in a way that had never been tried before in a production car. It was no fault of Citroen's considering the almost total ignorance of the subject in the motor industry before they started, that it took several years of further work and modification before the DS body eventually achieved its drag target. Needless to say the body construction was unitary just like that of the Traction Avant, but the suspension was different. The front wheels were each located by two curved arms that reached forward from the bulkhead, giving the same suspension geometry as equal-length wishbones but in a peculiar-looking way. The back wheels were attached to trailing arms. The whole layout meant that all the wheels leaned over at the same angle as the body when it rolled on cornering just as in the 2CV. The DS like its far smaller confrere offered excellent roadholding and secure handling at some cost in the willingness of the body to heel over when cornered hard. That did not stop the DS from becoming a formidable, if large, rally car, in the early 1960s.

However it was on close examination of the suspension mechanism that the wonders of the DS really came to light. There were no proper springs or dampers, instead the car had a completely new system in which both functions were fulfilled by small hydraulic struts, run at very high internal pressure, with a gas-filled space above the fluid. Many were the doubters until the first road tests showed how wonderfully effective this system could be. Eventually the DS came to be the standard by which the ride comfort of cars could be measured. Not content with this,

Citroen had taken the same high-pressure hydraulic supply delivered by an engine-driven pump and used it to power operate both the brakes and the steering! The history of the Traction Avant almost repeated itself in that the DS offered a rather odd automatic transmission, but eventually most of those sold had four-speed manual gearboxes of the traditional type.

The DS launched yet another highly significant motoring development, though it was almost lost amid the fuss caused by the car's shape and its high pressure hydraulics. The wheels carried a completely new type of tyre, the Michelin X. For 60 years, ever since the birth of the pneumatic tyre, the accepted method of construction had been to build up the tyre carcase with layers of rubberised cloth at an angle, forming a trellis-pattern in the sidewalls. Now Michelin offered this new tyre in which the cloth 'plies' ran radially from the centre of the tyre and were held together by a circumferential 'belt' around the tread. This new radial-ply tyre was one of the secrets of the DS ride and roadholding, and in the course of the next 15 years it completely usurped the traditional cross-ply tyre as far as cars were concerned. It was in its way a rather more significant feature of the car than any other, because no other manufacturer has yet gone so far as Citroen in adopting high pressure hydraulics as an effective and economical answer to the problems of suspension design, brake and steering operation. In that respect, the DS was a prophet without honour, at least for a while. However Citroen's own faith in the system has meant that they have included these innovations on the GS, CX and BX. Meanwhile the DS remains acknowledged as a pioneer in low-drag body design.

So what is to be learned from the DS? The car was by no means a failure, since it sold well over a million examples and remained in production for twenty years. That in itself is a tribute to the soundness of its design, especially as the car was considerably larger and more expensive than the average European model. Yet many of its advanced features have never been adopted by any other major manufacturer, and this suggests that if the car's anatomy is developed too quickly then there is a danger of outrunning the market and finding that the work is of less significance than one had hoped.

Citroën DS 19
Country of origin: France
Date: 1955
Engine: four-cylinders in-line; 75bhp at
4,500rpm push-rod operated overhead valve;
Zenith-type carburettor
Gears: four-speed; automatic clutch;
hydraulically controlled
Capacity: 1,911cc
Bore & Stroke: 78 × 100mm
Maximum Speed: 100mph (161km/h)
Chassis: front and rear suspension independent
with hydropneumatic units on all rear wheels;
built-in shock absorbers
Dimensions: wheelbase 10ft 3in (312cm);
track (front) 4ft 11$\frac{1}{16}$ in (150cm);
track (rear) 4ft 3$\frac{1}{4}$in (130cm);
Brakes: front/disc; rear/drum

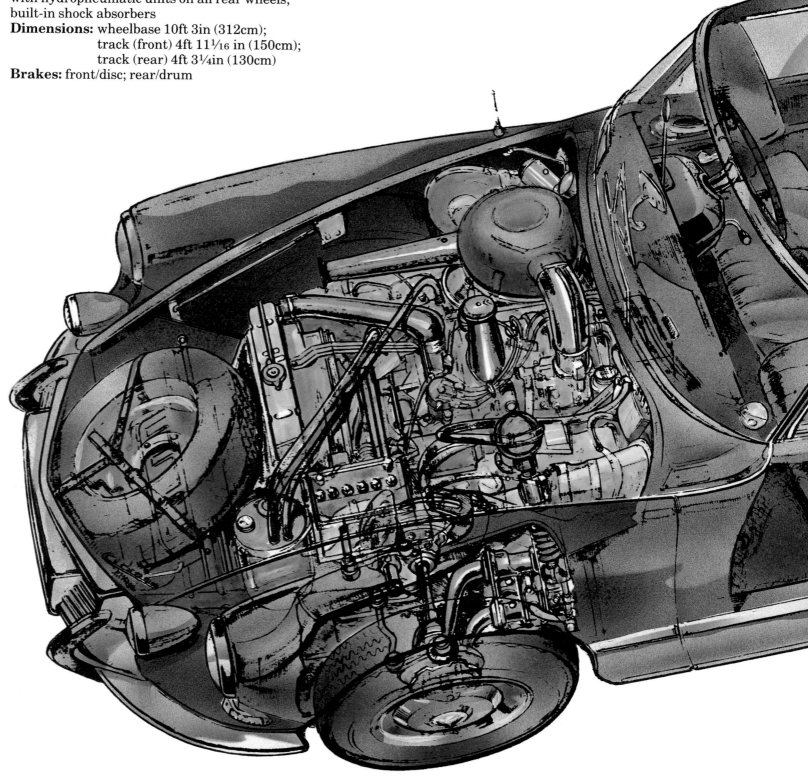

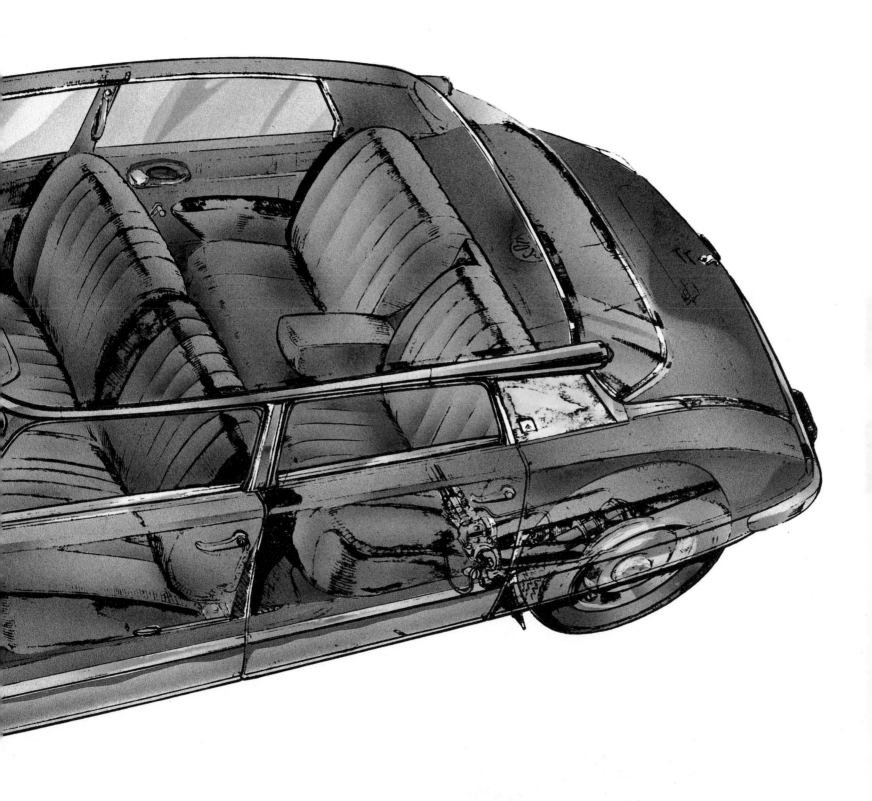

1958 TOYOTA CORONA

This is the first but certainly not the last Japanese car on the list. It is included mainly as an example of the kind of vehicle with which the Japanese built up their industry after the ravages of war. It was, at first sight, an extremely ordinary kind of car, with a simple pushrod ohv engine of modest output from its 1.3-litres, driving through a three-speed manual gearbox with a steering column gearchange, to a live back axle. That back axle was hung on leaf springs; the front suspension was double-wishbone. Drum brakes were fitted all round. The body was of unitary construction and its size places the car neatly alongside the middle-market European cars of its time: the Morris Oxford perhaps, or the Fiat 1300. Its anatomy was wholly unremarkable except to illustrate that the Japanese based the products of their recovering industry on existing, well-proven technology. They were not going to take any chances.

Like the Europeans, the Japanese feared after the war that the American car manufacturers would flood their country with cheap exports. They reckoned even then that it was less likely that the Americans would build smaller cars, so that was the area upon which the two Japanese giants-to-be – Toyota and Nissan/Datsun – concentrated. The cars which were imported to Japan during the first few years after the war were large American models. As as result the first Japanese cars resembled American vehicles shrunk to European size which certainly explains some of their main features and in particular the total lack of advanced features in the area of transmission or suspension.

Toyota's first post-war model proper was the Crown, launched in 1955 as a 1.5-litre medium-sized car. However, commencing a trend which has been constantly reflected within the Japanese industry, the Crown quickly began to grow. Today its successor is a large car by European standards with engines ranging from 2.0 to 2.8-litre capacity. As the Crown grew in popularity, it created the opportunity for another medium-sized model, the Corona, to be introduced into the market. Some time later both the Crown and the Corona had in their turn grown large enough to create space for the Corolla, which was destined eventually to become the best-selling single model motor car in the world.

At this stage, the Corona was hardly a suitable car for export. Toyota admits that when it tried to export the Crown to the USA in 1958, the venture failed miserably because the car simply was not engineered to withstand American conditions. The problem was that Japanese driving conditions (then as now) could hardly have been more different with narrow and badly overcrowded roads, generally short journeys, very low speed limits and lack of space for parking. Cars developed for such conditions were bound to fare badly in the land of the interstate freeway and the universal parking

The Toyota Corona 2000 Estate.

The Toyota Corona Saloon of the 1970s.

lot. Toyota's response to this failure provides an insight into the kind of practice that led to Japanese eventual success. The company withdrew from the USA for six years while it carried out a detailed study of American requirements and engineered new models to suit them. The Corona was a very early model and as it appeared before the programme was undertaken it therefore represents Japanese thoughts in their original form. Even at this early stage, all of the cars vital accessory parts were made in Japan. The carburettor, the coil ignition system and sparking plugs; the generator together with the rest of the electrical system and the telescopic dampers prove that Japan was quickly out developing a national industry capable of making its mark on the automotive anatomy.

Ultimately, the Japanese success was mainly due to their willingness to learn and adapt so as to be able to engineer cars for conditions which simply did not exist in Japan. Added to this was an appreciation of the reasons why the Volkswagen Beetle sold so well, especially in the USA. Consequently, Japanese engineers devoted themselves to quality control in order to achieve similarly high standards of reliability and produced cars which were not only more familiar in design but easier to drive than the Beetle. It was only later, when such goals had been achieved, that firms like Toyota and Nissan/Datsun sought to open completely new markets and to indulge in genuine technical advance with impressive results.

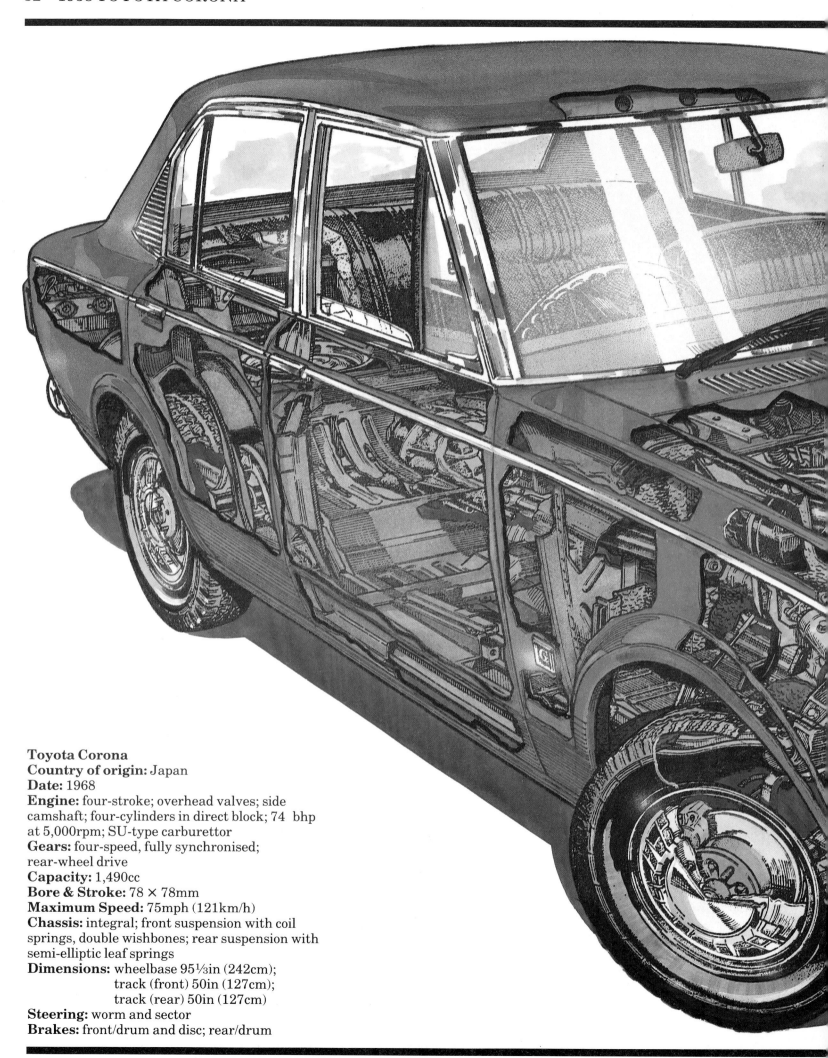

Toyota Corona
Country of origin: Japan
Date: 1968
Engine: four-stroke; overhead valves; side
camshaft; four-cylinders in direct block; 74 bhp
at 5,000rpm; SU-type carburettor
Gears: four-speed, fully synchronised;
rear-wheel drive
Capacity: 1,490cc
Bore & Stroke: 78 × 78mm
Maximum Speed: 75mph (121km/h)
Chassis: integral; front suspension with coil
springs, double wishbones; rear suspension with
semi-elliptic leaf springs
Dimensions: wheelbase 95⅓in (242cm);
　　　　　　track (front) 50in (127cm);
　　　　　　track (rear) 50in (127cm)
Steering: worm and sector
Brakes: front/drum and disc; rear/drum

1959 MORRIS MINI

The Mini was the result of the first great energy crisis of our time, caused by the Suez Canal crisis in 1956. At that time the management of BMC, the company formed by the amalgamation of Austin and Morris, decided that a new economy car was needed for the range and gave the task to Alec Issigonis, the designer of the Morris Minor. He decided the time was ripe to try a new approach to the question of the 'minimum car'. His aim was to build a full four-seater saloon which would nevertheless occupy no more road space than some of the tiny European economy-specials of the day. It was hoped that the car would also offer good performance and excellent roadworthiness – areas in which the bubble-car brigade were generally lacking.

The key to the project, as Issigonis saw it, was to ensure that the engine and transmission took up as little space as possible, leaving the rest of the car free for passengers. From this notion grew the idea of mounting the engine across the car and integrating it closely with the transmission. The engine/transmission pack would have to go at the front of the car, because enough was now known about the stability problems of rear-engined cars to dissuade Issigonis (himself a keen and skilful driver) to have anything to do with that layout. Besides, studies soon showed that more space was saved through having the engine at the front of the car than trying to stow it under the back seat.

The Mini therefore took shape between 1957 and 1958. Its engine was a version of the A-series four-cylinder pushrod ohv unit by then installed in the Morris Minor, driving through a single-plate clutch and a spur transfer gear arrangement to a four-speed manual gearbox installed in the engine's sump and sharing its lubricant. A further spur gear then took the drive aft to the differential, whence it was fed through shafts with constant-velocity joints to the front wheels. It was claimed afterwards that the layout was not entirely original – Fiat's chief engineer pointed to drawings he had made of similar layout in the late 1930's – but the fact remained that the Mini was in production and Fiat's principal rival of the time was the rear-engined 600.

The Mini's body was little more than a box for its four occupants, with another much smaller box attached to the front to house the engine. Construction was of course unitary, although the Mini also made use of 'sub-frames' bolted to the main body front and rear to act as the principal attachments for the engine and transmission assembly at the front, and the rear suspension. The chosen suspension geometry was double-wishbone at the front and trailing arms at the rear, while springing was by means of bonded rubber units invented by Alex Moulton. A feature of the car was its use of very small 10-inch (25cm) wheels with the object of taking up as little of the available space as possible with wheel arches. Considering the small overall size, the wheels actually looked well in proportion with the rest of the car. Drum brakes were used all round and an unusual feature of the system was the installation of a pressure limiting valve in the rear brake line to prevent premature locking of the lightly laden rear wheels. This system was later employed by most front driven cars. Given the effective forward weight transfer of a car under braking, the front brakes of a front-engined, front-driven car exert up to 80 per cent of the total braking effort. Issigonis did not hesitate to use rack and pinion steering for the Mini and his instincts as a driver led him to make it very 'quick' with well under three turns of the wheel between the extremes of a better-than average turning circle.

The Mini was a huge success not only in meeting its design aims but also in having an effect on the shape of cars to come. Thanks to its small size and consequently light weight, it did indeed achieve acceptable performance and excellent economy with an engine producing typical baby-saloon power (34bhp). Thanks to the ingenuity of its layout, it did indeed seat four adults in reasonable comfort, even if the luggage space left something to be desired. And

thanks to Issigonis' determination to buck the then fashionable trend and adopt front wheel drive, the Mini also managed to set new standards of stability and handling quality for cars in its class. The contrast with the rear-engined Beetle, Fiat 600 and Renault Dauphine could not have been more marked. It must have been profoundly upsetting for those European design teams with other rear-engined projects too far along the line to be halted. The next five years saw the launch of the Hillman Imp, the Fiat 850 and the Simca 1000 among others but none of these had the handling and stability of the Mini.

There was in effect a breathing-space while other designers took in what Alec Issigonis had achieved, but within a few years other major European manufacturers were building their own small and medium-sized cars with transverse engines and front-wheel drive, BMC itself embraced the concept wholeheartedly, perhaps too much so – in the next few years the company built another three larger cars with same mechanical layout. The first was an outstanding success but the latter were two arguable failures and not just because of the manner of engine installation.

If there was a single Mini feature, which was not accepted by other designers, it was Issigonis' use of a sump-mounted gearbox which gave rise to several problems, including those of intermediate gear noise and of access for service. In most respects though the Mini goes down as one of the few cars, even among those listed here

In most respects though, the Mini goes down as one of the few cars, even among those listed here, which have literally changed the shape of the motor car. Among its other achievements, it virtually was the demise of the small sports car like the successors of the MG M-type. The faster Cooper and Cooper S forms of the Mini could easily outperform and outhandle the Sprites and Midgets of their day and equally important, they were just as much fun to drive. The Mini was still in production three decades after its layout was finalised. It was a truly significant car.

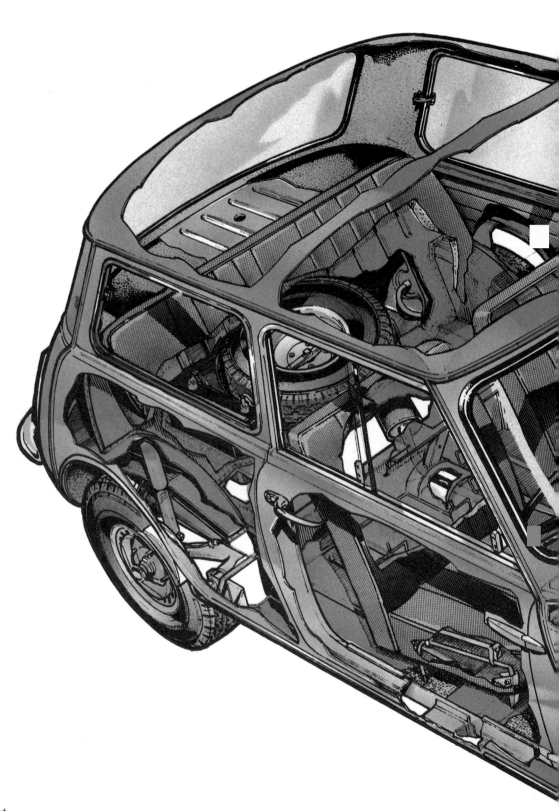

Morris Mini
Country of origin: Great Britain
Date: 1958
Engine: four-cylinder of 9.8bhp; 37bhp at
5,500rpm: SU-type carburettor
Gears: four-speed, synchromesh on 2nd, 3rd and
top
Capacity: 848cc
Bore & Stroke: 63 × 68.3mm
Maximum Speed: 70mph (113km/h)
Chassis: independent suspension front and rear
with rubber cones and tubular telescopic dampers
Dimensions: wheelbase 6ft 8in (203cm);
             track (front) 47¾in (121cm);
             track (rear) 45⅞in (116cm)
Brakes: front and back single leading shoe

1961 RENAULT 4

Where the French motor industry was concerned, Renault had spent many years in the shadow of Citroen. Even after the Second World War, when the company was nationalised and could count on whatever financial and moral support it needed, it tended to be outshone by Citroen's technical brilliance. Citroen won the heart of the French farmer with the 2CV, and then bolstered its reputation for technical leadership with the production of the DS. The majority of French policemen drove their patrols in the Traction Avant and even their villains were taken away in Citroen vans whose body panels bore the unmistakable corrugated-tin mark of the 2VC.

Against this background, post-war Renault set out to provide cars which fitted the yawning gap between the little Citroens and the big ones: it was never obvious to outsiders why for well over twenty years Citroen offered no car with an engine size larger than 602cc but smaller than 1985cc. Renault began by offering small family cars with neat four-cylinder ohv engines mounted at the rear, like the Volkswagen Beetle: the 4CV gained a lot of friends and the Regie Renault extended the formula to the Dauphine, an attractive four-door model which after its 1958 introduction quickly began to sell in very large numbers. Alas, the success of the Dauphine was illusory; its sales slumped almost as quickly as they had risen, especially in the USA, and alarming tales began to spread about its unreliability and the tendency of its body to rust. Renault continued to build medium-sized rear-engined cars for some years but it was obvious that a new approach was needed.

The company decided to break completely away from the Dauphine mould and to move towards Citroen's prime market – that of the 2CV. It was felt that after ten years of an improving national economy, many buyers would be ready for a car with the same essential utilitarian character, but also with a little more refinement and power such as would be offered

by a four-cylinder engine.

The car which emerged was evidence of that philosophy. Like the 2CV, it was built on a very strong 'pontoon' platform as the foundation for an essentially unstressed body built up from a few panels bolted together. Like the 2CV it had a very soft suspension system with plenty of wheel travel so that it could traverse bad roads and open country without discomfort. Like the 2CV – but for the first time as far as Renault was concerned – it used a front wheel drive. The car was simply called the Renault 4.

However, the Renault 4 was not a slavish copy of its Citroen rival and it introduced several new features of interest. Because Renault elected to use a water-cooled four-cylinder engine they could not, like Citroen, hang the unit ahead of the front wheels. Small and lacking in power it was surprisingly long and too heavy and it bore a close resemblance to the old rear-engined 4CV, having a capacity of only 747cc and an output of just 24bhp. Renault therefore tried the only solution which seemed possible and aped the arrangement seen in Citroen's bigger cars with the engine immediately ahead of the cabin, driving the front wheels forward through a transaxle. Consequently a Citroen-style gearchange also had to be introduced resembling an umbrella-handle sticking through the middle of the dashboard. The gearbox itself was a simple three-speed unit and spindly drive shafts with doubled-up universal joints carried the power to the front wheels.

Renault clearly could not bring themselves to adopt a suspension so simple yet so radical as Citroen's but instead proved that something more conventional could equally do the job. The Renault 4 was therefore given a double wishbone arrangement at the front which was more reminiscent of the Traction Avant than of the 2CV and which had simple trailing arms at the rear. Even more significant was Renault's use of torsion-bar springs which were set along the car at the front (rather like Issigonis' Morris Minor) and across it at the back. This was a major breakaway for the company, as they had previously stuck to coil springs for their rear-engined cars. The Renault suspension looked more conventional than Citroen's, but it soon proved that it was almost as capable of providing an uncannily smooth cross-country ride. Also, like the Citroen it allowed the car's body to lean over at alarming angles, yet the handing was safe and the roadholding good. The steering was rack-and-pinion and the R4 was an early convert to the Michelin X radial-ply tyre.

However, it was in the design of its body that the R4 was perhaps the greatest pointer of

The Renault 4CV was a predecessor to the Renault 4.

things to come. Its utilitarian shape included a large, top-hinged rear door. At the time people called it an 'estate car' because hitherto, all cars with opening rear doors had been saloon types converted to ease the loading of large and awkward items which would not fit in an ordinary boot. The R4 did not really fall into this category because there was not a saloon equivalent; they were not like that. Besides, the estate car convention demanded that the car's back end be squared off and often timber-framed to emphasise its particular status. Again, the R4 was not like that. Its back end shape was rather rounded and the door formed an integral part of it. It had been put there mainly as a convenience to the kind of Frenchman who was expected to buy the car because of the unstressed nature of the body, it was a very easy feature to incorporate in the car's design. Yet in this essentially practical arrangement lies the real root of the 'hatchback' which Renault were soon to exploit in a far more sensational way.

The Renault 4 was therefore a significant car in several ways. It may never have been a sensation for its performance was hardly calculated to impress. The 1961 car was flat-out at 60mph (97km/h) though it was economical enough to keep French farmers happy and could outrun the Citroen 2CV quite comfortably. Later it was given bigger engines, a four-speed gearbox and even disc front brakes to enable it to keep up with the increasing pace of motoring. Yet it remained a hut-on-wheels; a very successful one, since like the 2VC it remained in production into the mid 1980s and millions were made in a quarter of a century.

The car is also significant because it marked the conversion of one of Europe's major car manufacturers to front wheel drive; after the launch of the R4, Renault never again designed a car with its rear wheels driven. Just how much more might have been achieved if the R4 design team had looked at the Mini and thought to mount their engine transversely we shall never know; as it was, the R4 set the engineering pattern of Renault cars for many years to come.

Finally, the R4 pointed the way towards greater freedom for car body designers. Thanks to its influence, after 1961 the line of distinction between the saloon and the estate car was blurred, an event of major importance, as we shall see.

Renault 4
Country of origin: France
Date: 1961
Engine: four-stroke; overhead valves; side
camshaft; four-cylinder; Solex carburettor;
26.5bhp at 4,500rpm
Gears: three-speed; synchromesh on 2nd and
top; front-wheel drive
Capacity: 747cc
Bore & Stroke: 54.5 × 80mm
Maximum Speed: 60mph (96km/h)
Chassis: welded and bolted body panels on box
section platform; front suspension with torsion
bar and wishbones; rear suspension with torsion
bar and trailing arms
Dimensions: wheelbase N/S 7ft 10⅓in (239cm)
           wheelbase O/S 7ft 11⅕ in (244cm)
           track (front) 4ft 1in (124cm);
           track (rear) 3ft 11⅖ in (120cm);
Steering: rack and pinion
Brakes: front/drum; rear/drum

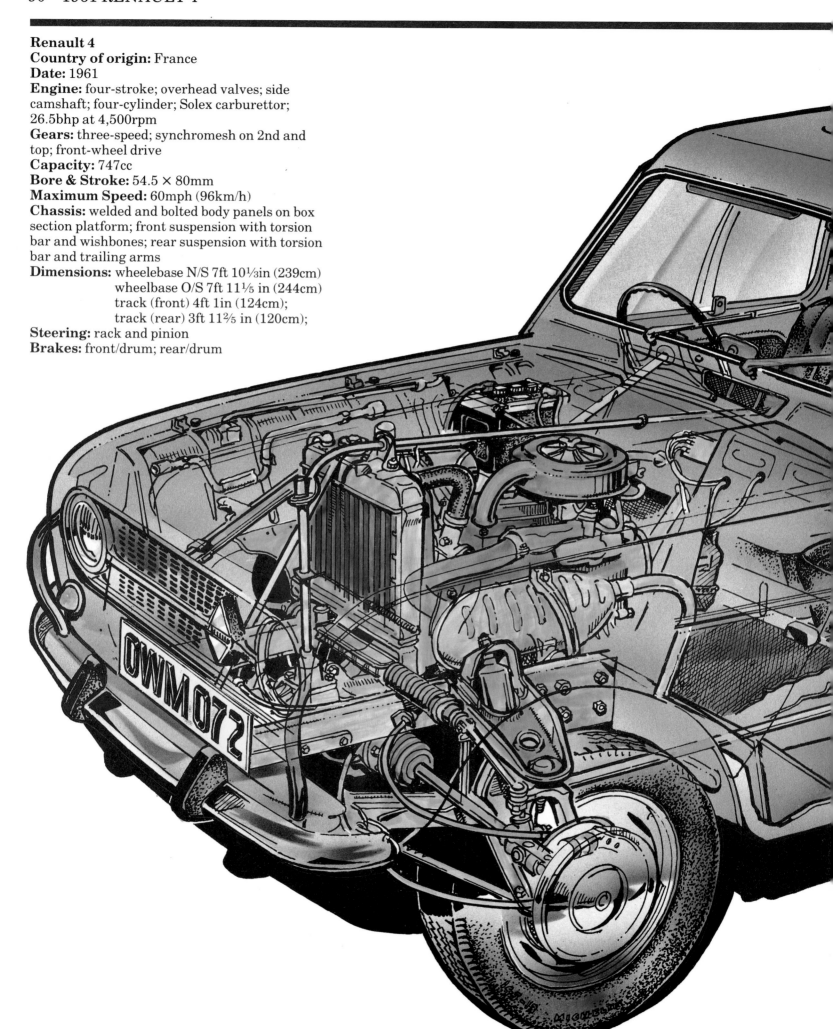

1961 JAGUAR E-TYPE

Can any high-performance sports model ever be regarded as truly significant in terms of the overall development of the motor car? The Jaguar can stake a fair claim for at least two reasons. Firstly, it has always been the function of the true sports car to show car designers, in general what may be possible in the way of performance and road behaviour: handling, roadholding, braking and so on. The best sports cars have always set targets for the more mundane saloons to strive after. Secondly, the E-type in particular showed that very high standards of performance can be achieved without a car being outrageously expensive.

For many years before the appearance of the E-type, Jaguar had already been in the business of achieving high performance. Their range was built partly on the strength of a single classic engine design, the XK, which entered production in 1948 and was still being produced 40 years later; in other words, it spanned more than a third of the total development life of the passenger car. Allied to this engine, which combined power and reliability to a remarkable degree, Jaguar could offer great skill in chassis engineering and an adventurous outlook towards new ideas: for instance, the company played a leading part in the development of the disc brakes without which the E-type's performance would have been difficult to achieve with safety.

The E-type arrived at a difficult point in the evolution of the sports car. The line of development that started with the MG M-type had run dry by the early 1960's because the new

breed of small saloon car, led by the Mini, proved capable of matching two-seaters in every respect while being more comfortable and cheaper. The most promising path open to the sports car specialist was to regain the advantage in performance and road behaviour at a reasonable cost for there was no point in chasing such goals if they resulted in cars which only a few could afford. Jaguar's own sports car record was impeccable. The company had built up a line of successful models from the XK120 of 1948 to the XK150 which was in effect a much improved version of the original. Jaguar had also built up a fund of racing development experience, not least as the result of winning Le Mans 24 Hours race five times in the 1950s.

All of this experience was thrown into the E-type which was intended as a completely new concept, not merely another progressive development of the XK cars. Yet the XK150 was already one of the standard-setters of the day. However there were three areas in which further progress was possible, as the later Le Mans cars had proved. Firstly, the car could be made lighter, since the XK150 followed tradition in having its body mounted on a chassis. Secondly the rear suspension could be improved since the XK150 like almost all the expensive classic cars of the time, retained a live axle mounted on traditional multi-leaf springs. Third, the shape of the body could be improved to cut down air resistance and achieve a higher maximum speed, and better high-speed stability. That was the basis upon which the E-type project proceeded, and it showed what could be achieved by a clear-sighted team seeking a way forward.

The E-type body was created in the form of a monocoque, a stressed-skin shell, for the centre section of the car. From the centre-section bulkheads, frameworks of welded tube extended fore and aft to accept the engine and front suspension, and the final drive and rear suspension. This technique certainly saved the desired weight, since although the E-type was almost exactly the same size as the XK150 (an inch (2.5cm) shorter, half an inch (1.3cm) wider) the new car was over 500 pounds (227kg) – or 17 per cent lighter. The centre-section mated with smooth nose and tail shapes to produce much less aerodynamic drag: the first E-type to be road tested managed a maximum speed of 150 mph (241km/h), compared with 134 mph (216km/h) recorded by the same test team for the XK150S.

As for the rear suspension, the Jaguar engineers were determined not to fall into the same trap as others who had sought to offer independent arrangements which did not cost too much, not take up too much space, and

whose cars often behaved extremely badly as a result. Instead they devised a cunning system which behaved like a proper double wishbone arrangement, though with the drive shaft to each wheel forming one of the 'wishbones'. As a final touch, they provided twin coil spring/damper units, one on each side of each rear wheel hub, to avoid any imbalance of forces. The E-type front suspension retained the well-tried double wishbone, torsion bar sprung system of the XK series although improved in detail: it had been obvious to keen drivers for some time that the XK's front end had needed an equally capable arrangement at the back to enable the car to achieve its full potential. In the E-type, this potential certainly was achieved and it was universally accepted that the car set standards of road behaviour just as astonishing as its performance.

The E-type was not the first production Jaguar to have disc brakes, for they were also fitted to the XJ150S. This is however an appropriate place to note that the design of brakes had hardly changed since the 1900s when the drum brake became universal. In the 1960s disc brakes rapidly came to the fore. Like so many things in vehicle engineering, the principle was far from new but had lain idle for at least as long as the drum brake had been in existence. From the 1930s onwards the makers of the fastest cars had always faced problems in providing adequate brakes but their answer had been to provide ever larger drums of exotic material, drums with fins to help dissipate heat and so on. The disc brake overcame most of these problems with its far better resistance to the old

problem of 'fade' and brake development quickly switched to the investigation of better brake lining materials. It should not be forgotten that the E-type was *the* car which brought the benefits of the disc type brake forcibly to the attention of the motoring world.

It may come as a surprise, considering the E-type's use of innovative brake systems, to discover that the car still ran on cross-ply tyres some six years after the Citroen DS had first launched Michelin's radial-ply X. The reason is twofold: the radial-ply tyres of 1961 would not withstand speeds as high as 150 mph (241km/h) and they lacked some of the qualities for which the Jaguar chassis experts were looking. The early radial-ply tyres were clearly dangerous when fitted to high speed cars because when the tyre lost its grip it did so suddenly and with very little warning. Even so, the radial-ply tyre would eventually make its mark in exactly the same way as the disc brake; it would just take a year or two longer to evolve.

Finally, there was the question of the E-type's price. In its year of introduction, 1961, the car cost £2,160 in Britain, less than three times as much as a mundane family saloon like the Ford Consul or the Triumph Herald. Some rival companies could never work out how Jaguar managed to produce a prestige sports car for the price. The E-type actually halted some rival projects such as a planned 4-litre GT successor to the Austin-Healey 3000, once it was realised that such cars could not match the Jaguar's performance or price. That, too, was a valuable lesson for everyone concerned with the development of the motor car.

Jaguar E-type (Series 3)
Country of origin: Great Britain
Date: 1971
Engine: 60-degree V-12; single overhead camshaft per bank; four Stomberg carburettors; 272bhp at 5,850rpm
Gears: four-speed manual
Capacity: 5,343cc
Bore & Stroke: 90 × 70mm
Maximum Speed: 145mph (233km/h)
Chassis: monocoque; independent front suspension by wishbones, torsion bars, dampers and anti-roll bar; independent rear suspension by wishbones, radius arms, coil springs and dampers
Dimensions: wheelbase 105in (267cm); track (front) 54¼in (138cm); track (rear) 53in (135cm)
Brakes: four-wheel drum brakes

1962 FORD CORTINA

In 1962, three years after the launch of the Mini, BMC launched its logical follow-on: a rather larger, smarter car called the Morris 1100. Other manufacturers were beginning to talk in terms of new and technically exciting models and it seemed a bad time for Ford's British arm to announce a car almost crushing in its apparent conventionality. The 'Consul Cortina' which quickly and understandably became simply the Cortina, was pitched very close in price to the Morris 1100 and offered much the same interior space and performance. The stage was set for a major sales battle and the struggle continued for many years. In the end the Cortina won, and it is highly instructive in the midst of any study of the motor car's development, to ask how this feat was achieved.

The Cortina grew out of the conviction on the part of some British Ford managers that a planned medium-sized, front-driven saloon car was not the answer to their market's needs. When such a car emerged in Germany as the Taunus 12/15M, the British team was proved right especially because they had already turned the Cortina into reality.

The Cortina was an act of deliberate rejection of the already proven virtues of front-wheel drive and indeed of advanced engineering as it was then understood. Yet the car finds its place in any study of vehicle evolution because it introduced two other concepts which have become increasingly important to all designers in the last twenty years. The Cortina succeeded in the first place because it was finely tuned to the needs and desires of its target market; and because it had a light and efficient structure.

Ostensibly, the first consideration has nothing to do with engineering, but in the present-day context the shape of any modern car is greatly determined by the findings of market researchers. They quiz the car-buying public about its tastes and then turn the answers into specifications for the designers and engineers. The Cortina was the first British car and arguably the first car anywhere, to be designed under the influence of these market-research techniques. The programme was master-minded by Ford's product planner Terry Beckett, who later received a knighthood for his achievements, as did Issigonis, the father of the Mini and the Morris 1100.

In essence, the Ford research found that despite the fashionable trend towards front-drive and adventurous engineering, there remained a large potential market among buyers who preferred a conventional, simple easily understood and serviced car. There was also a strong element of wanting 'as much car as possible for the money' which argued strongly against the Issigonis philosophy of making the car more compact. However, the buyer was not prepared to sacrifice performance or economy for the sake of his other needs.

The Ford team interpreted these findings in the only way possible, and produced their medium-sized saloon car using existing components combined into a body of exceptional lightness. The Cortina was therefore powered by the then-new Ford pushrod ohv engine, mounted· at the front of the car and driving through a conventional clutch, four-speed gearbox and propeller shaft (just as Renault had devised in 1899) to a differential housed in a rear live axle. The rear axle was carried on simple multi-leaf springs which would have been equally familiar in 1899, at least in principle; the Cortina's front suspension used the MacPherson strut.

was certainly an outstandingly light and all-drum brakes and narrow cross-ply tyres. All in several of its cars since the early 1950s and

Vincenzo Lancia, whilst working on the Lambda, had sketched almost every worthwhile variation on independent suspension geometry

except one: the MacPherson strut. Colonel MacPherson, a Ford consultant, realised that if a wheel was attached rigidly to the bottom of a telescopic strut with the strut flexibly mounted at its top, all that would be needed to locate the wheel sideways, fore and aft would be a single lower wishbone. The strut would of course almost inevitably double as the hydraulic damper, and would usually for the sake of tidiness have the coil spring wound round it. Ford of Britain had used the MacPherson strut in several of its cars since the early 1950's and proved that it worked well in practice. It had two particular advantages, first that it kept the change of wheel camber angle (the wheel's inclination to the vertical) to a minimum which was good for handling and stability. Secondly, it could be made to feed its loads into the body structure at three widely separated points which made for easy and efficient stressing. Like so many good ideas the MacPherson strut is not without its share of compensating drawbacks, nevertheless it has been widely accepted as a suspension medium for passenger cars.

Anything which promised easy and efficient stressing was of interest to the Cortina development team and without doubt the MacPherson strut made its contribution to what was certainly an outstanding light and adequately rigid body. The original Cortina was two feet (0.6m) longer than the Morris 1100 and three inches (7.6cm) wider thus living up handsomely the 'more car for the money' ambition lighter than the Morris 1100 which is why, given its near-identical power output, it achieved nearly identical performance. It had other advantages too. It was cheap and easy to service, just as had been anticipated, but it was also light and easy to drive. With less weight on its front wheels than the Morris 1100, its steering was notably lighter – though the early Cortinas had recirculating-ball steering, a system which gave too little 'feel' and an impression of slackness around the straight-ahead position. With its direct linkage to the gearbox, the Cortina had an excellent gearchange – something which was acknowledged to be not the best feature of the Morris 1100. Best of all perhaps, the Cortina proved that its simple layout gave it the capacity for 'stretch' so that it was easily developed into a long line of more powerful, capable and expensive versions. That should be enough to excuse the early Cortinas, from having all-drum brakes and narrow crossply tyres. All those who engineer new cars should understand the real lessons of the Cortina: build to satisfy the market, and make sure you can adapt your design to its changing needs.

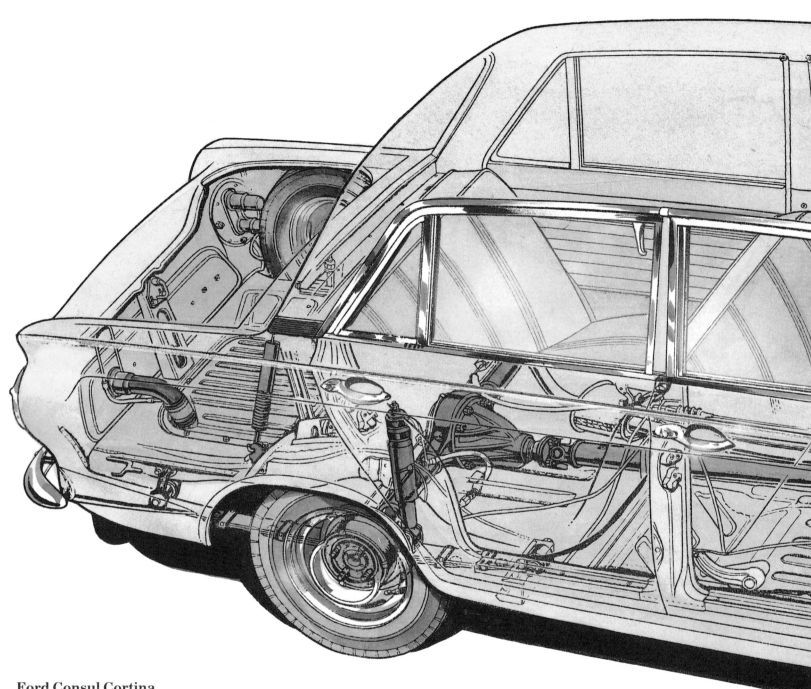

Ford Consul Cortina
Country of origin: Great Britain
Date: 1962
Engine: four-stroke; overhead valves; side
camshaft; four-cylinders direct in block;
53bhp at 4,800rpm; Solex carburettor
Gears: four-speed fully synchronized;
rear-wheel drive
Capacity: 1,198cc
Bore & Stroke: 80 × 58.17mm
Maximum Speed: 80mph (129km/h)
Chassis: integral; front suspension
independent with coil springs; rear suspension
with semi-elliptic leaf springs
Steering: recirculating ball
Brakes: front/drum; rear/drum

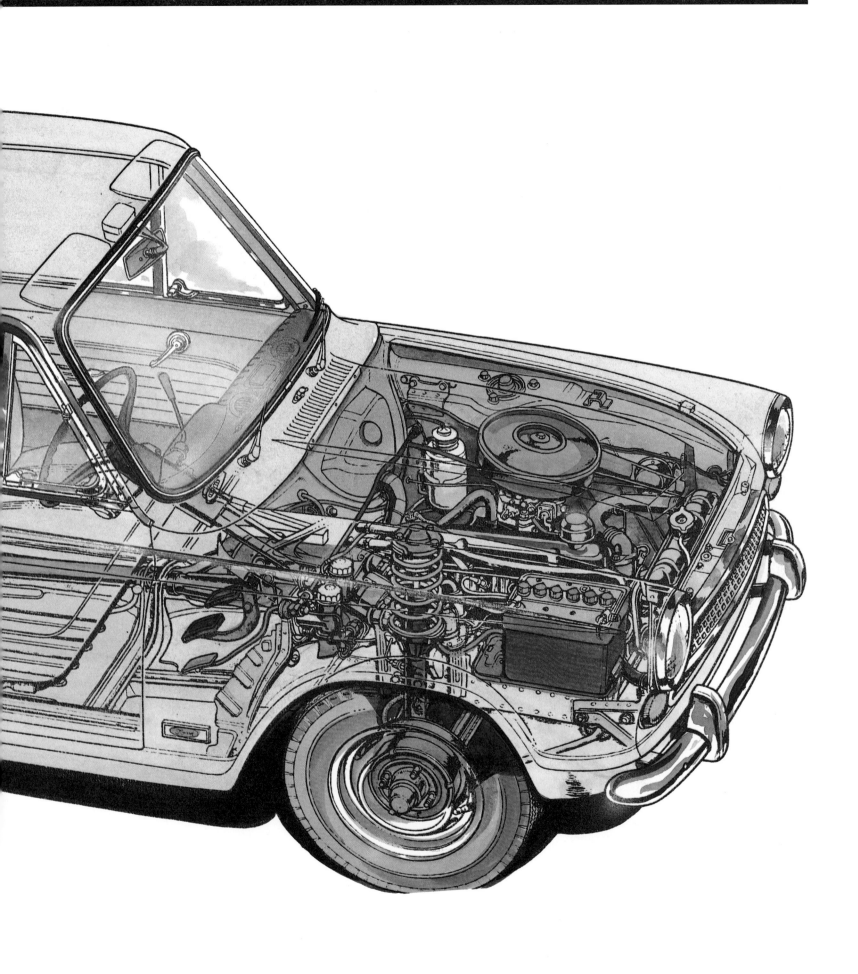

ROVER 2000

The Rover 2000 came from a company with a long tradition of building medium-sized and larger 'quality cars'. Despite its sometimes staid image – the typical Rover of the 1950's was often referred to as the 'Auntie' Rover – the company had its adventurous side too. It demonstrated some of the first, and most practical, gas-turbine powered cars in the world, and was perfectly well aware that in order to retain its position as a car manufacturer in the competitive world of the 1960's, it would have to apply that sense of adventure to its next new car, the intended replacement for its medium-sized range.

In one sense, therefore, the Rover 2000 is a lesson in how a design can set out to replace a worthy but outdated product with something new and exciting, and the lengths to which one must go in order to be sure of succeeding. Yet also, inadvertently, the Rover 2000 became the leader of a whole new generation of cars, the product of a philosophy which ran counter to the arguments used to justify the appearance of the Ford Cortina.

First, the straightforward story. Rover's engineers knew it would be no good trying to modify the existing medium-sized cars in their range, because these cars dated back to the 1940's, looked totally outdated and were above all, extremely heavy. To make matters worse, the engines were equally outdated, peculiar units with one side and one overhead valve, much better suited to the company's highly successful Land Rover than its luxury saloon. The brave decision was therefore taken to design a car completely new in every detail.

The first design decision had to concern the engine. Was it to have four or six cylinders? Although six cylinders would have been smoother, the Rover team opted for four because the engine would then be cheaper to make and would at least have advantage of a shorter, stiffer cylinder block. It was given an overhead camshaft and a capacity of 2 litres with exactly 'square' dimensions, that is the crankshaft stroke was exactly the same as the cylinder bore. It was easy enough to extract more power from the new engine than its predecessor had ever given: 90bhp compared with the 77bhp from the previous (2·3-litre) four-cylinder engine of the Rover 80. The drive from the engine was taken through a conventional clutch and four-speed gearbox to a differential at the centre of a de Dion rear suspension system.

The new body was unusual in its construction. It was built up in unitary fashion except that the end result was not the usual complete body shell, but rather a 'skeleton' to which unstressed body panels were then attached. Such a system offered several advantages. The Rover was certainly very strong and safe, it was easy to detach and replace the surface panels after a minor accident. It would also have been easier to restyle the car by changing the surface panels without having to worry about the skeleton beneath. However in 13 years of production, the shape of the Rover 2000 never noticeably changed. Conversely, the chosen system did make the car heavier than it need otherwise have been; but since it weighed 500 pounds less (227kg) than the Rover 80, most people were prepared to accept this.

The suspension system was also unusual. At the front, the independent mechanism was arranged with its upper arms feeding loads directly aft into the bulkhead of the structural skeleton, a much more complicated layout than double wishbones would have been. The reputed

object of this arrangement was to leave room under the bonnet for the gas turbine which Rover still hoped to be able to offer by the early 1970's. At the rear, the car used a system first invented by the Count de Dion, a contemporary of Panhard, Levassor and Renault designers who had all been active seventy years previously. De Dion devised a way of keeping the drive arrangement separate from the axle, joining together the driven wheels, by taking the axle tube around the differential and locating it independently. The Count's invention despite being expensive to engineer, managed to combine the best features of the axle (keeping the wheels parallel at all times), and of independent suspension (removing the weight of the differential unit from the unsprung weight and improving the roadholding and ride). Rover's de Dion system was itself unusual in certain details but it worked well, and the 2000 gained a good reputation for willing and safe cornering.

The Rover engineers were original in other respects too. After all, the 2000 was supposed to be an all embracing effort and it would be a long time before they were presented with another clean sheet of paper for the drawing board. The 2000 was therefore given disc brakes all round whereas the increasingly accepted compromise system was to have discs at the front and drums at the rear, and the car was designed to use the new radial-ply tyres. The late Peter Wilks was the confident design leader but there were, nevertheless, features of the Rover 2000 which drew criticism. The boot certainly too small; the back seat was divided into two properly shaped places and the car was never offered with an overdrive like so many of its competitors, even though it would have helped its cruising refinement and economy. Despite this, the Rover 2000 became a firm favourite, sold well and remained in production for well over a decade.

Why did the Rover 2000 become a favourite? It was by no means cheap; in 1963, a much bigger car with similar performance like the Austin Westminster, Ford Zodiac, or Vauxhall Cresta could be bought for the same price. Many people, perhaps because of the Suez Crisis of 1956 and the petrol rationing which followed, decided that quality was quite distinct from size. It became much smarter, more socially acceptable, to drive the Rover 2000 – or its rival the Triumph 2000 which emerged within weeks of the Rover – than to own one of the traditional big 3-litre saloons. The Rover proved significant because it showed car designers that as long as they got the quality and image right, they need no longer worry about the size of their vehicle. The Rover's four seats were enough.

Rover 2000
Country of origin: Great Britain
Date: 1963
Engine: four-stroke; in-line overhead valves;
single overhead camshaft; four-cylinders;
SU-type carburettor; 90bhp at 5,000rpm
Gears: four-speed fully synchronized;
rear-wheel drive
Capacity: 1,978cc
Bore & Stroke: 85.6 × 85.6mm
Maximum Speed: 95mph (153km/h)
Chassis: skeleton base unit, body panels
bolted on; front suspension with coil springs,
hydraulic shock absorbers, anti-roll bar; rear
suspension with de Dion tube, coil springs,
hydraulic shock absorbers
Dimensions: wheelbase 8ft 7⅜in (262cm);
                track (front) 53⅜in (132cm);
                track (rear) 52½in (133cm)
Steering: worm and roller
Brakes: front/disc; rear/disc
Body: bonnet and boot lid aluminium; others
steel

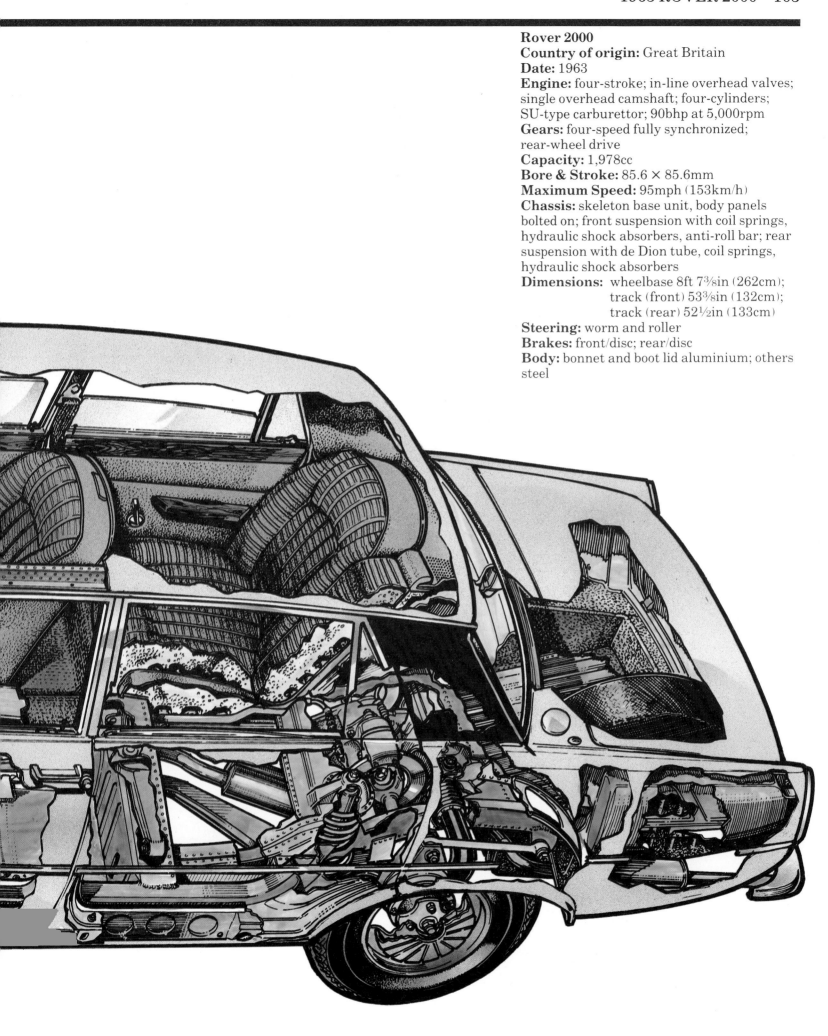

PORSCHE 911

Thirty years after Dr Porsche set about designing the Volkswagen Beetle, another rear-engined car was launched, this time to bear the name of his own factory. The 911 finds a place in this study because, more than any other car, it illustrates the way in which a car of character can survive despite admitted and major faults.

The 911 story started in Porsche's temporary war-time factory in Austria where Ferry Porsche built two-seater sports cars using Volkswagen Beetle components. The Beetle had less than perfect stability and handling, and this became even more apparent in Porsche's first production car, the 356, as it was given more power in search of better performance. The rearward weight bias and swing-axle rear suspension, combined with two or three times more power than was available to the Beetle, made the 356 an 'expert's' car to drive. Thus it was that by 1960 or so, the Porsche's team began to consider replacing it with something better.

Remarkably, the team decided to remain faithful to the concept of a rear-mounted, air-cooled engine. It believed the wayward handling of the 356 could be cured in the replacement car by adopting a new suspension system, wider wheel track and longer wheelbase. That was the basis of the 911 which appeared first in 1963 – though it did not enter production until later – with an outstandingly beautiful sports coupé body, built in true unitary fashion and owing nothing to Volkswagen. The swing-axle rear suspension system had given way to semi-

trailing arms, an arrangement in which the member that determines the wheel's path during suspension movement is hinged at an angle from the rear bulkhead of the body. The wheel is thus independent of the drive shaft angle – which was at the root of the trouble with the swing-axle. Wishbone suspension was retained at the front, and the springs were Volkswagen-type torsion bars.

The 911 power unit was an air-cooled flat-six engine mounted aft of the back axle and driving forward through a transaxle. The original engine size was 2-litres but the unit proved to have more built-in 'stretch' than almost any other in history. In the course of long development it has been opened to 3.3-litres and produces very high power output – 230bhp even without the turbocharging that is offered in some versions.

The car had not been in production very long before it was realised that the new rear suspension layout was by no means the complete answer to rear-engined handling problems. Four years later, the 911 was almost completely redesigned with a brand-new front suspension (changed to MacPherson struts) and an even longer wheelbase. It remained unusually difficult to drive fast and safely, and still does; but the beauty of the early cars and their reputation gained through a large number of sporting successes including the Monte Carlo Rally, have established Porsche as an enthusiast's car. Measures taken to improve the handling and stability included the fitting of

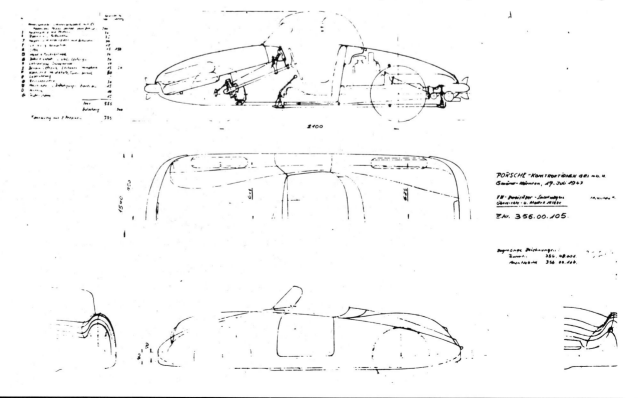

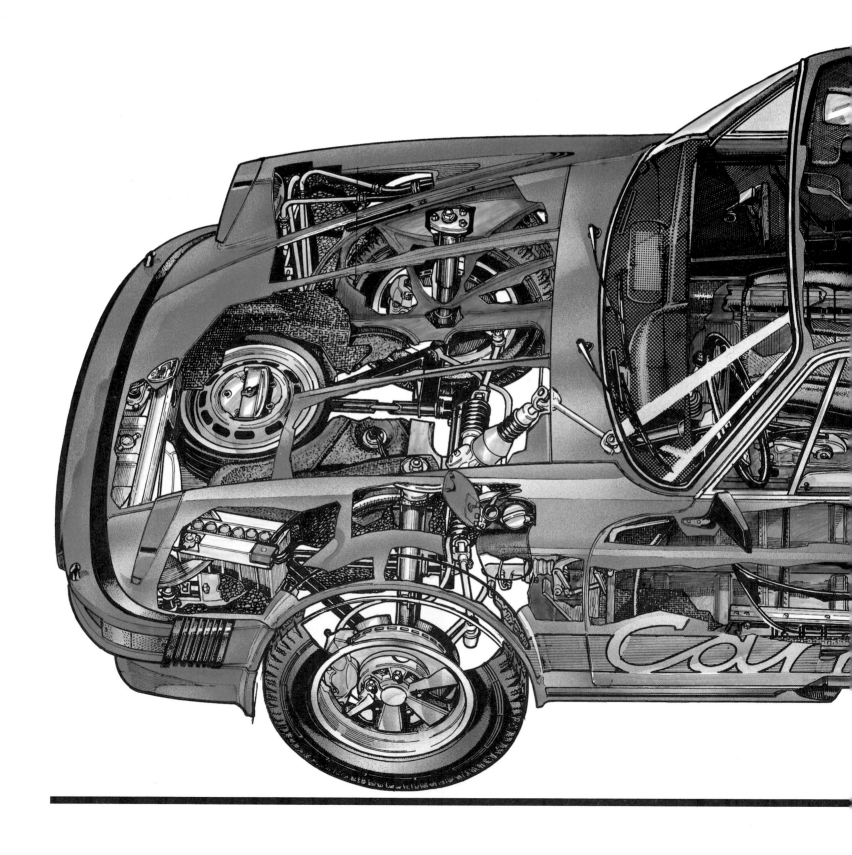

Porsche 911
Country of origin: West Germany
Date: 1965
Engine: flat-six; single ohc per bank; six Solex carburettors; 130bhp at 6,100rpm
Gears: five-speed manual, with optional four-speed manual or sportomatic semi-automatic
Capacity: 1,991cc
Bore & Stroke: 80 × 66mm
Maximum Speed: 130mph (210km/h)
Chassis: integral steel; front suspension independent by MacPherson struts, transverse wishbones, torsion bars and anti-roll bar
Dimensions: wheelbase 87in (221cm); track (front) 53in (134cm); track (rear) 52in (132cm)
Brakes: four-wheel disc brakes; drum handbrake

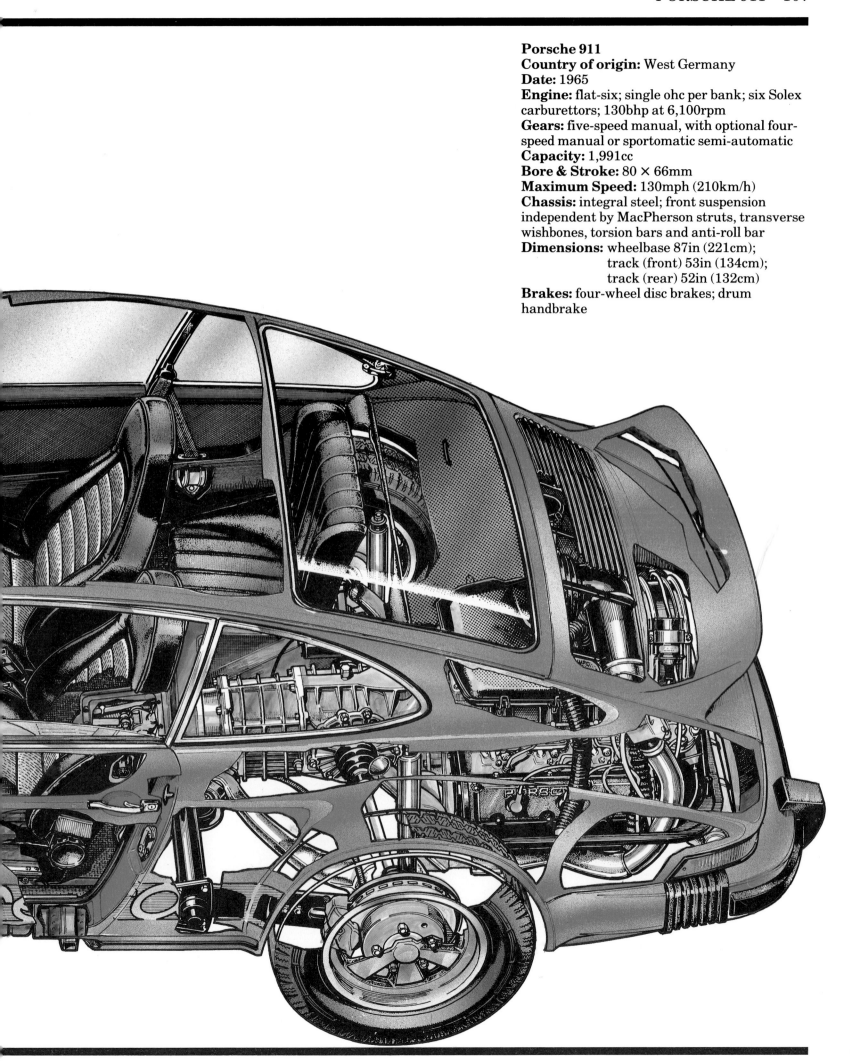

wider tyres at the rear of the car than at the front. Also, spoilers were fitted to the front and rear of the car, to redistribute the aerodynamic forces. Nevertheless the problems remain because nothing can altogether overcome the fundamental disadvantage of having so much of the car's weight so far aft.

Porsche has long since started building cars with their engines at the front, driving the back wheels; these cars, the 924, 944 and 928, seek the best possible balance by having their gearboxes mounted together with the differential and final drive unit. All three models have sold well and yet demand for the 911 continues despite the very high price asked for a car which is not only tricky to drive, but cramped and old fashioned in its interior appointments.

The 911, demonstrates to car designers and engineers that it is possible for a car to survive and prosper even if it suffers from major faults. In order to do so, that car must have some very positive virtues – like the 911's performance, and the lightness and precision of its rack and pinion steering, the excellent traction afforded by its rearward weight bias and the good braking balance; but a good deal of luck is also needed to survive so precariously for over twenty years.

1964 LOTUS ELAN

As already described in previous pages the conventional small sports car was overtaken by the arrival of the highly capable small salooon car, but it continued to sell mainly because of tradition. We have also seen how Jaguar showed it was possible, with a suitably thorough engineering approach, to set new standards of performance and road behaviour well beyond those of any saloon car of the 1960's. The Elan was another, smaller sports car in the same mould as the Jaguar, but also interesting for a number of other reasons. In particular, it is the first car in this study list to have had a body made principally from anything other than metal.

The Elan was the brainchild of Lotus Chairman Colin Chapman, who brought to car design a new understanding of suspension behaviour and the fresh analytical approach of an aeronautical engineer. The car was the road-going expression of principles also embodied in Lotus Grand Prix racing cars, but at the same time it was intended to be, and indeed succeeded in being, a comfortable and practical vehicle. The car was an extremely clean, aerodynamically-shaped two-seater and its interest from the point of view of car anatomy lay in three main areas: the body construction, the engine and the suspension.

Lotus has always been a small company and never in a position to spend millions of pounds on tooling to produce stamped sheet-metal parts for car bodies. Its chosen alternative material was glass-reinforced plastic (GRP): a matrix of woven glass-fibre sheet moulded into place within a layer of polyester resin. The company actually tried using the material to produce complete, fully-stressed bodies in one earlier application (the Lotus Elite) but decided that too many problems were involved – not least, those of attaching metal parts to a plastic body. For the Elan, which could be said to have replaced the Elite, a different system was therefore chosen. The car was given a chassis – not the ladder type chassis of old, but a carefully stressed 'backbone' with branched ends to provide mounting points for the engine, transmission and suspension. The moulded GRP body was placed upon and bolted to the chassis and the system proved extremely satisfactory, even if the Elan remained more costly than a mass-produced, metal-bodied car. Since the advent of the Elan, and other cars from small, specialised makers, the industry has retained an interest in plastic body construction and Lotus especially has devised new and more efficient ways of making such bodies.

The Elan engine also showed a new approach to the question of obtaining satisfactory performance at reasonable cost. It was a skifully engineered version of the then-current 1.5-litre Ford ohv powered unit, as used in the Cortina 1500. The standard cylinder head was replaced by a completely redesigned one with twin overhead camshafts, directly operating the valves in hemispherical 'cross-flow' combustion chambers (that is, the inlet ports are on one side of the head, while the exhaust ports emerge from the other side). The camshafts were chain-driven from a sprocket on the crankshaft nose

and as many of the original Ford engine parts as possible were used to keep the overall cost to a minimum. This conversion proved extremely successful, producing 105bhp which was enough to give the Elan extremely good performance. The drive was taken through a clutch and four-speed gearbox to the final drive unit, and then by drive shafts with simple rubber 'doughnut' joints to accommodate flexing, to the rear wheels.

As for the suspension, the Elan naturally enough used independent suspension on all four wheels. Double wishbones were used at the front, while the rear suspension used a strut and wishbone system of Colin Chapman's own devising, which gave very well-controlled and advantageous changes of wheel angle with suspension movement. The front end was probably more notable for the steering geometry which Chapman employed. For sixty years, car designers had accepted without question the need to use Ackermann geometry – designing the steering linkage so that the inner front

wheel turns through a greater angle than the outer because it is turning on a small-radius circle. Chapman was the first to question the wisdom of this approach for use with wheels equipped with pneumatic tyres that deform at the point of contact with the road to generate their own 'slip angles'. The steering geometry of the Elan and later Lotus cars was therefore arranged on a different basis, giving a rather peculiar feel at low speed but greatly improving the precision and response in normal driving.

The significance of the Elan is apparent in many ways. It clearly demonstrated the possibility of making high-performance cars out of materials other than metal; it showed that a high performance engine could be created out of a very ordinary mass-production unit; and its suspension had enough new features to be of major interest in themselves. The Elan also, like the Jaguar, proved that there was scope to further improve road-going standards of car behaviour – though it seemed that the mass manufacturers were not interested.

Lotus Elan S.2
Country of origin: Great Britain
Date: 1965
Engine: four-stroke; twin overhead camshafts; four-cylinders direct in block; two Weber carburettors
Gears: four-speed, fully synchronized; rear-wheel drive
Capacity: 1,558cc
Bore & Stroke: 82.55 × 72.75mm
Maximum Speed: 110mph (177km/h)
Chassis: separate body unit on welded steel backbone chassis taking all loads; front suspension with wishbones and coil spring/ damper units; rear suspension independent with Chapman struts, coil spring/damper units, wishbones
Dimensions: wheelbase 84in (213cm);
track (front) 47³⁄₃₂in (119cm)
track (rear) 48⁷⁄₁₆in (121cm)
Steering: rack and pinion
Brakes: front/disc; rear/disc
Body: glass-fibre – reinforced plastic

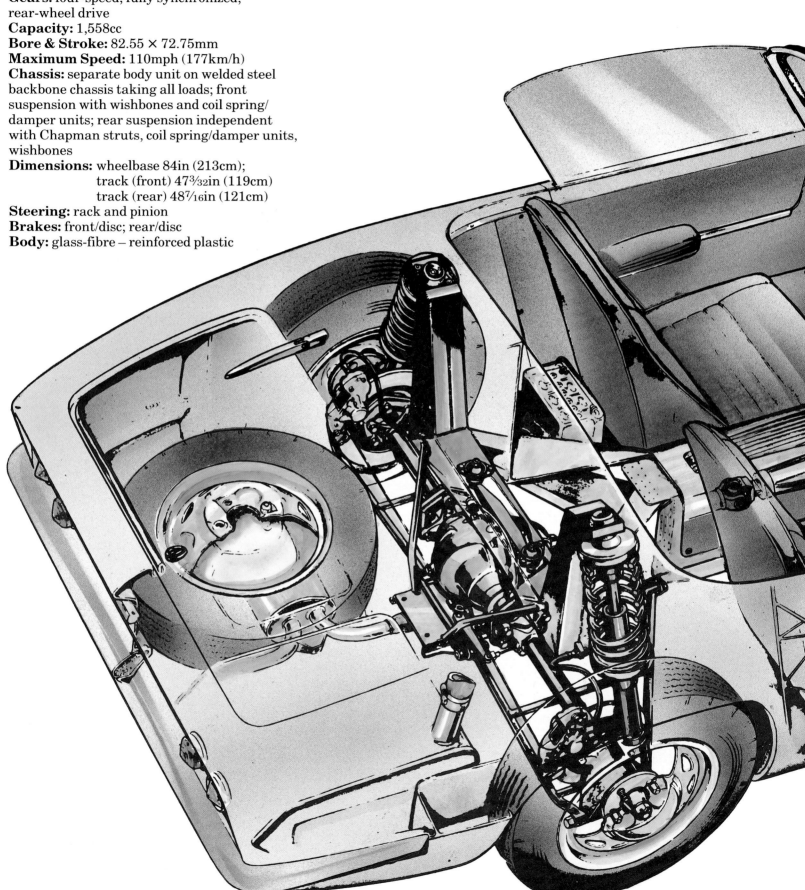

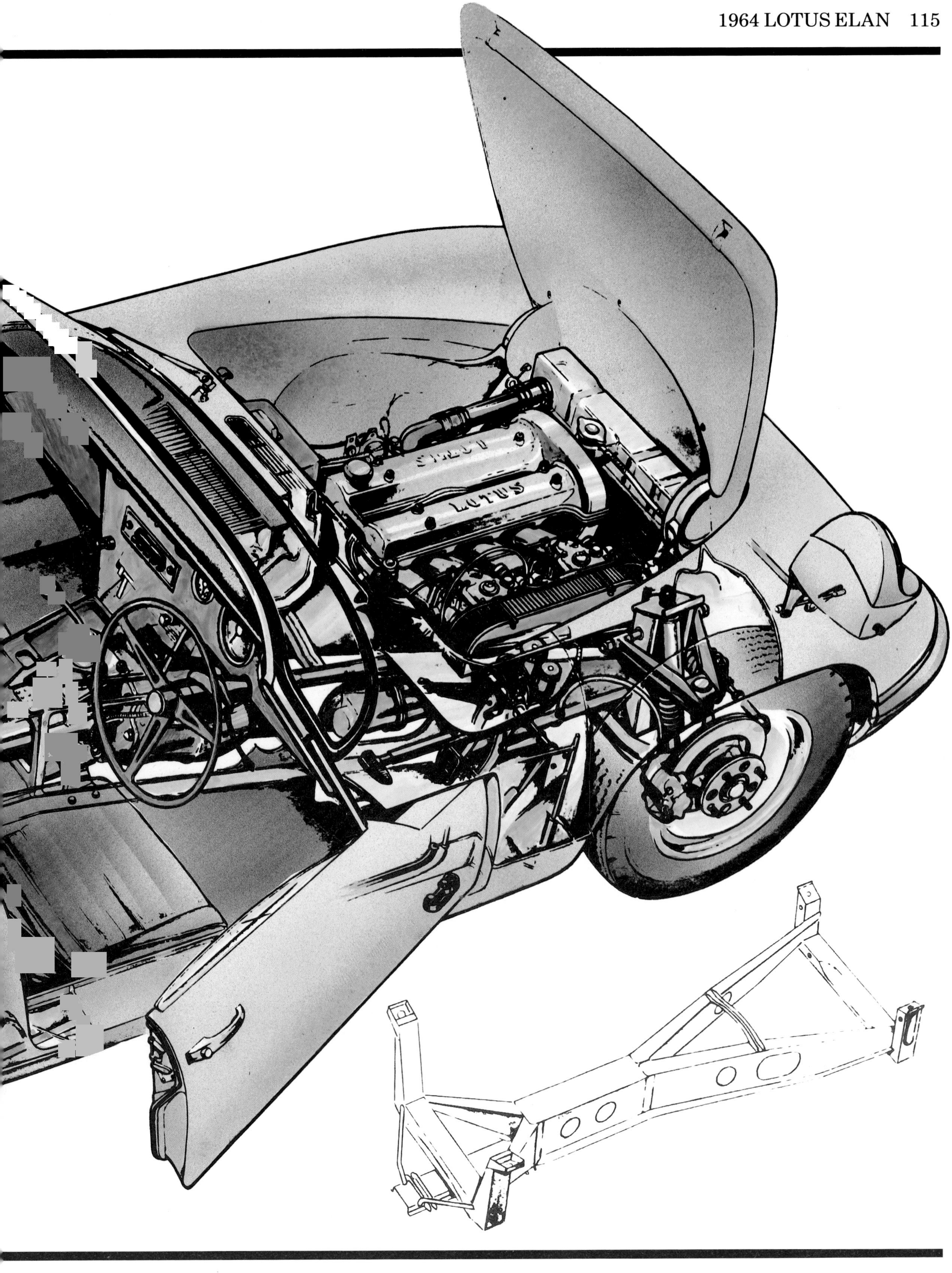
LOTUS

1965 RENAULT 16

After the success of the R4, Renault sought to make a fresh impact on the European 1.5-litre car market, because its existing offerings were extremely old, conventional and not very attractive. There was no doubt in the minds of Renault engineers that, like the R4, the new car should have front wheel drive. That in itself would make the vehicle – the Renault 16 – highly significant because it would be rather bigger and more powerful than any front-driven car then successfully demonstrated though BMC's bigger 1800 was in almost parallel development. However, a further decision turned the R16 from an interesting car into a highly significant one, and that was the adoption of a second idea from the R4: the rear loading door.

Renault decided to retain the R4 mechanical layout for the R16; that is, to instal the engine aft of the front axle, with the gearbox of the transaxle at the front of the car. However it was clear that they needed a bigger engine and they elected to design a completely new one. This emerged as a four-cylinder ohv unit of 1.5-litre capacity, notable mainly for being made mostly of light alloy rather than cast-iron. Renault wanted to minimise the weight on the front wheels of the R16 for the sake of better balance and lighter steering, and one way to achieve this was to make the engine as light as possible. Since the gearbox was, as in the R4, at the very front of the car it needed a special type of gearchange linkage. Renault provided an arrangement which had been imported from America in the post-war years and incorporated without a great deal of logic in many European cars during the 1950's. At least, in the case of the R16, such a system was as logical as devising a linkage from a floor-mounted lever round the engine to the very front of the car.

The Renault body design looked extremely unusual by the standards of the day, partly because its back end sloped to contain the rear door, but also because its roof gutters were raised into extremely prominent ridges, which were exaggerated by the addition of bright trim

strips. These were the result of a Renault decision to make the body (though in now-conventional unitary fashion) out of very large panels welded together at roof-edge joints. It was actually a very clever piece of production engineering which helped to reduce the cost of the car and was the first of many such examples from Renault. However it raised some eyebrows in 1965 even if it gave the R16 a highly distinctive shape.

The suspension was similar in principle to that of the R4, with double wishbones at the front and trailing arms at the rear, everything being sprung by torsion bars. Like its smaller forebear, the R16 proved to have an exceptionally comfortable ride, and managed to avoid excessive body roll on cornering. The car was fitted with front disc brakes, and smaller drum brakes at the rear: this was to become standard practice in the future as more saloon cars adopted front wheel drive, and the highly

capable disc brakes were installed. Also, needless to say, the R16 was equipped with radial-ply tyres from the outset.

The 16 was a highly successful car for Renault, remaining in production for over ten years and even then not being directly replaced but rather 'squeezed out' between the 18 and the 20 models. It proved that front wheel drive worked well for larger cars but, more than anything else, it is significant as the first model in which the hatchback rear door made a huge sales impact. It might have done better still if Renault had given it every possible variation of back seat arrangement including the straightforward estate-car type fold, but it seems that the company was afraid of producing a vehicle which may have been taxed as a 'commercial vehicle'. Even so, it made everyone realise that it was possible to combine the saloon car with the versatile load carrier and from that point, the stylists and engineers never looked back.

Renault 16
Country of origin: France
Date: 1966
Engine: four-stroke; overhead valves; side
camshaft; four-cylinder; 65bhp at 5,000rpm;
Solex carburettor
Gears: four-speed, fully synchronized;
front-wheel drive
Capacity: 1,470cc
Bore & Stroke: 76 × 81mm
Maximum Speed: 90mph (145km/h)
Chassis: integral; front suspension with
torsion bar, wishbones, telescopic shock-
absorbers, and anti-roll bar; rear suspension
with torsion bar, trailing arms, telescopic
shock-absorbers, anti-roll bar
Dimensions: wheelbase N/S 104⅓in (265cm)
                    wheelbase O/S 106⁷⁄₁₀in (271cm);
                    track (front) 52⅖in (133cm);
                    track (rear) 50⅖in (128cm)
Steering: rack and pinion
Brakes: front/disc; rear/drum
Body: welded

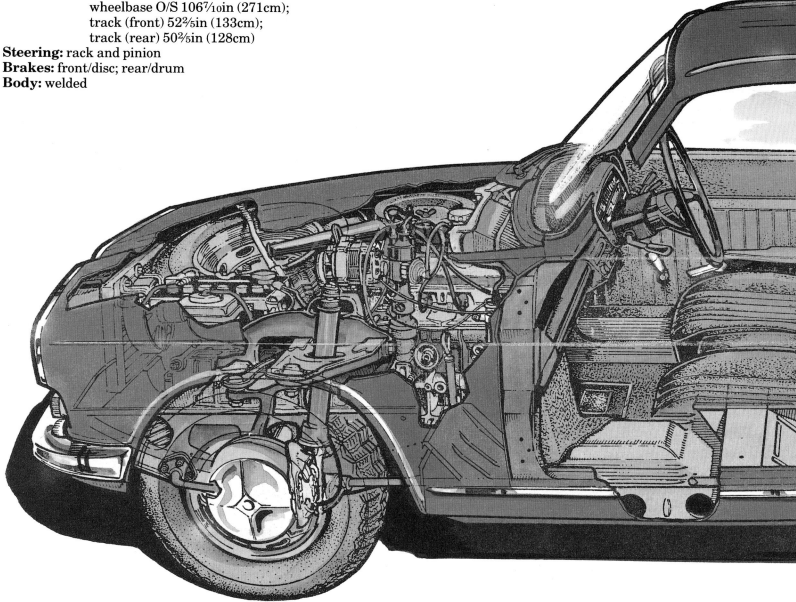

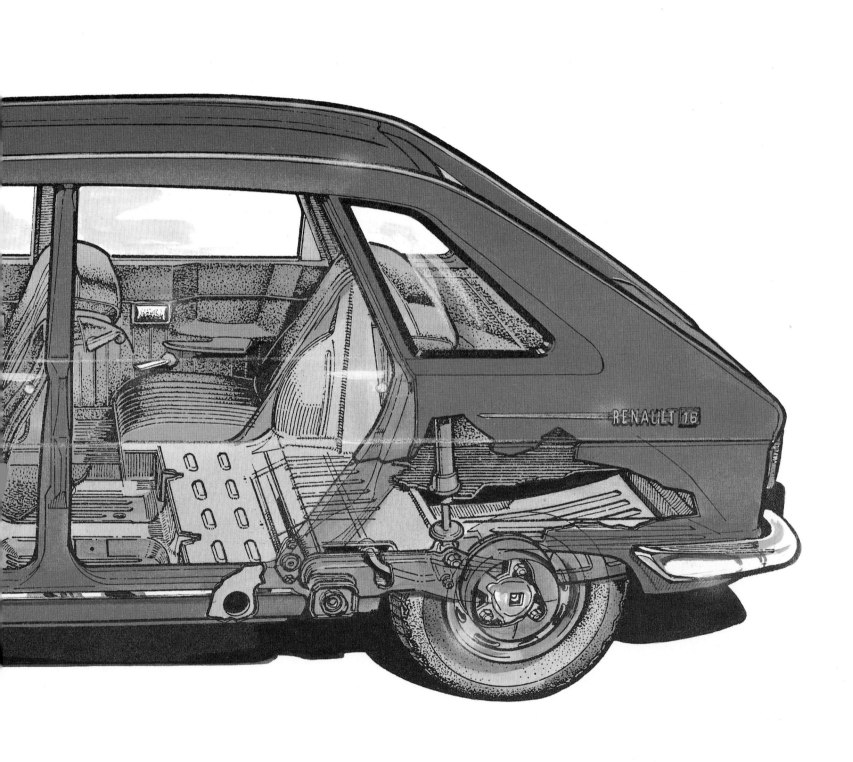

1966 RELIANT SCIMITAR GTE

The Scimitar GTE amalgamated features from some of the cars already discussed, for example it combined the plastic body material of the Lotus Elan with the originality of layout of the Renault 16 – and features of some such earlier cars as well.

Like Lotus, Reliant Motors was a small-volume specialist which could not afford tooling for metal body panels. The company had entered the car business as a manufacturer of light three-wheeled vehicles but gradually it began small-scale production of larger four-wheelers with a sporting flavour. Using GRP as the principal body material, these were built on a ladder-type chassis frame onto which was also mounted the engine and transmission (using standard Ford components) and the suspension for which Reliant made their own parts. By the early 1960s, production of the Scimitar sports car was ticking over slowly but it was by no means evident what should be done next.

The answer was supplied by the styling firm of Ogle Design, who first adapted a single Scimitar as a glass-roofed 'special' for the Triplex company to use as a demonstrator and followed suit with a redesigned Scimitar body that had a major impact on car styling in general and on the world of the sports coupé in particular. The key feature of the new version, the Scimitar GTE, was the rearward extension of the roofline into a low-set and nicely shaped

adaptation of an estate car back end. If the Renault 16 showed it was possible to have a saloon car with estate car convenience, then the GTE did the same thing for the sporting car. From that point on, it quickly became almost unthinkable that a sports coupé should not have the fashionable fastback shape complete with upward-opening rear hatch. The advertising image would have us believe that this made it easier to load up fishing tackle, shotguns and working dogs – or at very least, golf clubs and picnic hampers.

Beneath this new skin the GTE remained very much the Scimitar as before, powered by an untuned Ford 3-litre V6 engine driving through four-speed manual or three-speed automatic transmission to a live rear axle located both crosswise and fore and aft by rod linkages. By the late 1960s the faithful multi-leaf spring was increasingly seen as an undesirable feature and engineers sought other less hit-or-miss ways of achieving rear axle location. The Scimitar front suspension used double wishbones, and the rest of the car was fairly unremarkable except that it managed to offer good performance and solid, safe handling despite the apparent crudity of its chassis and the unrefined nature of its engine and transmission. However, it was the GTE body that extended its active life by fifteen years or so and added another dimension to people's perception of what the ideal car should look like.

1966 JENSEN FF

By now it will be apparent that many of the advances in motor car thinking during the 1960s were achieved by small, specialised British companies. That is certainly true of Jensen Motors who had built up a promising business building large, luxurious, Italian-styled GT cars in small numbers. By the early 1960s the staple product of the company was the Interceptor, an extremely powerful machine with a large American V8 engine and automatic transmission as standard. At this point, two problems faced Jensen. The first was how to extend its limited model range, and the second was how to render the Interceptor's prodigious power safer to use in adverse road conditions.

One feature promised the answer to both problems. A British company specialising in transmission developments, Ferguson Research, had devised an ingenious system to permit four-wheel drive to be used for high-performance road cars. Hitherto, the problem of dividing the drive torque between the front and rear of the car to avoid tyre scrub, had largely confined the system to off-road vehicles like the Jeep and the Land Rover; Ferguson's centre differential overcame this drawback. Jensen therefore adopted the Ferguson Formula (FF) by adding the necessary centre differential and installing the necessary arrangements to drive the front wheels.

The result was a modified Interceptor of outstanding capability. To further improve its safety, Jensen added another new feature, anti-lock brakes. The company used the Maxaret principle which the Dunlop company had already successfully applied to high-performance aircraft. Using this system it was possible to detect any sudden slowing of a wheel implying an impending skid and this was countered by a brief release of brakes. The driver could thus apply the FF brakes as hard as he liked, even on sheet ice, and know that he would not skid.

Thus the Jensen FF had two unique features, its four-wheel drive system and its anti-lock brakes. In other ways Jensen typified the approach adopted by several European manufacturers of 'Grand Touring' cars such as Bristol and Gordon Keeble in Britain, Facel Vega in France and de Tomaso and Iso in Italy. The approach was to take one of the very large, but relatively cheap V8 engines being used in huge numbers by the American car manufacturers and install it complete in a high-quality European chassis topped by an equally high quality body. In Jensen's case the chosen engine was the Chrysler V8 of 6.3-litre capacity, producing about 300bhp. This drove through the Chrysler Torqueflite three-speed automatic gearbox; no manual gearbox was offered. The gearbox in turn drove directly into the centre differential of the Ferguson system, from which propellor shafts ran fore and aft to the conventional differentials driving the front and rear wheels.

The FF chassis was essentially the same as the Interceptor's, with double-wishbone front suspension and a de Dion system at the back. Oddly, the de Dion tube was located by two old-fashioned looking multi-leaf springs. To cope with the improved cornerning ability of the FF, it was given an addtional linkage to make sure it could not move sideways relative to the chassis – such a linkage is known as a Panhard rod, after the man who first suggested it in the 1890s. The car had a substantial chassis frame to carry the massive steel-panelled body; no matter what the tooling cost, GRP was not considered suitable for so expensive and prestigious a car. Like most of its rivals, the FF was almost if not quite a four-seater, and its dimensions and weight are typical of its class: all but 16 feet (4.9m) long, nearly 6 feet (1.8m) wide, scaling 3,800 pounds (1,723kg). Any such car needs power assisted steering, at least when wide, modern radial-ply tyres are fitted, and the Jensen's was rack-and-pinion. Four very large disc brakes formed the 'sharp end' of the Maxaret system.

Unfortunately the extra cost of these features added over 30 per cent to the cost of the standard Interceptor and while people were prepared to admire the FF, they generally bought the rear-driven car which offered just as much performance and visible prestige. In fact the FF seemed to prove yet again the contention of one American motor industry chief who explained – or perhaps complained – that 'safety does not sell'. Any hope the car might have had of longer-term sales success was destroyed by the energy crisis of the 1970's. Despite that, work on the four-wheel drive and anti-lock braking concepts continued and to good effect.

Jensen FF
Country of origin: Great Britain
Date: 1966
Engine: (Chrysler) four-stroke V8; overhead
valves; two side camshafts; 325bhp at 4,600rpm;
eight-cylinders bored direct in block
Gears: four-speed automatic; four-wheel drive
Capacity: 6,276cc
Bore & Stroke: 107.9 × 85.7mm
Maximum Speed: 130mph (209km/h)
Chassis: tubular ladder frame; front
suspension independent with wishbones and
coil springs (dual compression); rear
suspension with semi-elliptic leaf springs
Dimensions: wheelbase 109in (277cm);
             track (front) 56⅞in (142cm);
             track (rear) 56⅞in (142cm)
Steering: rack and pinion
Brakes: front and rear discs and
'Maxaret' anti-skid unit

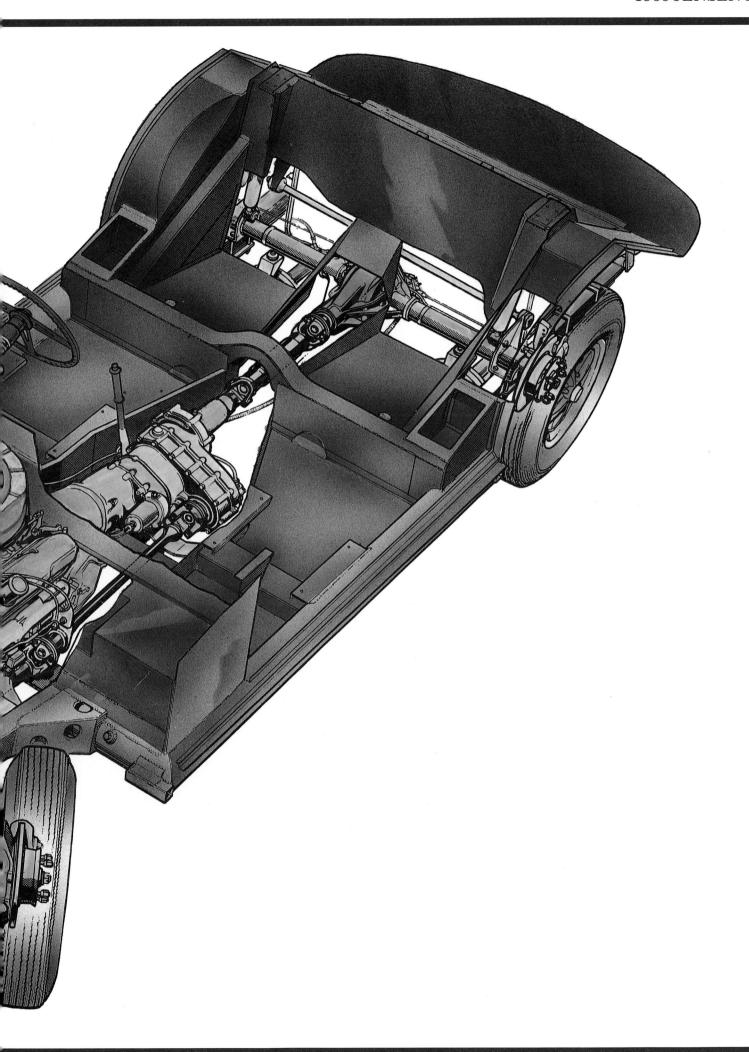

1968 JAGUAR XJ6

In the early 1960s Jaguar cars realised they would soon need a new range of saloon cars to replace the existing S-type and 420. The car which was announced in 1968 to fulfil that need, the XJ6, proved immediately successful and is still in production 17 years later; indeed, demand for it has never been stronger. The XJ6 is worthy of close study to discover the particular ingredients of a luxury car which not only had immediate success on its launch but also remained accepted as the best in its class for many years.

Jaguar had already established the necessary design principles in the big 420G saloon and followed them closely in the XJ6. Some of those principles, especially in the area of suspension design; had been introduced for the E-type sports car. The company was eager that the E-type's prestige should be more fully reflected in its saloons and that was one reason why the XJ6 eventually showed such a high standard of road behaviour.

The XJ6 body was of conventional unitary construction, though it was provided with front and rear sub-frames for the mounting of the main mechanical components. Comparing the car's dimensions with those of its predecessor 420, we find that while the XJ6 was rather longer and wider, but nearly five inches (12.7cm) lower, reflecting the strong styling and engineering trend of the time. It was a period when the engineers were seeking to lower the car's centre of gravity for ever-better stability and handling while the stylists (who do not always see eye to eye with vehicle engineers) were keen on lower, sleeker looks. The XJ6 was the last Jaguar to be styled under the direct influence of Sir William Lyons, the company's founder, who had always had a sure touch in matters of appearance. There was general agreement that the car had avoided the rather dated, slim-tailed shape of the old 420 whose rear wheel track, like that of other earlier Jaguar saloons, was notably narrower than the front. However, the new car retained the distinctly Jaguar image.

However successful the body might have been, it was lacking in two areas even it its faults were not immediately appreciated. It was strong, but it was also heavy, so that the car weighed over 250 pounds (113kg) more than the 420 and it lacked sufficient interior space. Eventually, Jaguar offered a version with a further four inches let into the wheelbase and the cabin legroom. Such were the benefits that before long, this version became standard although little could be done about the weight.

Jaguar's power unit was once again, inevitably, the six-cylinder XK engine with its twin overhead camshafts. By this time it had been further extended in capacity and power, from the 3.8-litres introduced with the E-type, to 4.2-litres and well over 200bhp. However, Jaguar was anxious that the XJ6 should sell well in Europe, and also produced a version of the engine with its capacity reduced to 2.8-litres (and the power output to well under 200bhp) for those markets in which larger-engined cars were heavily penalised by taxation. This latter move was not a success. Not only did the smaller engine prove to lack some of the XK unit's traditional reliability but it also attracted fewer buyers than was anticipated. Eventually the company restored the smaller engine to the former XK capacity of 3.4-litres, and also made amends in 1972 by offering a further version of the XJ6 and the XJ12 which was powered by a completely new and remarkable V12 engine of 5.3-litre capacity. This engine also became the standard fitting in the final versions of the Jaguar E-type.

The XK engine drove through either a four-speed manual or three-speed automatic gearbox and a propeller shaft to the rear differential unit. The majority of XJ6 buyers opted for the automatic transmission, a preference even then becoming very strong among luxury car buyers and the XJ12 when it emerged was offered with the automatic transmission as standard. The XJ6 suspension closely resembled that of the E-type, using double wishbone geometry at both ends of the car, the drive shafts forming the upper links at the rear, running between double coil spring and damper struts at each side. As in the E-type, the result was a standard of reliability and handling which could not have been achieved with any simpler form of independent rear suspension. A major improvement was the adoption of power-assisted rack and pinion steering in place of the

JLM 372K

recirculating-ball system of earlier saloon Jaguars. Four large disc brakes were fitted to complete a formidable-looking chassis.

The XJ6 was a big car in most of its details, indicating that little thought had indeed been given to weight reduction. The design team's priorities lay elsewhere. For instance, the fuel capacity was 23 gallons (104.5l), carried in twin tanks in the rear wings, while the wheels were 15-inch (38.1cm) and wide enough to carry the new lower-profile radial-ply tyres. The first generation of such tyres followed long-established cross-ply tyre practice in making the height of the tyre cross-section about 82 per cent of its width. By the late 1960's it had been realised that better grip and quicker steering response could be obtained by making tyres with an 'aspect ratio', the ratio of section height to width, of 70 per cent or even less, although changes in the aspect ratio usually resulted in some small loss of ride comfort. Surprisingly the Jaguar used these tyres without its ride

suffering in any way, indeed, the car's ride, comfort and freedom from interior noise became legendary. This was partly the result of its otherwise excessive weight since, as we have seen, the heavier the sprung parts of a car compared with the unsprung parts like the wheels and suspension components, the better its ride will be. As for the quietness, this was mainly the result of excellent insulation between the engine and suspension and the cabin, largely due to the clever use of rubber mountings for the front and rear sub-frames.

Thus, despite several partial drawbacks, the XJ6 quickly established an excellent reputation as a car which combined high performance and good handling with remarkable comfort. It was one of the last cars in its class to be designed with that order of priorities, since the time was fairly close when successive energy crises would result in every kind of car reflecting the need to save fuel by achieving better economy.

Jaguar XJ6 2.8 litre
Country of origin: Great Britain
Date: 1968
Engine: four-stroke; overhead valves; twin
overhead camshafts; six-cylinders; 180bhp at
6,000rpm; two SU carburettors
Gears: four-speed manual
Capacity: 2,792cc
Bore & Stroke: 83 × 86mm
Maximum Speed: 120mph (193km/h)
Chassis: integral; front suspension
independent with coil springs, wishbones,
telescopic dampers, anti-roll bar; rear
suspension independent with coil springs and
hydraulic dampers
Dimensions: wheelbase 108in (276.5cm);
         track (front) 58in (147.3cm);
         track (rear) 58⁵⁄₁₆in (148.1cm)
Steering: rack and pinion, optional power
assisted
Brakes: front/disc; rear/disc

1970 DATSUN 240Z

By 1970, the Japanese motor industry had progressed far and fast from starting points like our 1958 Toyota Corona. There was a feeling of immense confidence and in particular the Japanese had realised the advantage they might hold in the lucrative market on the West Coast of the USA, including California. The era of learning how to make a car which would survive in American conditions was long past, and a new generation of Japanese designers was eager to exploit evident gaps in the market on the other side of the Pacific Ocean.

One of those gaps was caused by the lack of a truly modern sports car at a realistic price. As we have seen, the traditional British sports car had become outmoded, and the only cars which had tried to extend the sports car concept into new areas were models like the very expensive Jaguar E-type and the relatively fragile, low volume Lotus Elan. The way was certainly open for any new car which could combine good performance with a real improvement in road behaviour and the kind of looks which would last into the 1970s. It was a market opportunity which especially appealed to Nissan, Toyota's great rival in Japan. Nissan had already offered the Americans a two-seater sports model adapted from their existing saloon cars and bearing something of a resemblance, at least in principle, to the MGB. However, their experience with this model was enough to convince Nissan that something better was needed, and the result was the Datsun 240Z.

Unlike its predecessor the Datsun 2000 sports, the 240Z was a new car 'from the ground up' and owed nothing to any of Nissan's saloon cars. Its designers realised that styling was extremely important but that the car must also be capable of an adequate performance. Therefore, it needed a chassis advanced enough so as to leave drivers in no doubt as to its superiority over traditional sports cars with stiff springs and live back axles.

The chosen body style was a smooth and well-proportioned two-seater hardtop coupé whose lines were reminiscent of some Ferrari models of the day. The nose needed to be long because the engine was an in-line six-cylinder unit, while the sloping tail panel included a useful rear loading hatch, and there was enough room inside the cabin for two very comfortable seats which could easily accommodate people well over six feet (1.8m) tall. The 240Z might be a Japanese car, but one of the lessons the Japanese had learned at an early stage was that export models must be designed for much bigger people. Equally evident as the result of their studies was an excellent control and instrument layout, which showed that the sports car market was indeed being taken seriously.

The 240Z was often compared in spirit with a much respected BMC sports car, the Austin-Healey 3000, which had just been taken out of production without being replaced. It is interesting to compare the 240Z with the Healey 3000 especially where body engineering is concerned. The 240Z was rather bigger than the Healey – six inches (15.24cm) longer, four inches (10.2cm) wider – but it weighed nearly 300 pounds (136kg) less, thanks to efficient

unitary construction in which many of the bending loads were taken through the roof. Another interesting Japanese decision was that the 240Z should be a closed coupé rather than a soft-topped convertible. The saving in weight helped to compensate for the 240Z's slightly lower power and torque; so did its superior aerodynamics.

The 240Z engine was, as the name implied, a 2.4-litre unit. It had a single overhead camshaft for its six cylinders and was a notably strong and well-tried unit producing about 150bhp – quite enough to confer 120mph (193km/h) maximum speed and excellent acceleration. The drive was taken through a manual gearbox – four speeds for the USA, five speeds wherever Datsun thought it was needed, including Britain – via a propeller shaft aft to the differential unit. Here we encounter another reason for the 240Z's superiority: it was given independent rear suspension.

Poorly designed independent suspension can be a snare and delusion, but the 240Z design team adopted an excellent solution. They used MacPherson struts at the back of the car, as well as the front. It was not quite the first car to use the arrangement – among others, its Japanese compatriots at Honda had early realised its advantages – but at the time it was certainly the highest-performance car to have done so, and the results were rewarding. The 240Z offered a very good ride, adequate road-holding and good handling due to rack and pinion steering.

The 240Z claimed a large part of the American sports car market when it was launched. This was hardly surprising, since Nissan had bravely decided to price the car on the assumption that it would justify volume production as it had avoided the 'specialist' premium which would have dramatically reduced its sales. But there is no doubt the 240Z's success also owed a lot to the quality of the product itself. Success emphasised that the best sports cars are designed as such, not adapted from saloons; the good sports car must avoid being too conservative in its engineering, but rather use sufficiently advanced ideas to achieve its intended specifications.

Datsun 240Z
Country of origin: Japan
Date: 1969
Engine: straight six; single ohc; twin Hitatchi (SU) carburettors; 157bhp at 5,600rpm
Gears: five-speed manual, with sychromesh
Capacity: 2,393cc
Bore & Stroke: 83 × 73.7mm
Maximum Speed: 125mph (200km/h)
Chassis: unitary; independent suspension both front and rear, with wishbones, and MacPherson struts
Dimensions: wheelbase 90½in (230cm);
            track (front) 53½in (136cm);
            track (rear) 53in (135cm)
Brakes: disc/front; drum/rear
Body: fastback, two-seater coupé

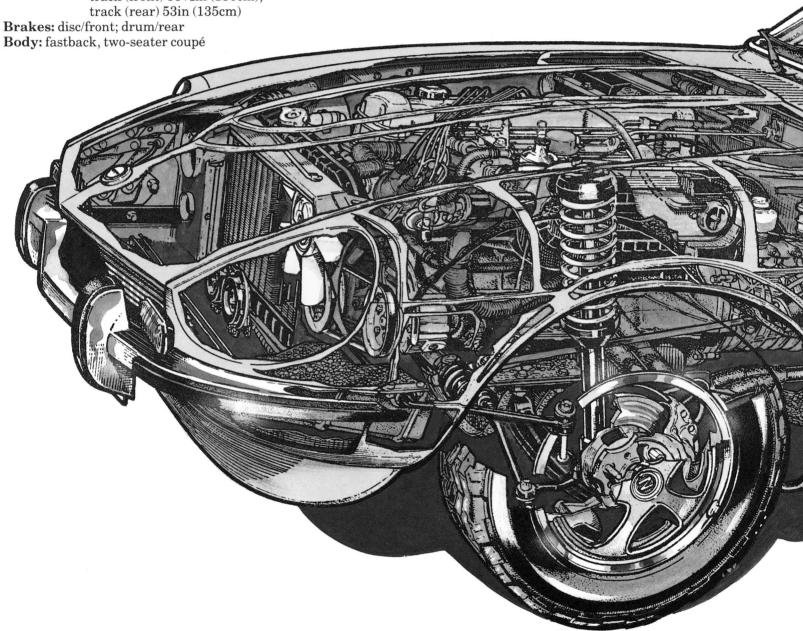

1971 FIAT 127

We have already seen how the BMC Mini created a sensation among car designers by showing how an economical but eminently roadworthy, roomy four-seater could be created within a much smaller space. This was achieved by turning the engine sideways, integrating it closely with the transmission and driving the front wheels. It was a concept which greatly appealed to those European designers trying to create family cars for the continent's increasingly crowded roads and work began in French, German and Italian drawing offices to study its application.

From the outset, each team had to take two critical decisions. Did it accept Issigonis' transmission arrangement, with the gearbox in the engine sump, or did it opt for an alternative system? Second, but even more fundamental: just how big should such a car be?

Fiat was quicker off the mark than any rival, although to begin with it launched a series of small front-driven saloons under the name of its subsidiary manufacturer, Autobianchi. It seemed that Fiat's management wanted to make sure that the front-drive layout had no hidden snags before it was put into a car that bore the company's own name. Hence the restricted distribution and Autobianchis were sold only in Italy and one or two other export markets. In the meantime Fiat itself launched one final small rear-engined saloon, the 850, which resembled an enlarged and generally developed version of the long-standing 600. The results of the Autobianchi experiment were reassuring, and little time was lost in planning not just one, but two Fiat models with transverse engines and front wheel drive.

The first of these models, the 128, was launched in 1969 as a replacement for the aged 1100R and was widely acclaimed as an excellent product which combined space and performance with a surprisingly comfortable ride. The 128 was shortly followed by the 127 which offered similar virtues but was by far the more significant car. This was surprising since it used an old engine whereas the 128's was brand-new and technically more advanced. The 127 established the basic shape of what has since become one of the most prolific classes of European and Japanese cars: the 'supermini'.

The term supermini was only coined later when it became clear that every major manufacturer felt it was necessary to build a model in this class, but each new introduction has stayed remarkably close to the Fiat 127 concept. Although the BMC Mini had demonstrated the advantages of the transverse engine, front-drive layout, the 127 proved that a great deal could be gained by making a car that was about 10 per cent bigger overall. In fact

BMC's own follow-up to the Mini, the Austin Morris 1100 came very close to the idea but emerged too early to be considered as such: in 1962 the 1100 was thought of as a medium-sized family car but the increasing affluence of the European car buyer meant that by 1971 the Fiat 127 was considered just one step up from the most basic type of vehicle.

We must begin by comparing the 'supermini' with the Mini. The Fiat 127 was nearly two feet (0.6m) longer than the BMC Mini, and 4½ inches (11.4cm) wider. Although the Mini was thought of as a miracle of compression it could only squeeze in four adults partly by adopting an uncomfortable sitting position for those in front. Therefore it seemed quite natural that the 127 should offer four comfortable seats and a great deal more luggage space. It says a good deal for the advance of structural design during the 1960's that for all its larger size, the 127 weighed only 200 pounds more than the Mini – 14 per cent more weight for 28 per cent more floor area.

The 127 engine, like the Mini's, was a conventional pushrod overhead-valve unit, developed from that used in the rear-driven 850. Although its capacity was not much greater than that of the Mini's (903cc compared with 848cc), it was tuned to produce a lot more power (47bhp compared with 34bhp). This gave the Fiat a tolerable performance with a maximum speed of well over 80mph (129km/h). The way in which its transmission was arranged was also different. Instead of having its gearbox in the sump, the Fiat used what appeared to be a conventional in-line gearbox hung off the end of the engine, in line with the crankshaft. In fact the two-shaft Fiat gearbox 'turned round' the power just like the gearboxes used in earlier transaxle arrangements, to drive a differential housed just aft of the engine itself. This system enabled Fiat to use the gearbox from the rear engined 850 but meant that the differential could not be in the centre of the car, instead it was noticeably offset to one side, but Fiat simply fitted a longer drive shaft on one side than the other – viewed from the driving seat, the right-hand shaft is the longer – and proved that it worked. After that, the same arrangement was used for the majority of superminis as well as for larger front-driven cars.

Fiat's approach to suspension design was also different. Both the 128 and the 127 used MacPherson struts for all four wheels, again proving that such a system can be extremely satisfactory, especially in conjunction with light and accurate rack and pinion steering. The rear suspension was especially neat since, instead of the customary coil springs, Fiat used a single crosswise leaf spring which also acted as an

anti-roll bar to resist the body roll in cornering. While the Mini was notable for its small wheels, the Fiat 127 was given standard 13-inch (33cm) ones with radial-ply tyres. The wheel arches took up more of the body space as a result but not enough to be a nuisance, while the car's appearance was certainly better balanced than it would have been with 10-inch (25cm) Mini-size wheels.

Only one more thing was needed to turn the Fiat 127 into what we today would call a typical supermini, and it was not long in coming. Two years after its original introduction, the car was also offered with a hatchback rear door and a back seat which folded in the manner of an estate car. It was a move which proved extremely popular and set the seal of success on the 127 which remained in production for 12 years until it was replaced by the Fiat Uno – a supermini of the second generation.

Fiat 127
Country of origin: Italy
Date: 1971
Engine: four-stroke; transverse; overhead valves; push-rod operated; Weber carburettor
Gears: four-speed manual, fully synchronized; front-wheel drive
Capacity: 903cc
Bore & Stroke: 65 × 68mm
Maximum Speed: 85mph (137km/h)
Chassis: integral; front suspension with coil springs, lower swinging arms, anti-roll bar; rear suspension with transverse leaf spring with lower swinging arms
Dimensions: wheelbase 87⅔in (222.5cm); track (front) 40 4/10in (128cm); track (rear) 50 9/10in (129.5cm)
Steering: rack and pinion
Brakes: front/disc; rear/drum

1971 DATSUN CHERRY

The late 1960s were extremely productive for Nissan in Japan. At one extreme, as we have already seen, the company produced the admirable 240Z; at the other, it was busy designing its own supermini, the 100A Cherry, which was announced almost at the same time as Fiat's 127 and might almost have been designed to the same specification. Although the Fiat is generally given the credit for starting the supermini trend, the Cherry was also strong evidence for the rightness of the concept.

Perhaps the most interesting thing about the Cherry is that while Fiat played its Autobianchi experiment before going ahead with the 128 and 127, Nissan launched off into what was for it unexplored territory, and got the car right first time. The design team under Mr Goto was actually given a brief to produce a car with a certain passenger space and performance. They quickly realised – due to the example of the Mini — that by using a transverse engine and front wheel drive, the specification could be met by a car which was lighter and smaller, and therefore cheaper and more economical. It was daring thinking by the Japanese standard of time, as the domestic market still tended to judge cars by

their size and sure enough the Cherry never sold as well in its own country as the cramped, rear-driven and technically inferior Toyota Publica. Elsewhere, and especially in Europe, it was another matter.

Like the Fiat 127, the Cherry was powered by a well-tried engine with pushrod-operated overhead valves, and directly comparable with the Italian car in power output and performance. However, the transmission was arranged like the Mini's, with the gearbox in the engine sump, the differential immediately aft, and equal-length drive shafts. Where the suspension was concerned the Nissan engineers trod something of a middle way, using MacPherson struts at the front (like the Fiat) but trailing arms at the back (like the Mini). Another daring move, at least by Japanese standards, was to use rack and pinion steering.

The Cherry body was a neat two-door saloon which was even more structurally efficient than that of the Fiat 127. Again, the comparison is illuminating: the Cherry was exactly the same length as the Fiat, and just two inches (5cm) narrower. It weighed 150 pounds (68kg) less than the Fiat, or if you prefer, just 50 pounds

(23kg) more than the Mini. Japanese compromise was again reflected in the choice of 12 inch (30cm) wheels for the Cherry, smaller than the Fiat's, bigger than the Mini's: and cross-ply tyres were standard equipment because the radial-ply revolution was late reaching Japan (and indeed America).

In common with most Japanese car models, the Cherry was steadily developed and, in the process, became bigger and heavier as well as more technically advanced. An overhead camshaft engine was eventually adopted and more significantly perhaps, the original transmission arrangement gave way to that pioneered by the Fiat, which seems now to have become accepted as the best method. Now there has emerged into the space left by the growth of the Cherry a new and typically 1980's supermini, the Micra, whose specification looks remarkably similar to that of the first Cherry except in a few important respects. It is, for example, a few inches wider, but even lighter . . .

If the Cherry had lessons to teach they might be these. In the first place, it is clear that the thinking process which led to the Cherry differed notably from that which gave rise to the Fiat 127, yet the two cars were in the end remarkably similar and emerged at much the same time. Obviously there is more than one way of arriving at a good new idea. The Japanese car should also act as a warning to any European still insular enough to think that all original thought and advanced vehicle engineering, especially where small cars are concerned, starts in Europe. It is ironic then that the Japanese industry was terribly slow to realise just how good a concept the Cherry was, and failed to exploit it properly. The supermini has established itself more firmly than any other motoring idea of recent years. Since the Fiat 127 and the original Cherry started the ball rolling, something like a dozen other designs have followed the same path. Most significant of all perhaps, the British Leyland design which started out as a Mini replacement ended up instead as yet another supermini — the Austin Metro. Every car which now competes in the class has certain things in common: the transverse engine, the front-wheel drive and the compact body with the rear hatchback door. It may yet be some time before we see an idea sufficiently original to reshape this area of car design.

Datsun Cherry
Country of origin: Japan
Date: 1971
Engine: four-stroke in-line ohc four-cylinder;
Hitachi carburettor; 59bhp at 6,000rpm
Bore and stroke: 73 × 59mm
Capacity: 988cc
Transmission: front-wheel drive; four-speed
manual gearbox
Chassis: integral
Suspension: front, independent with coil
springs; rear, independent with trailing arms,
coil springs
Steering: rack and pinion
Brakes: drum, front and rear
Dimensions: wheelbase 92in (234cm)
          track (front) 50in (127cm)
          track (rear) 48.6in (123cm)
Maximum speed: 87mph (140kmh)

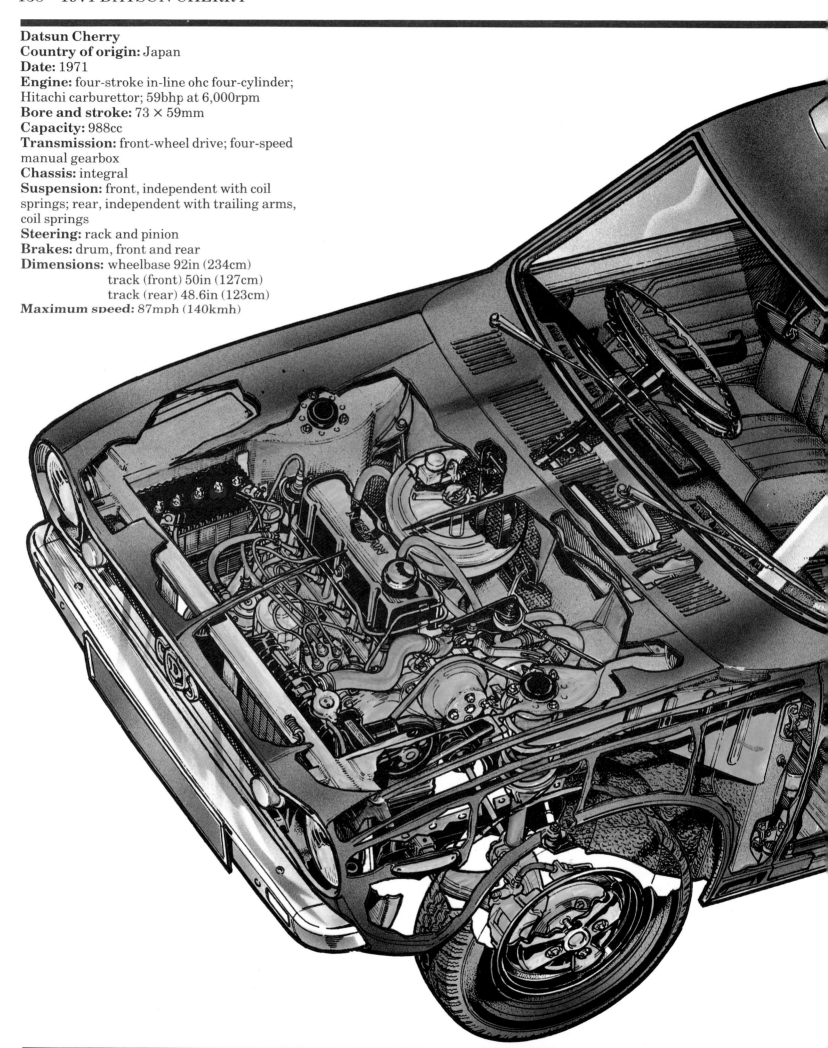

1972 RENAULT 5

In the late 1960s the Regie Renault decided that it too needed a supermini in its range. At the time the gap between the Renault 4 and the newly introduced Renault 12, both of them front-driven, was less than satisfactorily filled by the rear engined 8 and 10 which were really no more than rebodied developments of the old Dauphine. However, it was not easy for Renault to conclude that a supermini was what it needed because it had a tradition of only building cars with four or five doors. It felt doubtful that the French market would welcome a two-door car but eventually the appeal of a small, smart city 'runabout' won the day.

There were two important respects in which the new design, the Renault 5, failed to conform with the supermini mould. Firstly, Renault did not immediately accept the logic of the transverse engine installation. Secondly, the reason for the huge success of the 5 lay not so much in its specification as in its appearance.

In the beginning, Renault had too little confidence in the idea of the 5 to commit a very large engineering effort to it. Instead of designing a new engine or even adapting an existing one for transverse installation as BMC and Fiat had done, it preferred a layout which to all intent and purposes was borrowed from the existing Renault 4. Consequently, the 5 had an engine in-line but immediately forward of the cabin, which drove the front wheels through a transaxle in which the gearbox was right at the front of the car. By doing this Renault was able to use a large number of existing components and keep down the development cost. On the other hand it sacrificed the valuable compactness of the transverse engine and, as in

the 4 and 16, left itself a problem with gearchange design.

Like BMC and Fiat, Renault had a well-tried small engine available and, given the chosen layout, even more reason to use it. Again like its rivals, it was a simple four cylinder power unit with pushrod-operated overhead valves. Renault offered a number of engine sizes for the 5 especially in France, where the size makes a difference to the amount of licence fee paid by the car owner, but in Britain the most familiar unit was of 956cc delivering 43bhp. This was marginally less than the Fiat 127 engine but a good deal more than the basic Mini unit. A four-speed gearbox was standard from the outset and later on, unlike most of the superminis, the 5 was also made with an original answer to the gearchange problem was to use a linkage similar to that in the 4, with an 'umbrella handle' emerging from the centre of the dashboard, but this did not fit the smart image of the 5 as well as it did the utiliarian 4 and caused adverse reaction in some important export markets. Before long Renault devised a tortuous linkage to a conventional-looking floor lever but the 5's gearchange was never one of its better points.

By far the strongest point of the Renault 5 was its body styling. In the world of car fashion it is very difficult to achieve a shape which is both universally pleasing yet immediately different from any other car, but the Renault designers managed it. In particular, it emerged that the body's softly rounded lines had a particular appeal for women owners, and a notable pioneering feature was the 5's use of very large reinforced plastic bumpers which

The Renault 5 of the 1980s.

blended in with the main body lines and were also able to survive minor parking knocks without damage – an advantage anywhere, but especially in Paris. Despite Renault's marketing misgivings the 5 was given just three doors; the 5 therefore beat the Fiat 127 in offering the rear hatch which became an essential part of the supermini formula. What is more, the French car had it as standard, but that was hardly surprising since the 4 and 16 were already hatchbacked designs.

Renault's engineering preoccupations were reflected in other aspects of the 5 body design which comprised relatively few individual steel pressings and was by the current standards outstandingly economical to build. Another of its pioneering features, like the bumpers, was a semi-rigid, pre-formed interior headlining which simply stuck into place (it was discovered that it also made the cabin notably quieter). Both bumper and headlining techniques have since become commonplace. Despite its sound engineering the body weighed more than the Fiat's. This was largely due to the fact that in order to obtain sufficient cabin space with the in-line engine, the Renault team had to use a wheelbase which was longer by more than six inches (15cm). In the circumstances it did them credit that the 5 was slightly shorter than the Fiat 127 overall, and that the weight penalty was only 30 pounds (14kg) or so.

The 5's close engineering connection with the 4 could be seen in the suspension design which, like the earlier car, used double wishbones at the front and trailing arms at the rear. One odd feature common to the 4, 5, and 16, was that in order to allow the rear torsion bars to run the full width of the car without fouling each other, the car's right-hand wheelbase was about an inch longer than on the left! Like Fiat, Renault opted for 'proper' 13 inch (33cm) wheels for the 5, and the car was equipped with radial ply tyres and front disc brakes. It also used rack and pinion steering, though this proved surprisingly heavy until Renault substantially revised the details of their front suspension geometry, such as the wheel castor angle – the forward inclination of the steering axis.

For the student of the motor car anatomy, the Renault 5 holds two somewhat contradictory lessons. From the strictly engineering point of view, it proved that a supermini-class car could not be designed with an in-line engine without making some important sacrifices, especially of interior space. In a broader context however, it proved that the right kind of styling can bring success to a car despite apparent drawbacks and that it is possible to create high-impact styling without slavishly following fashion.

The 5 remained in production for 12 years and was extensively developed in that time, receiving bigger and more powerful engines and eventually, a complementary five-door version. In 1984 it was finally replaced by a 'superfive' whose styling remained as close as possible to the admired original – but whose engine and transmission were installed transversely!

Renault 5L
Country of origin: France
Date: 1972
Engine: four-stroke in-line ohc four-cylinder;
Solex carburettor; 35.5bhp at 5,500rpm
Bore and stroke: 58 × 80mm
Capacity: 845cc
Transmission: front-wheel drive; four-speed
manual gearbox
Chassis: integral
Suspension: front, independent with
wishbones, torsion bars and anti-roll bar; rear,
torsion bar and trailing arms
Steering: rack and pinion
Brakes: drum, front and rear
Dimensions: wheelbase (left) 95.7in (243cm)
                    wheelbase (right) 94.5in (240cm)
                    track (front) 50.4in (128cm)
                    track (rear) 48.8in (124cm)
Maximum speed: 85mph (137kmh)

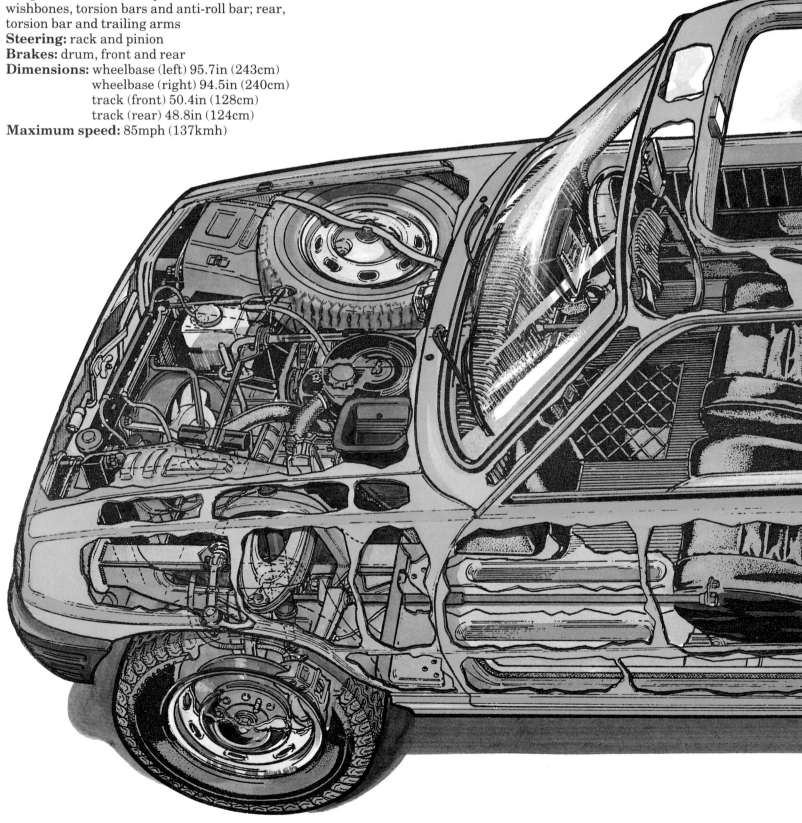

1974 VOLKSWAGEN GOLF

By the early 1970s the Volkswagen concern was in deep trouble: history had repeated itself. In 1927 Ford almost paid the penalty for having assumed the Model T had so secure a place in the public affection that it would sell forever; in 1974 the same thing happened over the Volkswagen Beetle. Dr Porsche's formula had worked for over 20 years but quite suddenly a lot of Beetle buyers decided that the car demanded too many sacrifices in exchange for its virtues. The Beetle had its devoted adherents but, by the early 1970's there were no longer enough of them to make the large scale manufacture of the car an economic proposition, especially in an expensive labour market like Germany. A replacement was needed.

Volkswagen had already tried to move up-market by applying the Beetle formula to larger cars but with diminishing success. It took over the ailing NSU company but that failed to give it the product it needed; it absorbed the Audi company and that at least was start. By the late 1960s Audi engineers had built up substantial experience with front-driven cars, an experience that went back to small-scale beginnings in 1932 when cars were powered by efficient, water-cooled engines: the antithesis of the Beetle, in fact. The main Volkswagen management had long been unwilling to accept the idea that salvation would only be found in a complete break with tradition; there was also a school of thought which argued that any Beetle replacement would have to be at least as revolutionary as the Beetle itself had been at the time of its introduction. This line of argument led to the building of prototypes with mid-mounted engines compact enough to be mounted under the floor, but costs were rising and time was running out. In the end a new Managing Director, Rudolf Leiding, threw out all the existing work and set his engineers severe but realistic targets to be met with a highly efficient front-driven car along Audi lines. The result was a Golf.

The Golf was not a supermini because it was too large and it had to replace the Beetle which, however cramped inside, was not a small car with its overall length of more than 13 feet (4m). Its designers set out to make a comfortable four-seat car with better economy, comfort, performance, stability and handling than the Beetle and they succeeded. The key to that success was the decision to adopt a transverse engine and transmission. Since they could hardly have used the flat-four Beetle engine even if they had wanted to, the engineers faced a choice: how to use the latest Audi engine and transaxle assembly which had already been transferred to the first 'new generation' Volkswagen, the Passat. In this car a light, efficient, four-cylinder 1.5-litre engine with overhead camshaft had been installed ahead of the front wheels, driving them through a transaxle of the type with which we have become familiar. However, this solution meant the body must have a long enough nose to house the engine, and given the constraints in the Beetle-replacement specification it simply would not do, even though it worked well in the Passat.

A completely new engine was therefore designed along the same lines as the Passat unit, but suitably smaller and lighter, with a capacity of 1.1-litres. It was intended from the outset for transverse installation and was kept compact enough to enable it to sit well to the right (viewed from the driving seat) within the engine compartment. This meant that a Fiat 127-type transmission – gearbox in line with the engine, returning the drive to a differential housed immediately aft of the crankcase, could be used while still having equal-length drive shafts. The engine showed several details which have since become familiar in other recently introduced units, including the use of a distributor driven directly from the end of the overhead camshaft. With a capacity nearly 10 per cent less than that of the basic Beetle engine, the Golf unit produced 50bhp compared with 34bhp, and almost matched the torque output of the flat-four as well. Having gone to the trouble of designing a new engine, the Golf engineers adapted the 1.5-litre Audi unit for transverse installation anyway, so that they could use it in their car's more up-market versions. A very important detail design point in both engines was the use of wide, toothed rubber belts rather than chains to drive their overhead camshafts – a technique which had just begun to come into use and which was destined to spread very widely.

The Golf body was designed as a five-door hatchback, making the most of the compact engine and transmission layout. It had exactly the same wheelbase as the Beetle but was a full foot (0.3m) shorter overall, while offering more cabin space. It is also structurally highly efficient, weighing for instance hardly any more than the Renault 5 despite being a good deal bigger and having two more doors. This close control of weight was another key to the Golf's performance and economy.

Having chosen the front-drive layout, the Golf's designers would have had a difficult task not to come up with a car infinitely more stable and better-handling than the Beetle. Here again there emerged a key design feature which was to become very widely accepted in small and medium-size cars of the next ten years. While the front suspension used the now-familiar

MacPherson struts, the location of the rear wheels was new and ingenious. At first sight the system was no more than a pair of simple trailing arms joined at their 'roots' by a transverse beam of carefully designed shape. In fact this beam turned the whole assembly into a U-shaped 'dead' axle, sufficiently flexible at its centre to allow the two arms a degree of independent movement but not too much, while also acting as an anti-roll bar and taking some of the suspension loads out of the body mounting points. It was light, it was simple and it proved extremely satisfactory, since the Golf had excellent stability and handling. Subsequent designs (including that of the Golf's smaller cousin the Volkswagen Polo, a true supermini) moved the cross-beam part-way along the trailing arms towards the wheels to create what is now known as the 'H-beam' rear suspension.

In other respects, the Golf was conventional. It saved further space compared with the Beetle, by using 13 inch (33cm) wheels instead of 15 inch (38cm); it was naturally equipped with radial-ply tyres and front disc brakes.

Beyond doubt, the Golf saved Volkswagen from the threat of extinction. It was immediately accepted by its target markets and sold so well in the USA that Volkswagen set up an American factory to build versions of the car adapted to meet the USA's safety and exhaust emission regulations, which were by then becoming a serious problem for European car manufacturers. In 1983, after a production run of nine years, the Golf was replaced by a car bearing the same name, and with a striking resemblance of styling and engineering features, but further refined.

Golf 1 Volkswagen
Country of origin: West Germany
Date: 1975
Engine: four-stroke; front, transverse; overhead camshaft; four-cylinders (direct in block); 50bhp at 6,000rmp; Solex carburettor
Gears: four-speed manual, with synchromesh; front-wheel drive
Capacity: 1,096cc
Bore & Stroke: 69.5 × 72mm
Maximum Speed: 90mph (145km/h)
Chassis: integral; front suspension with coil spring/struts with lower wishbone; rear suspension with trailing arms on T-section torsion beam
Dimensions: wheelbase 95½in (240cm);
track (front) 54⅗in (138.7cm);
track (rear) 53½in (135.8cm);
Steering: rack and pinion
Brakes: front/drum; rear/drum

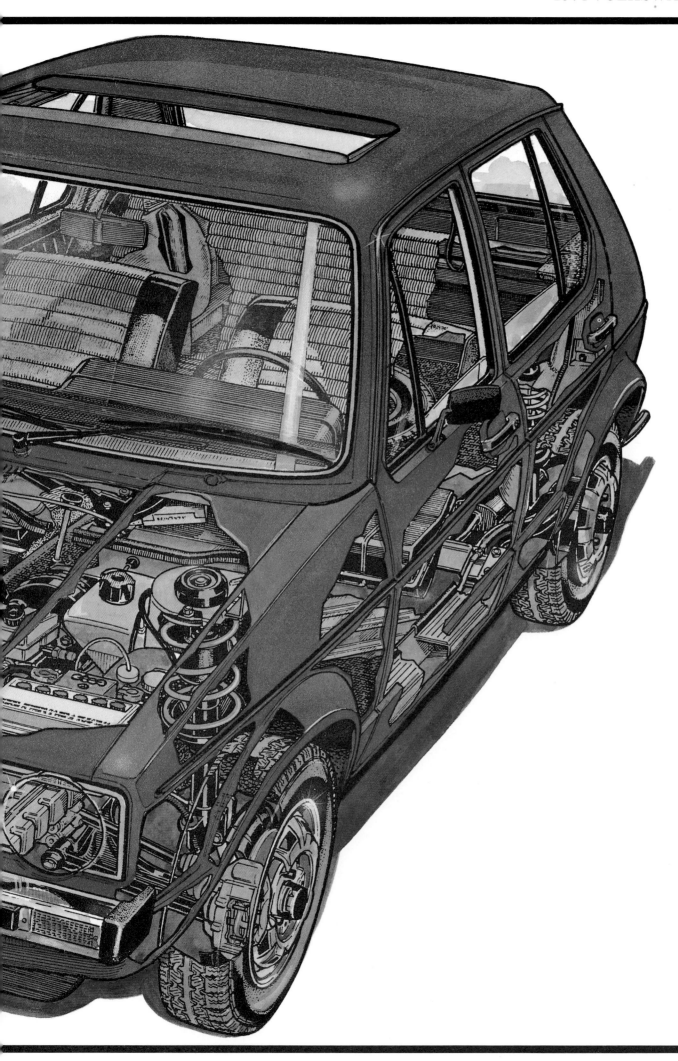

1974 RELIANT ROBIN

The Robin is well out of the mainstream of motor car development, which is why it finds a place in our list of significant cars. Models which differ so drastically and which appeal to a minority audience however enthusiastic, deserve attention if only to see whether they hold ideas which might benefit the industry more generally.

Strictly speaking the Robin is barely a car at all, since it owes its existence to regulations drawn up in Britain to favour motor cycle combinations – the almost-dead assembly of motor cycle and side-car. The regulations are written in such a way that they can be met by any vehicle with three wheels, a sufficiently low weight, and the facility to blank off the reverse gear (if one is fitted) to render it inoperative – this last requirement being called for so that the vehicle can be driven by anyone holding a motor cycle licence.

The Reliant Motor Company, which we have already encountered as the manufacturer of the GTE 'sports hatch', actually came into being specifically to build three-wheeled vehicles taking advantage of these regulations. It had prospered on that basis for many years. During the late 1960s it became clear that the product would have to be made more attractive if it was to survive the increasing affluence of society and the rapid spread of small, cheap cars like the Mini. A new design was therefore prepared by Ogle Design, the same styling organisation which had shaped the GTE, and this proved good enough to carry Reliant's traditional three-wheeler on into the 1980s.

The most crucial decision in designing a three-wheeled vehicle is whether to put the two wheels at the back or at the front. There is no agreement about this: Reliant chose a single steered front wheel and two driven rear wheels while the idiosyncratic Morgan company enjoyed many years of modest success with vehicles in which the two front wheels were steered while the single rear one was driven. Reliant's philosophy was that the paired rear wheels were essential to support a four-seater body which, through diligent engineering, could just be squeezed under the official weight limit of eight hundredweight (896 pounds) (406kg) for the vehicle.

From an engineering point of view, the new Robin did not greatly differ from its predecessor the Regal. A simple chassis of welded, square-section tube served to carry the engine, mounted at the front but of necessity a long way back to leave room for the front wheel, the transmission and suspension. Upon the chassis sat the newly styled body, moulded from GRP and, naturally, made as light as possible. Structural efficiency was helped by its neatly rounded lines. It had two doors, plus a large, sloping rear window which hinged open at its top to give much of the hatchback loading convenience of a supermini.

Reliant had to be at pains to make everything as light as possible because of the severe weight limitation which was little more than two-thirds the weight of the basic Mini. At one time the company had used a side-valve Austin engine but, by the time the Robin arrived, it had switched to an overhead-valve unit of its own design. This was made largely out of light alloy in the interest of weight-saving and was capable of producing Mini-type power from its 750cc (later increased to 850cc). The engine drove through a gearbox also of lightweight Reliant design and manufacture, through a short propeller shaft to the differential of a live rear axle. The axle was suspended on simple leaf springs while the front wheel was located on a leading arm.

The Robin had mostly predictable characteristics. To begin with, being outstandingly light yet possessed of reasonable power, it had good performance allied to excellent fuel economy. These, together with its lower tax liability and small dimensions, were its main plus points. On the debit side there was first and foremost the immense handicap of only having one wheel at the front when it came to handling and stability. Despite some enthusiastic claims to the contrary, the Robin could not be driven in safety along any kind of winding road at a speed even approaching that of a typical four-wheeled supermini. It also suffered from a poor ride, partly because of its very low sprung weight but also due to its short wheelbase and the inability

of its central front wheel to straddle bumps or potholes in the manner of a four-wheeler. Its cabin was cramped because the rearward mounting of the engine created a large and awkward hump in the front bulkhead, which in turn made the footwells narrow and uncomfortable. Finally, the choice of materials needed to meet the weight limit, plus the small scale of production made it inevitable that the Robin would actually be markedly more expensive than a Mini.

Despite these drawbacks the Robin sold reas bly well, helped by the two great energy crises of the 1970s which focussed attention on its outstanding economy. As though to place the vehicle fully in focus, Reliant also engineered a four-wheeled version, the Kitten, which proved — not unexpectedly — to have infinitely better stability, handling and ride plus one of the tightest turning circles of any production car, an attribute certainly not shared by the three-wheeler. The Kitten was a complete failure commercially, because it begged direct comparison with cars like the Mini and was very

expensive for what it was.

What lessons does the Robin hold for the motor car anatomist in general? Three things, certainly. Firstly, it is possible to build vehicles that are very light indeed. The Robin's ability to creep under 900 pounds ought to give other vehicle designers serious pause for thought. Secondly, it is very difficult indeed to make a three-wheeled vehicle that competes on every technical basis with a four-wheeled equivalent and the most likely qualities to be sacrificed are stability and handling. Thirdly, if a vehicle is sufficiently different from everything else available, people will find it difficult to make value comparisons and may buy it anyway on the strength of its uniquely good points. The Robin's advantage of lower annual tax was barely significant in terms of its overall cost, but it probably won the car more sales than any other factor.

The Robin survived for several years in a 'facelifted' form called the Rialto. It will be interesting to see if any fundamental replacement is ever forthcoming.

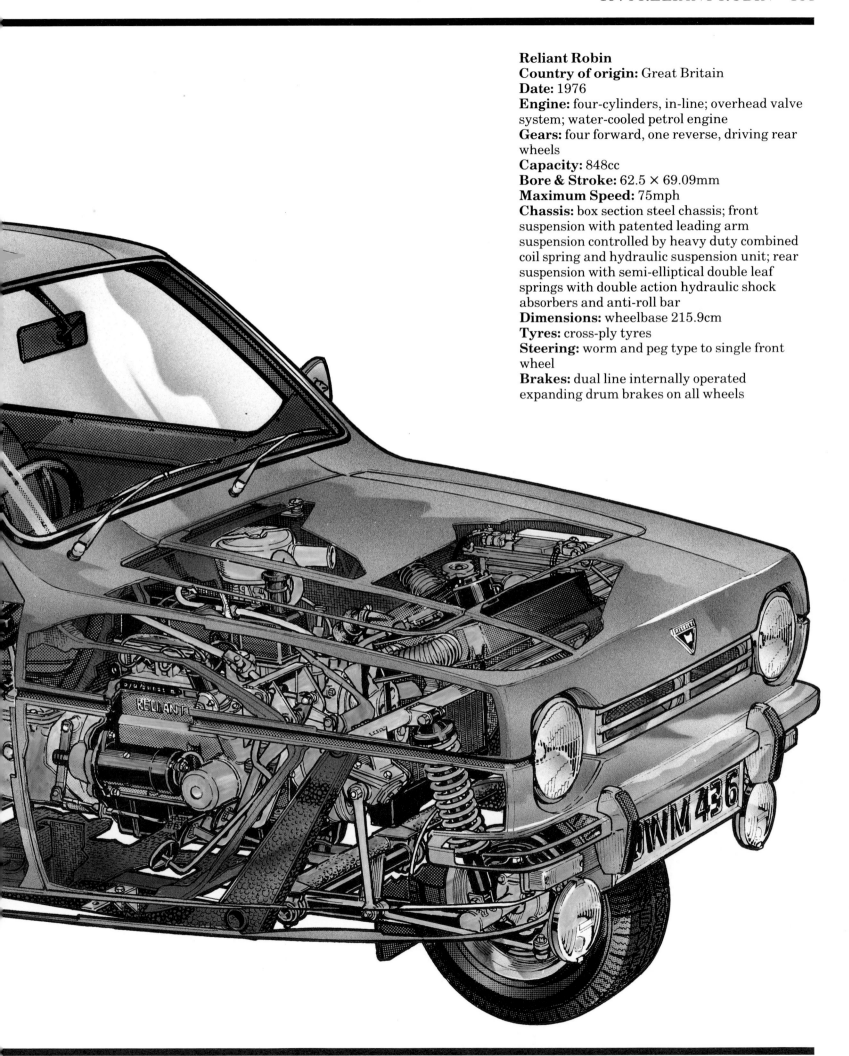

Reliant Robin
Country of origin: Great Britain
Date: 1976
Engine: four-cylinders, in-line; overhead valve system; water-cooled petrol engine
Gears: four forward, one reverse, driving rear wheels
Capacity: 848cc
Bore & Stroke: 62.5 × 69.09mm
Maximum Speed: 75mph
Chassis: box section steel chassis; front suspension with patented leading arm suspension controlled by heavy duty combined coil spring and hydraulic suspension unit; rear suspension with semi-elliptical double leaf springs with double action hydraulic shock absorbers and anti-roll bar
Dimensions: wheelbase 215.9cm
Tyres: cross-ply tyres
Steering: worm and peg type to single front wheel
Brakes: dual line internally operated expanding drum brakes on all wheels

1974 VOLVO 200

Although Sweden has a small population, the country is technically advanced and prosperous. It is not surprising therefore that it can support a small but capable motor industry. Nor is it surprising, given the traditional Swedish interest in the quality of design and in safety, and the severe Swedish winter weather, that its industry builds cars which are seen as tough and long-lasting.

The Volvo company has been involved with car manufacturing for many years but its products were hardly known outside Sweden until the 1950s when a trickle of strong but hardly beautiful saloon cars began to be exported. There followed two major changes of styling, and a steady increase in available engine size and power, until by the early 1970s Volvos were well known and generally respected for their safety and longevity even though they were less than inspiring to drive. Then in 1974 the company launched its new 200-series in a clear attempt to win world-wide recognition and sales.

The most important thing about the 200-series was that it broke very little new engineering ground but was a progressive development of what had gone before. In particular that meant the car was rear-driven and, as a matter of deliberate policy, it retained a live axle rather than moving to any form of independent rear suspension: Volvo designers have long cherished the value of parallel rear wheels on gravel roads and ice.

It is worth comparing the Volvo 200-series with the previous 100-series in some detail, if only to see how a company which believes in evolution rather than revolution sets about creating a new model which offers worthwhile

improvements. Volvo's object was to achieve more space, better performance and even greater reserves of safety without upsetting any of the established 100-series virtues. Thus although the 200-series body was completely restyled, it bore a close and obvious resemblance to the 100-series, the main distinguishing feature being a rather more 'shovel' nose and bigger bumpers ready to meet the latest American regulations. These made the 200 series five inches (13cm) longer than before, though its body was actually an inch (2.5cm) narrower despite the provision of new side-structures to resist impact penetration through the doors. The new body was also 1½ inches (3.8cm) longer in the wheelbase, which was translated into useful extra legroom inside the cabin.

The 100-series cars had been powered by in-line engines with pushrod operation of their overhead valves, and with capacities of 2-litres (four-cylinder) and 3-litres (six-cylinder). For the 200-series Volvo was seeking more choice for the buyer. Thus, while the basic 2-litre engine was retained, a second version was created with 2.1-litre capacity and an overhead camshaft driven by a toothed belt. It is worth noting at this point that the toothed belt proved especially valuable to several designers of the 1970s who wanted to update their engines by redesigning them with overhead camshafts. Since a toothed belt needs no lubrication it is much easier to install as an afterthought, the only penalty being to add an inch or so to the unit's overall length. In Volvo's case, the 2.1-litre engine offered worthwhile extra power to fill the gap between the most basic model and the new top of the range, the 264.

The 264 was powered by a completely new engine, a 2.7-litre V6, jointly developed by Volvo, Renault and Peugeot for use in each of the companies' new larger models – the Volvo 264 was first, the Renault 30 and Peugeot 604 followed later. The new engine was in detail, built mostly of aluminium alloy for lightness and equipped with overhead camshafts, but its real significance lay in the fact that three companies had pooled their resources to undertake a task which any of them would have found too expensive to tackle alone. This was a trend which was to grow in Europe during the next decade.

From Volvo's point of view, the compact shape and lightness of the V6 meant it could use the same chassis for both four cylinder and six-cylinder engines, while the old six-cylinder 164 had been a longer and heavier car than the 144. All versions of the 200 series received two worthwhile chassis improvements, the adoption of MacPherson strut front suspension instead of

wishbone, and rack and pionion steering in place of the previous worm-and-roller system. The rear axle was located by trailing arms and a Panhard rod, and coil springs were fitted front and rear. Volvo also used disc brakes on all four wheels, those at the front being ventilated through internal air passages for improved cooling and better fade resistance. The wheels were reduced from 15 to 14-inch (38 to 35cm) diameter and the 200-series suspension was developed with radial-ply tyres in mind.

When it was introduced, the Volvo 200-series was generally admired but it was still felt that the cars were uninspiring to drive. Volvo began an exhaustive study of the relation between chassis design and handling which resulted in the introduction of several changes in 1980, the most notable being the use of antiroll bars at front and rear. Power-assisted steering was also made standard on all 200-series cars in response to a shift in market taste. The result was that the handling of the cars was greatly improved, something which is still not generally recognised. That has not stopped the 200-series from being a considerable success for Volvo and the design was still in production more than ten years after it was launched.

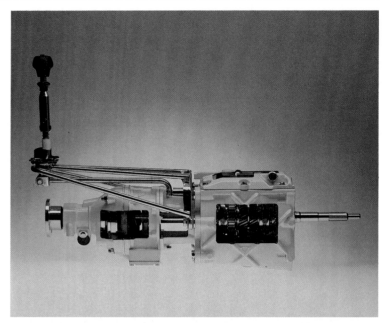

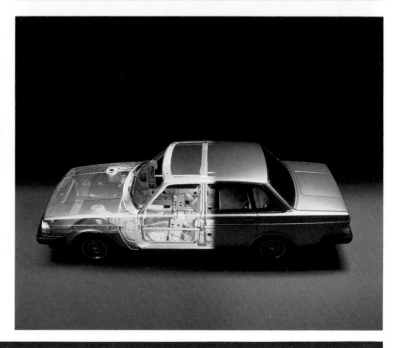

1978 SAAB 900

Saab is a Swedish company that is equally famous for building aeroplanes; SAAB originally stood for Svenska Aeroplan AktieBolag (Swedish Aircraft Company). Soon after the end of the Second World War the company decided to enter car manufacturing to expand its industrial activities. Saab's cars have always been designed by engineers with aircraft experience and this shows in their sometimes unusual but always highly efficient shape, and in particular, their characteristic deeply-curved windscreens.

At first the company built small cars powered by two-stroke engines but gradually found it more profitable to build bigger models in relatively small numbers. In the mid-1970s they launched their biggest car yet, the 900. Like all Saab's cars, it used front-wheel drive. The 2-litre overhead camshaft engine was mounted in-line, sitting partly above the gearbox and final drive unit. This was not so compact an arrangement as might have been managed with a transverse engine but Saab was familiar with the layout, having used it in the earlier 96 and 99, and

knew it worked well. The engine itself was an almost totally redesigned version of a unit originally developed for Saab by Triumph in England and used in the early 99 model. By the time it reached the 900 it was an altogether tougher and more powerful engine producing comfortably over 100bhp with the aid of electronically controlled fuel injection. Its power was taken through a three-speed automatic, or a four-speed or five-speed manual gearbox according to model.

The 900 body was offered originally as a five-door hatchback, but Saab realised there was a market for alternatives; today the 900 may also be had with two, three or four doors as well as with original layout. In its hatchback form the 900 was notably roomy and useful, with a low loading sill in estate-car style. Needless to say the shape had been carefully studied to reduce aerodynamic drag and improve high-speed stability; the structure was also extremely strong but efficient enough to ensure that the 900 weighed no more than the equivalent 99 model despite being over a foot (0.3m) longer,

with a longer wheelbase which helped to make it roomier inside. As in the 99, double wishbones were used for the front suspension and Saab tradition continued with the retention of a well-located 'dead' axle at the rear. It is interesting to note that while Sweden's two car manufacturers totally disagree on the question of whether to drive the front or rear wheels, they both agree that for safe and predictable handling in poor conditions, the rear wheels need to be kept parallel. Again like Volvo in the 200-series, Saab used disc brakes for all four wheels and rack and pinion steering. The company continued to pin its faith in big wheels and the 900 was fitted with 15-inch (38cm) wheels carrying radial-ply tyres.

However, undoubtedly the most interesting technical aspect of the Saab 900 was the fact that it brought the turbocharged engine to a high state of development and did more than any other car to make it acceptable to the car-buying public. The turbocharger has the appeal of a 'something for nothing' device as it extracts energy from the exhaust which would otherwise vanish down the exhaust pipe, and used it to pump fuel/air mixture into the cylinders rather than leaving it to be sucked in. In practice, the exhaust gases drive a small turbine wheel which in turn drives the inlet air compressor. The system enables an engine to produce a good deal more power without undue stress – the Saab 2-litre Turbo manages 145bhp, which could only otherwise be achieved by turning the engine to the point where it would start to become difficult to drive. With other recent improvements including the use of twin overhead camshafts driving four valves per cylinder, it now manages 175bhp without strain. There are drawbacks to turbocharging, including the very high temperatures reached by the turbine from which the rest of the engine compartment must be shielded and the problem of preventing the compressor from pumping so much air into the engine that it becomes overstressed. Saab developed a control system which was especially neat, not only preventing too much boost but even making automatic allowance for whatever grade of petrol the engine was using.

The Saab 900 continues in production, though it had now been joined by an even larger new model, the 9000, in which the engine is installed transversely. However, Saab models tend to be long-lived – the previous 99 is still produced in modified form as the 90 – and it seems that the 900 could be offering the student of motor car anatomy lessons for some time to come. It is worth looking at for several reasons, not simply the fact that it is so strongly associated with the advanced engineering of the turbocharger. It is one of the few cars in which aircraft engineers have had a direct and real influence; and it also demonstrates how a relatively small company can succeed by picking the right product in the first place, and then developing it well.

Saab 900
Country of origin: Sweden
Date: 1978
Engine: four-stroke in-line ohc four-cylinder;
twin Zenith-Stromberg carburettor; 108bhp at
5,200rpm
Bore and stroke: 90 × 78mm
Capacity: 1985cc
Transmission: front-wheel drive; four-speed
manual gearbox (three-speed automatic
optional)
Chassis: integral
Suspension: front, independent with
wishbones, coil springs; rear, dead axle with
Panhard rod, coil springs
Steering: rack and pinion
Brakes: disc front, drum rear
Dimensions: wheelbase 99.4in (252cm)
           track (front) 54.5in (139cm)
           track (rear) 55in (140cm)
Maximum speed: 103mph (166kmh)

1980 AUDI QUATTRO

The Audi Quattro created a sensation when it was first announced, because its combined use of two advanced technical features enabled it to offer a degree of performance and road-worthiness hardly encountered in any previous production car. The two features were four-wheel drive, and turbocharging.

Audi, taken over by Volkswagen in the late 1960s, proved to be the technical inspiration that saved the group from possible disaster. By the late 1970s Audi was well established as the 'prestige' arm of Volkswagen, making the group's bigger and more expensive models. The company had already created a great deal of technical interest in the mid-1970s when it sought extra power beyond what it could find from its four-cylinder engines, not by going to six cylinders as might have been expected, but by adding a fifth cylinder to create the first production in-line 'five'. This engine, complete with electronically controlled fuel injection, was to become the basis of the Quattro power unit.

Audi became interested in four-wheel drive mainly because it had ambitions in the rallying world. It seemed to the Audi engineers, who were faced with the problem of transmitting a lot of power through the front wheels of their cars, that driving all the wheels might be a better solution. Studies soon indicated that given the right detailed engineering, the solution was a good one.

The adaptation was easy for Audi because their engine lay ahead of the front wheels, driving through a transaxle. All that had to be done was to take a second power output from the rear of the transaxle gearbox, into a centre differential unit and then aft via a new propeller shaft to a rear differential which would in turn power the drive shafts to the back wheels. As in the Jensen FF, it was intended that four-wheel drive would be permanently in use, with no provision to return to two-wheel drive whether front or rear. Audi provided locks for the centre and rear differentials but these were really for use in very difficult conditions and were certainly not recommended for normal road use, as they could have led to rapid tyre wear and possibly also to serve handling problems.

In order to achieve the performance it sought, Audi decided to use turbocharging with the five-cylinder engine, thus boasting the 2.1-litre unit to produce 200bhp in standard form and more in the works rally cars. The drive was taken through a five-speed manual gearbox. The front wheels retained the standard Audi MacPherson strut suspension but at the rear, where there would normally have been undriven wheels on a 'dead' axle, MacPherson struts were again fitted to accommodate the movements of the drive shafts. Given the high performance of the car, it was natural that it should have been fitted with disc brakes for all four wheels, together with some of the latest low-profile radial-ply tyres. Indeed, by the end of the 1970s, tyres with aspect ratios of 60 per cent were readily available and becoming popular for many high performance cars.

The Audi body was a three-door sports Coupé of generous size, and a much simpler Coupé model was announced which used the same basic shape but without the four-wheel drive or the turbocharging. This car was large enough to be considered a comfortable four-seater, which meant in turn that the original Quattro eventually proved to be too big and heavy to make it virtually a two-seater.

Audi by no means wasted the experience of turbocharging and four-wheel drive which the Quattro brought to the company. Before long, turbocharging was offered on its top standard saloon model, the 200, and plans were realised to offer four-wheel-drive versions of every car in the Audi range, in addition to the standard front-driven models. The four-wheel-drive system has also been used by Volkswagen itself in some models.

The Quattro must be judged a success, not only for the effect it has had on the world of rallying but also because it has done what the Jensen FF failed to do: convince the world of motor car engineering that four-wheel-drive needs to be taken seriously and that it offers a way forward to a generally higher standard of road behaviour.

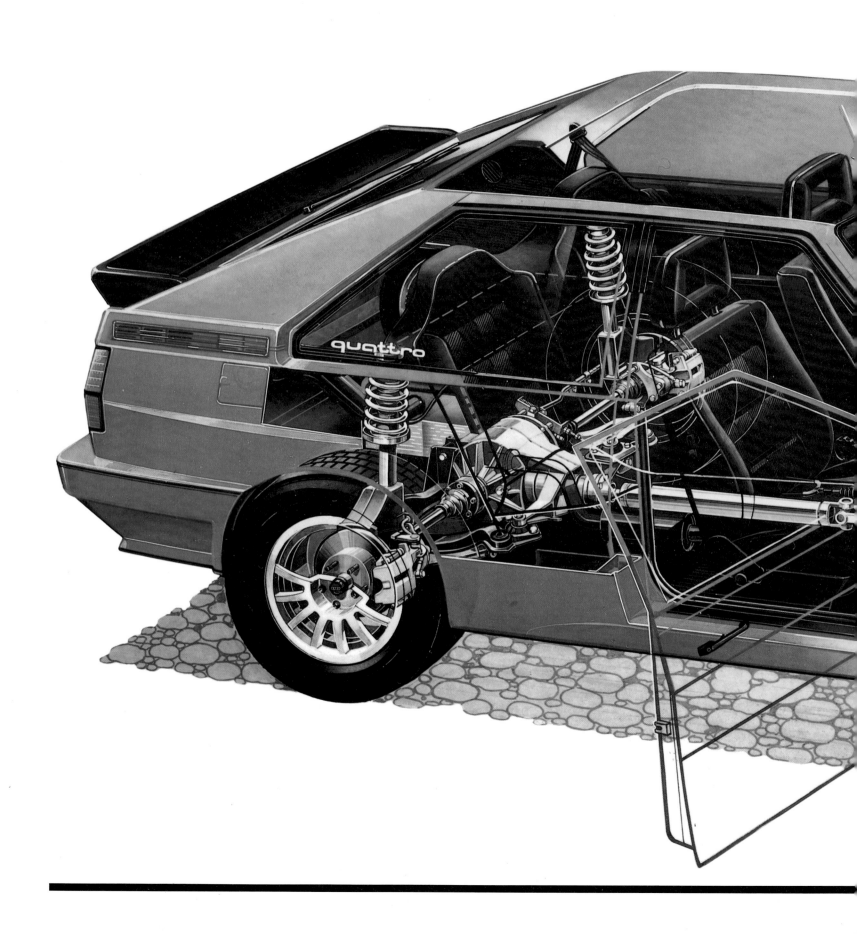

Audi 200 Quattro
Country of origin: Germany
Date: 1984
Engine: four-stroke in-line ohc five-cylinder; Bosch K-Jetronic fuel injection; 182bhp at 5,700rpm
Bore and stroke: 79.5 × 86.4mm
Capacity: 2144cc
Transmission: four-wheel drive; five-speed manual gearbox
Chassis: integral
Suspension: front, independent with MacPherson struts, coil springs, anti-roll bar; rear, independent with wishbones, transverse upper link, coil springs
Steering: rack and pinion
Brakes: discs, front and rear
Dimensions: wheelbase 105.8in (268.7cm)
track (front) 57.8in (146.8cm)
track (rear) 57.8in (146.8cm)
Maximum speed: 139mph (224kmh)

1980 FORD ESCORT

Despite the success of so many small family cars with front-wheel drive, the American-owned European companies – Ford and General Motors Opel/Vauxhall – seemed for a long time to fight against the trend. In Ford's case this may partly have been because the thoroughly conventional Cortina overshadowed its front-driven equivalent in the early 1960s. It was only in 1976, when the Mini was already 18 years old, that Ford launched its Fiesta supermini with front-wheel drive. However it was still another four years after that before the company directly replaced one of its successful rear-driven model lines with a new front-driven design and that new car was the Escort.

The Escort was an extremely important range for Ford, even though it was a smaller car, and sold in somewhat fewer numbers than the Cortina. Its predecessors stretched back in an unbroken line through the Anglia of the 1960s, and the Prefect of the 1950s, all the way to the Ford Popular which was one of the few genuinely '£100' cars of the 1930s. It faced strong competition in the market from rival European designs ranging from Austin's Allegro to Volkswagen's Golf and it was vital that any new Escort design should do well. By the late 1970s most of the Escort's market rivals already had front-wheel drive – the only major exceptions being GM's Opel Kadette/Vauxhall Chevette, the Morris Marina and sundry Japanese models – and it was clear that Ford would have to follow the same path in order to remain competitive.

The Escort was interesting for a number of reasons. It showed even more clearly the particular features which design teams were putting into front-driven cars. Ford elected to make its new Escort almost the same size as the rear-driven car it replaced – in length, width and wheelbase. In addition, a completely new engine was developed which powered most of the model in the new Escort range.

Once the decision had been taken to use front-wheel drive it was inevitable that Ford would also adopt the 'Fiat 127' solution of the transverse engine, in-line gearbox, and final drive unit aft of the crankcase. This layout had already been used in the smaller Fiesta and many of its components could be 'carried across' together with a lot of useful service experience. Like Fiat, but unlike Volkswagen, Ford used drive shafts of unequal length – the left-hand one being substantially shorter – between the final drive unit and the front wheels. To begin with, Ford offered only four-speed manual gearboxes in the Escort, but quickly extended the range to include five-speeds for some models in line with a rapidly growing European trend.

Eventually there was also an optional automatic transmission, once the problems of squeezing it into the limited space available had been solved.

Needless to say, the use of a transverse engine and transmission meant that within its same-size body, Ford could offer a great deal more interior space in the new Escort than there had been in the old one. In this case the difference was all the more obvious because while the old rear-driven car had been cramped for four large adults, the front-driven replacement had comfortable space. Equally, Ford fell into line with the new European trend by fitting a larger rear loading door as standard. Later, to meet a demand from customers who wanted more of a traditional layout, Ford also launched a modified Escort with a longer, 'booted' body under the name Orion. Apart from the gain in interior space, Ford had been seeking two major gains in the new Escort body design and both were achieved: a notable weight saving by comparison with the previous car, and much lower aerodynamic drag. Efficient structural analysis, plus the advantage of grouping all the main mechanical components at one end of the car, enabled the designers to make the new Escort over 250 pounds (113kg) lighter than the old one, model for model, while the new shape resulted in the drag coefficient being reduced by some 16 per cent, with immediate gains in acceleration and maximum speed.

The Escort's performance was also improved by the fitting of a completely new engine design, the so called 'CVH' unit, with a layout based on achieving highly efficient combustion through the use of a chamber of complex shape. This chamber used valves with axes which were offset at different angles from the centre-line of the engine's crankshaft, but partly opposed to each other so that the gas flow could be across the cylinder head: Compound Valve angles in a Hemispherical chamber, whence the CVH. In order to operate the valve at such awkward angles. Ford used a single overhead camshaft, driven by the increasingly popular toothed belt, together with rocker levers and hydraulic tappets. These tappets had long been a popular way of operating the valves in big American engines: because they use hydraulic pressure instead of direct mechanical contact they are quiet in operating, self-adjusting and can be designed to set an automatic limit to the speed of the engine without risking damage. Their use in a small European engine was new, however, though they have become more frequently used since Ford's lead. The new engine helped to improve performance too, since it produced rather more power, and slightly more torque

than the older engines of similar capacity.

Ford chose to fit the new Escort with MacPherson strut suspension for all four wheels, again reflecting the engineering trend in that direction. However, while the front suspension layout looked familiar, that at the rear differed significantly in detail. Its telescopic dampers were placed as far outboard as possible so as not to intrude into the rear load platform any more than necessary, while the coil springs were separately located further inboard, between the forks of the lower wishbones and low enough to be housed beneath the floor of the platform. Positive fore and aft location of the rear wheels was provided by trailing arms. In other chassis respects the Escort closely followed the pattern set for cars of its class, with 13-inch (33cm) wheels shod with radial ply tyres of moderate section, and front disc brakes combined with rear drums. The steering was rack and pinion: by 1980 it would have been unthinkable to find a new, small European car that used any other system.

The Escort was an immediate success, to the extent that it became Ford's best-seller in Britain and other European markets rather than the rear-driven Sierra, which soon afterwards replaced the mid-range Cortina. It showed yet again how the advantages of front-wheel drive for smaller cars were too great to be ignored, and with its introduction only two of the world's major car manufacturers, General Motors and Toyota, seemed still to need convincing of that.

Ford Escort 1.6
Country of origin: Great Britain
Date: 1980
Engine: four-stroke in-line ohc four-cylinder;
Weber carburettor; 84bhp at 5,500rpm
Bore and stroke: 80.98 × 77.62mm
Capacity: 1598cc
Transmission: rear-wheel drive, four-speed
manual gearbox
Chassis: integral
Suspension: front, independent with
MacPherson struts, coil springs, anti-roll bar;
rear, live axle with leaf springs, anti-roll bar
Steering: rack and pinion
Brakes: disc front, drum rear
Dimensions: wheelbase 94.5in (240cm)
　　　　　　　track (front) 51in (129.5cm)
　　　　　　　track (rear) 50in (127cm)
Maximum speed: 98mph (157kmh)

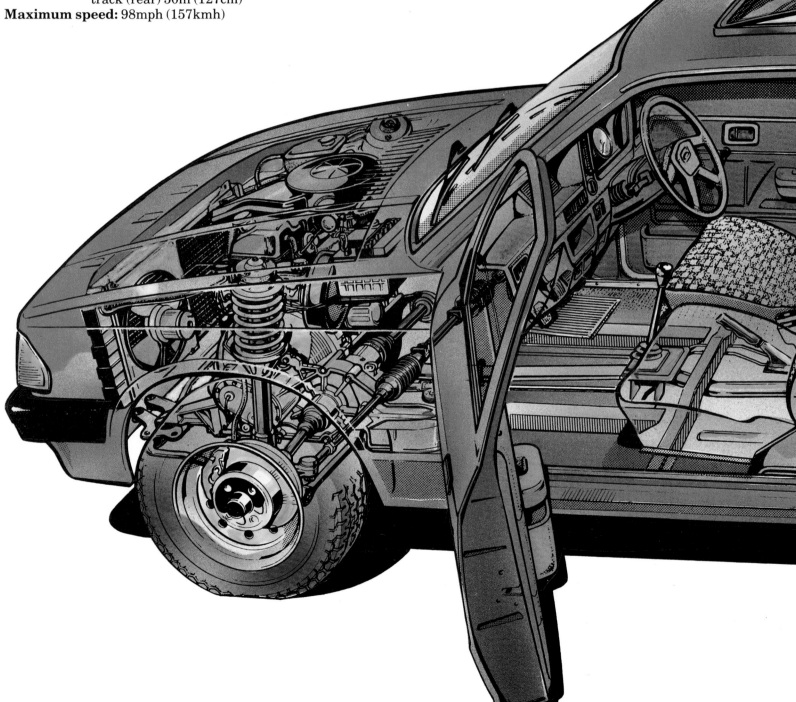

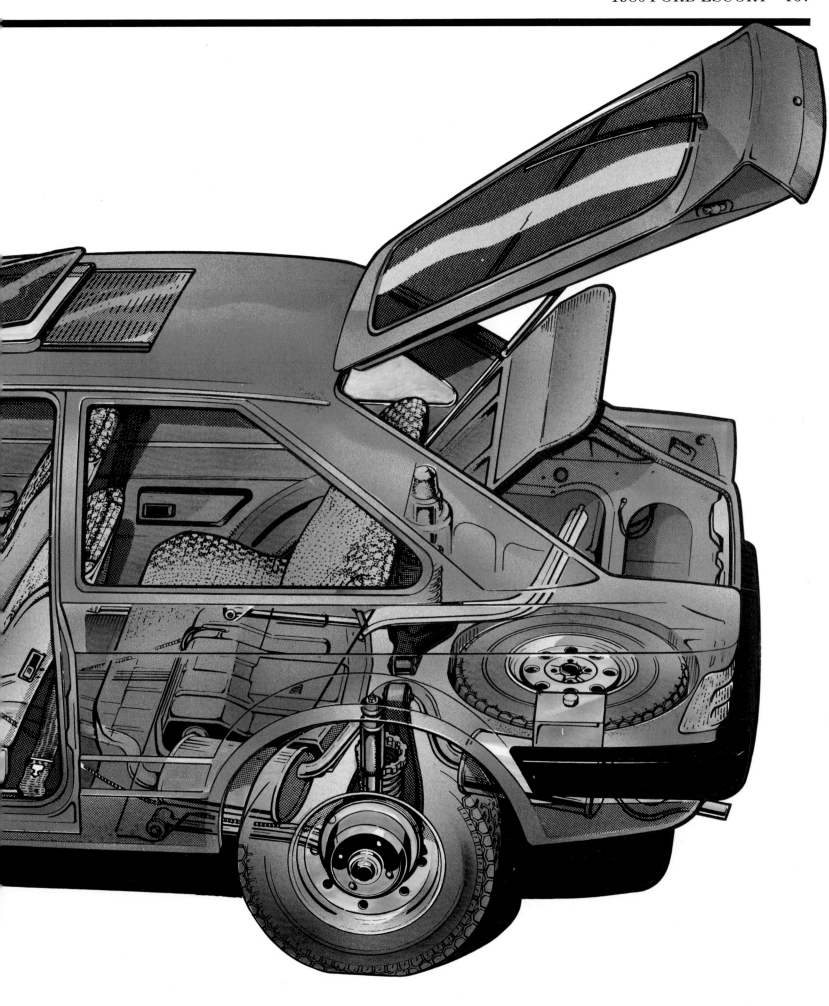

1982 BMW 3-SERIES

From the late 1950s onwards, the Bayerische Motoren Werke (BMW) of Munich proved that it was possible to start with a single well-conceived mechanical layout and develop it into a number of car models spanning a wide variety of customer requirements. BMW had been famous before the Second World War as a manufacturer of high-quality sports and touring cars, but in the early 1950s it had scant success trying to put the old cars back into production and then failed dismally with an excursion into the short-lived market for ultra-small economy cars. Then BMW introduced the 1500 saloon, which was an instant success and the company has adhered to its basic formula ever since.

The 1500 was a medium-sized four-door saloon powered by an efficient four-cylinder engine with a single overhead camshaft, driving the rear wheels and using MacPherson strut front suspension with semi-trailing arms at the rear. The original model was soon given bigger engines and more power, while the company extended its range in both directions by designing a slightly smaller two-door model, with the same type of four-cylinder engine and a rather larger one with six-cylinder power (that engine being in many respects one-and-a-half times the four-cylinder). All three models had a close and obvious family resemblance, as did the engines; and all three model lines were steadily developed as BMW made its mark as a 'prestige' manufacturer. At the time of writing, the 3-series is the latest stage in that development process and shows, better than any other current car, the extent to which the same basic idea can be made to last for nearly 30 years.

The first BMW 3-series replaced the original two-door 1602/2002 cars in the mid-1970s, bringing BMW's smallest model up to date and into line with the styling trends already established with the bigger 5-series and 7-series. Then, in 1982 there came a replacement design, again known as the 3-series and continuing the designations of the previous cars in most cases. This latest 3-series reflected a growing trend, seen particularly in Germany, which sought to avoid making the replacement models for successful cars look markedly different from their predecessors – a principle BMW had already adopted for the 5-series cars. Thus, while the new 3-series differed considerably in detail from that which had gone before, it took an expert eye to tell the cars apart on the road. The two most significant statistics about the new car were that it was over an inch wider, though actually marginally shorter overall, and about 150 pounds lighter. The extra width was reflected not only in cabin space but also in wider wheeltrack especially at the rear,

and the suspension had been greatly changed to answer criticisms of the semi-trailing arrangement used in the previous model. Naturally, the lighter weight reflected more efficient structural design while the new body, despite looking remarkably unchanged actually gave a useful improvement in aerodynamic drag.

There was no question of BMW adopting front-wheel drive, even for its smallest car. To do so would have been to put at risk the carefully developed balance and 'feel' which had become so familiar to customers over the years. It would also have meant embracing a completely new concept which ran the risk of having less of an appeal to such customers: as the 'bread and butter' medium-sized saloons adopted front-wheel drive, it was less likely that companies like BMW would follow suit even if it meant interior cabin space in relation to the overall size of the car – and the BMW 3-series has no more cabin space than the Ford Escort which is a clear foot shorter overall. All BMW engines are therefore mounted in-line, driving through either a five-speed manual or an automatic gearbox and a propellor shaft to the final drive unit, whence drive shafts power the rear wheels.

Almost as soon as the first 3-series cars replaced the original 1602/2002 cars, the four-cylinder engines were supplemented by six-

cylinder units. These were not notable for their power but for their exceptionally smooth operation. Thus while the basic 3-series car, the 316, has a four-cylinder unit, its bigger brothers use six-cylinder engines of 2.0 or 2.3-litre capacity, with electronically controlled fuel injection. An even more recent addition to the range is a 2.5-litre engine specially tuned for maximum economy rather than the highest obtainable power. All BMW engines, other than some exceptionally powerful versions used in their sporting cars, retain single overhead camshafts.

It is perhaps most remarkable of all that BMW has made no major change to its suspension layout in many years. Of course, there are many advantages in staying with a familiar layout and developing it progressively and the MacPherson strut front suspension has never given cause for complaint. The semi-trailing arm rear suspension, on the other hand, allows the rear wheels to assume camber angles which can in some circumstances adversely affect the handling of the car – a fault which can be avoided with a De Dion layout, double wishbones or rear-mounted MacPherson struts. Thus far, BMW has dismissed all these alternatives in favour of modifying many aspects of its semi-trailing system, most notably the manner in which the arms themselves are able to move slightly within their mounting bushes. It remains to be seen if there is any further development potential within the basic layout. If there is, it seems certain that BMW will find it. One significant move which the company did make when engineering the

current 3 series cars was to adopt wider wheels of generally lower profile. Thus the 320i was equipped with 195/60 section tyres in place of the 185/70 tyres of the previous model. By reducing the section height of the tyre it was possible to use a larger diameter 14 inch (36cm) instead of 13 inch (33cm) wheel, within the same size wheel arch; this is a recent trend among many cars, reversing the tendency of many years for car wheels to become smaller. One of the advantages of a larger wheel is that it makes room for bigger and more effective brakes, an especially welcome feature for the manufacturers of high-performance cars seeking to fit the biggest front disc brakes they can.

The BMW policy of evolution, not revolution, has clearly paid off if sales of the 3-series are any guideline. In 1983 the company broadened the appeal of the car, in some markets, including Britain, by offering the car with four as well as two doors. It remains to be seen what can possibly be done to effect major improvements for the 'next generation' 3-series without embracing more fundamental changes of engineering concept; yet the current car stands as evidence that determined and competent engineering teams, when subjected to marketing pressures to retain certain layouts and features, can still always find ways to keep improving a conventional chassis.

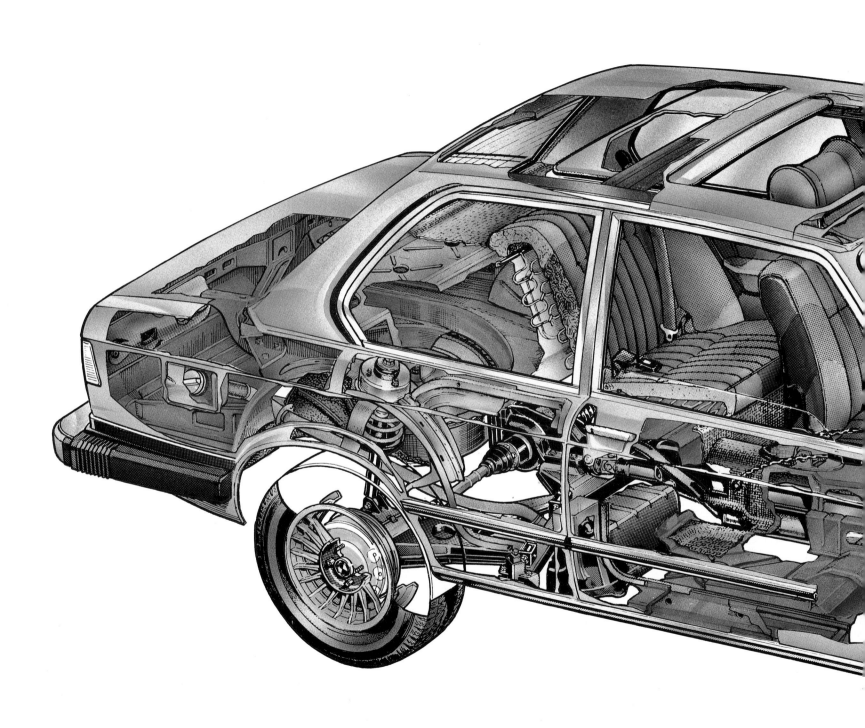

BMW 323i
Country of origin: Germany
Date: 1983
Engine: four-stroke in-line ohc six-cylinder; Bosch L-Jetronic fuel injection; 139bhp at 5,300rpm
Bore and stroke: 80 × 77mm
Capacity: 2316cc
Transmission: rear-wheel drive; five-speed manual gearbox
Chassis: integral
Suspension: front, independent with MacPherson struts, lower wishbones, coil springs, anti-roll bar; rear, independent with semi-trailing arms, coil springs, anti-roll bar
Steering: rack and pinion
Brakes: discs, front and rear
Dimensions: wheelbase 100.3in (254.7cm)
                track (front) 55.8in (141.7cm)
                track (rear) 55.5in (140.9cm)
Maximum speed: 124mph (199.5kmh)

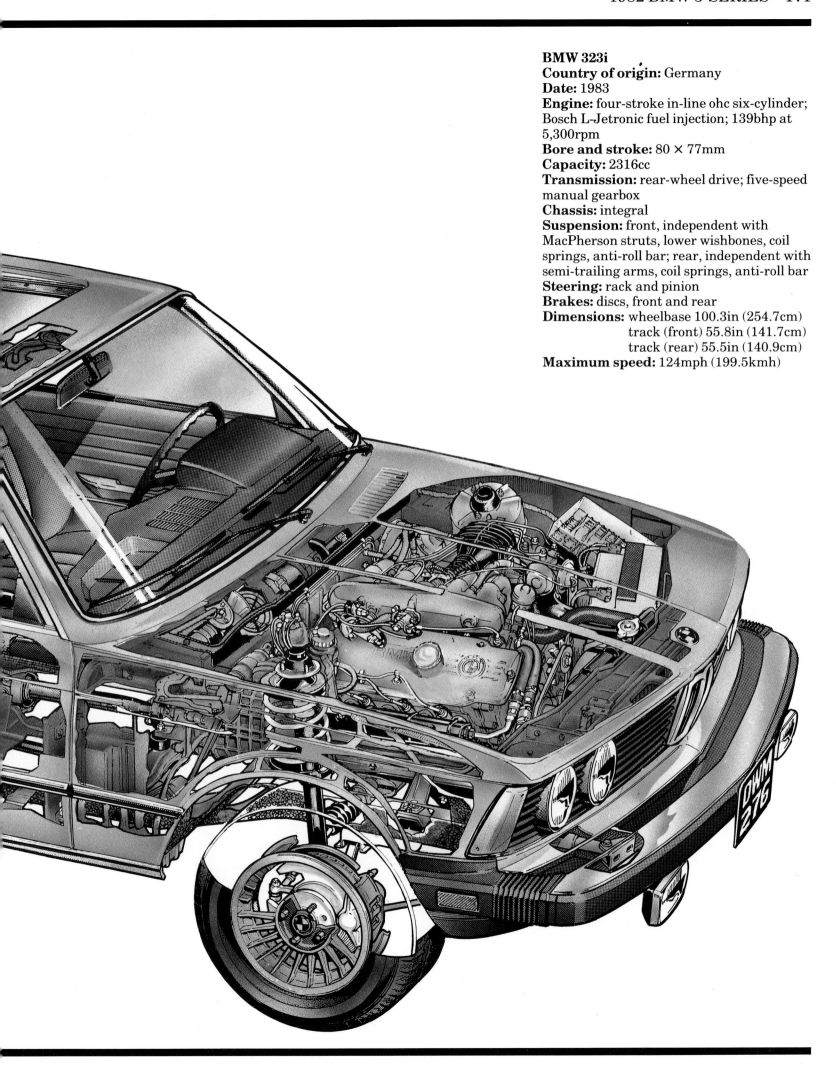

1982 OPEL CORSA/ VAUXHALL NOVA

General Motors took a long time to adopt front-wheel drive for any of its European cars, and even longer to decide the time was ripe for an entry in the supermini market. By the late 1970 s the trend of sales towards smaller cars could not be ignored. The company took the appropriate steps to design a car that would compete strongly among the 'second generation' superminis like the Fiat Uno and the Peugeot 205. In line with GM marketing policy, two slightly different versions of the car were prepared: the Opel Corsa and the Vauxhall Nova, distinguished only by small changes of styling, mostly at the front end.

There were points of interest in the way the GM car resembled other superminis and in the few significant points where it differed. The first obvious resemblance was in size, because the Corsa/Nova in three-door hatchback form was extremely close to the original Renault 5 in every respect but overall length (where it was 4 inches longer). In wheelbase, body, width and weight it was astonishingly close. More obviously, the GM car had a transverse engine and 'Fiat 127' transmission layout. The most basic engine was a pushrod-operated overhead valve unit with a very long development history; this 1-litre engine produced 45bhp, very much in line with the most basic current versions of other superminis. The cars were also offered with 1.2-litre and 1.3-litre engines of much more modern overhead-camshaft design.

One of the major differences between the Corsa/Nova and other superminis was that the car was immediately offered not only as a three-door hatchback but also as a small two door saloon car of conventional 'booted shape'. In this form the car was more than a foot (0.3m) longer. Yet hardly any heavier, an interesting pointer to the weight which must be devoted to engineering a strong supporting frame around a large rear hatch opening, and to provide enough strength in a short tail to meet the legal requirements for resistance to rear-end impact. In other respects the car was mostly conventional by 1980s standards, using MacPherson strut front suspension and a 'compound crank' rear suspension which was in effect another variation on the Volkswagen idea of a trailing H-beam. GM saved extra space by using clever 'Minibloc' springs coiled into a pyramid form so that they could be squeezed almost flat; thus they were compressed very short while retaining a long operating length.

In most respects the Corsa/Nova remained faithful to the chassis details established by other superminis. For instance, it was equipped with disc front and drum rear brakes, 13-inch (33cm) wheels and rack and pinion steering. The standard gearbox was a four speed manual, with five speeds optionally available; there was (and is) no automatic transmission offered although it is possible that the Corsa/Nova will eventually be offered, like some other

superminis, with a continuously-variable transmission (CVT). This is a unit in which the drive is transmitted by a belt running between two pulleys of variable radius, so that instead of a series of gears with fixed ratios, the ratio is able to assume any value within upper and lower limits. This system has the advantage of always allowing the engine to be run as close as possible to its point of maximum efficiency; but until now its development has proved troublesome and has taken rather longer than expected.

The Corsa/Nova is most interesting, perhaps, because it confirms the rightness of the typical European supermini package. When a company like General Motors with all of its resources produces a car similar to the products of other design teams, it is strong evidence that the concept is close to the ideal. It will be interesting to see if other companies agree with GM's conclusion that there is a market for a small 'three-box' saloon alongside the widely accepted hatchback. Volkswagen offers a booted version of its Polo but at the time of writing it is the only other supermini to have moved in this direction. However, future technical development may still result in Europe's small-car design teams breaking away from the transverse-engine, front-wheel drive layout which has become so standardised during the 1980s.

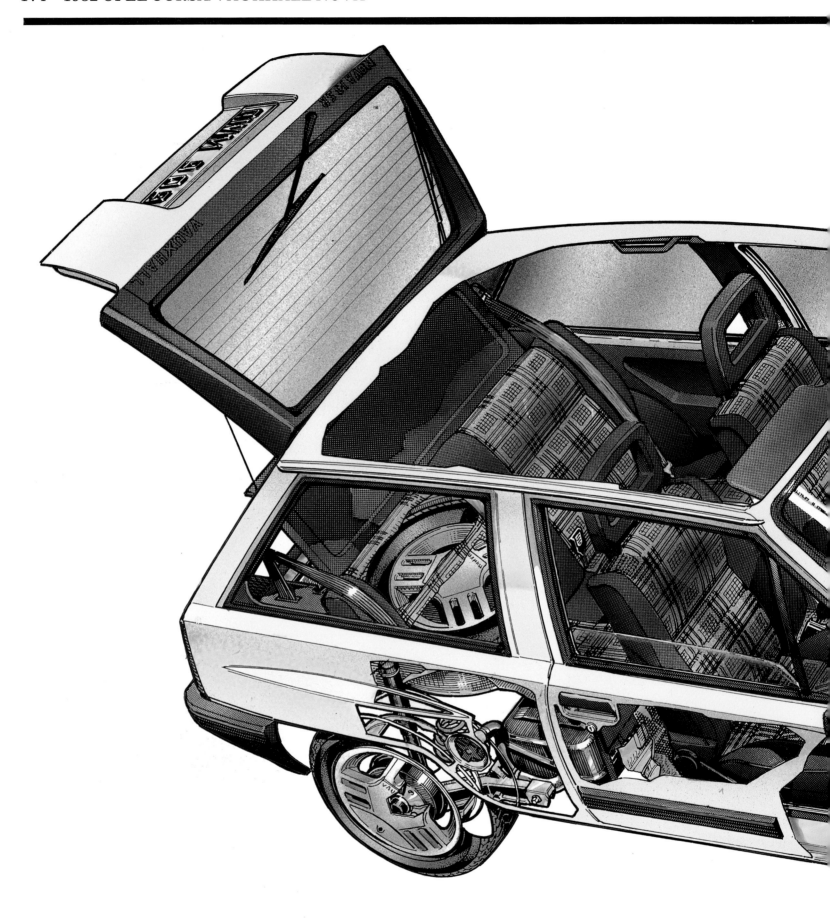

Vauxhall Nova
Countries of origin: Great Britain/Spain
Date: 1983
Engine: four-stroke in-line pushrod ohc four-cylinder; Weber carburettor; 45bhp at 5,400rpm
Bore and stroke: 72 × 61mm
Capacity: 993cc
Transmission: front-wheel drive; four-speed manual gearbox
Chassis: integral
Suspension: front, independent with MacPherson struts, coil springs; rear, trailing arms, coil springs
Steering: rack and pinion
Brakes: disc front, drum rear
Dimensions: wheelbase 92.3in (234.4cm)
　　　　　　track (front) 52.3in (132.8cm)
　　　　　　track (rear) 52in (132cm)
Maximum speed: 84.3 mph (135.6kmh)

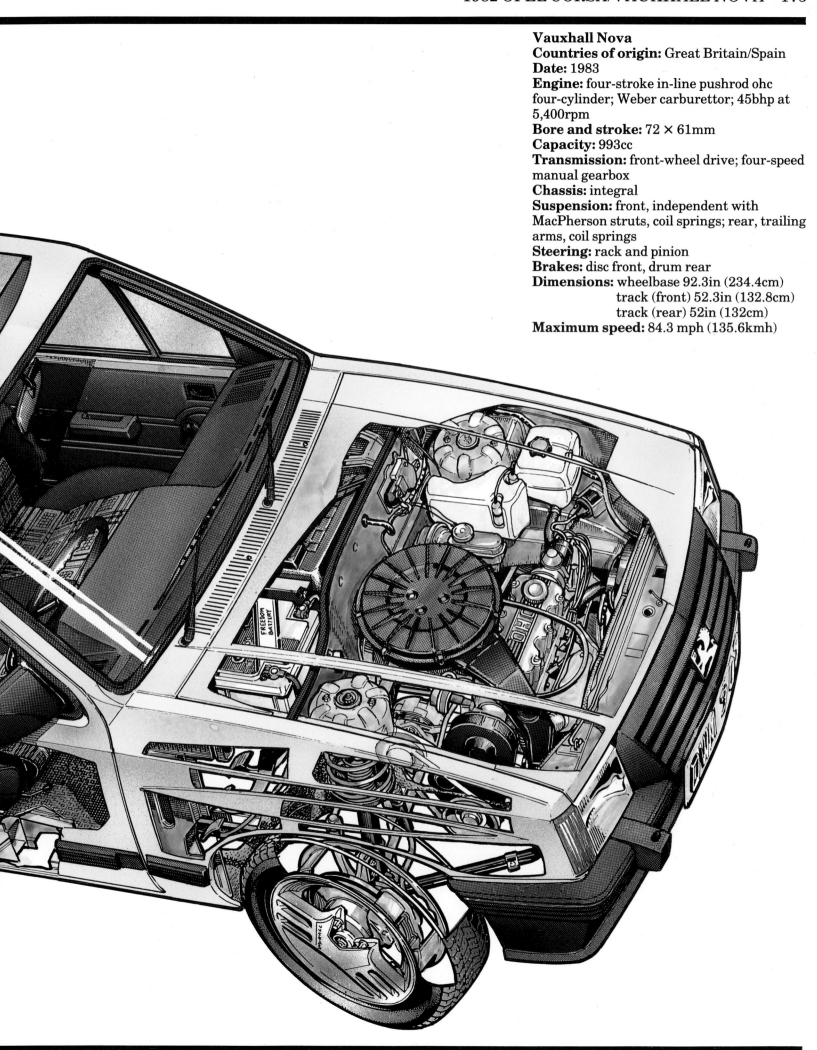

1983 MERCEDES 190

The reputation of Mercedes-Benz has always been as a maker of big cars, even though in the 1930s they did venture to produce something smaller. During the 1970s the company's range grew and included some of the largest models built in Europe, if not the world. It was clear that the Mercedes car production could only be significantly expanded if they designed a model smaller than anything they already produced.

The key decisions facing the Mercedes product planners were many. Just what size should the new car be? How much smaller than the smallest of the existing range? Should the mechanical layout be that of the traditional Mercedes or front-wheel drive? And finally, should the new car be powered by the smallest of the existing engines, or by a completely new unit?

The question of size was easily solved; the new car should be smaller than was necessary to establish it in a lower bracket than the smallest existing Mercedes model, the 200. Since the 200 and its higher-powered sister models up to the 280 were some five inches (2.7cm) shorter overall than the 'big' Mercedes – the 280S and upwards – cold logic suggested the new car should be the same amount smaller, and cold logic has never been in short supply at Mercedes. Accordingly, the new car was given a wheelbase of 105 inches (267cm) and a body

with an overall length of 174 inches (442cm), which made it far from small in absolute terms but rather a competitor for the larger cars from manufacturers like Ford, General Motors and Renault. It was decided to call the new car the Mercedes 190, another deliberate link with the past since that number had been a long standing part of the Mercedes range until the most basic model was elevated to 200 status.

Considering the size of the car and the 'prestige' buyer's loyalty to traditional engineering, there was no question of Mercedes forsaking the front-engine, rear-drive layout which characterised all their cars. As for the engine itself, it would be sufficient to take the 2-litre, lightweight, single overhead camshaft design recently introduced to the 200 and develop it for the 190. In fact, the engine was 'detuned' from its original 109bhp to just 90bhp for the most basic 190 model; but it was also given electronically controlled fuel injection to help increase the power to 122bhp so that there could be a better-performing 109E version of the car.

Since the 190 was both smaller and a more recent design than the 200 it was only to be expected that it would be substantially lighter. The designers were helped towards this aim because the body was not only shorter but narrower than the 200, nine inches (23cm). A huge margin where width is concerned. Consequently, the team managed to make the 190 over 500 pounds lighter than its bigger brother. They did not compromise Mercedes' reputation for huge margins of strength above that necessary to meet existing legislation.

Like so many car manfacturers, Mercedes had previously accepted the logic of the MacPherson-strut front suspension and used it in the 190. Working at the rear of the car they moved further away from the semi-trailing arrangement that had been a feature of their earlier 1970s cars and adopted their ingenious system of five articulated links. This gave most of the advantages of double-wishbone geometry without taking up nearly so much of the space needed for luggage and fuel tank. Unlike the bigger 200, the 190 was given drum rear brakes but its wheels remained 14-inch (36cm), though the fitting of lower-profile radial ply tyres enabled some space to be saved in the wheel arches.

The Mercedes 190, like the BMW 3-series, shows how a design team can wring further improvement from an existing framework especially in more prestigious areas of the car market, and that this may be a better way forward than adopting the latest mechanical layout.

1983 TOYOTA COROLLA

It could be argued that of all the world's mass-producers of family cars, none is as conservative in its design approach as Toyota of Japan. This approach has made the company the second-biggest car manufacturer in the world, General Motors being the first. If that is the result of cautious, step-by-step evolution, it is a good commendation. However, after so many years of building cars with front engines driving through live rear axles, Panhard/Renault fashion, Toyota began a surprising wholesale conversion of its range to front-wheel drive. The seal was set on this shift of policy when in 1983 the new Corolla was launched with transverse engine and front-wheel drive. The Corolla was and remains the world's biggest-selling single model and the cornerstone of Toyota's massive success.

The Corolla had grown up by stages since the early 1960s but had remained stoutly conventional in layout. By Toyota's standards the 1982 version of the car was almost as revolutionary, due to its new rear suspension, with links replacing its leaf springs, and rack and pinion steering in place of the recirculating-ball system which had lingered so long in Japan. Yet, late in 1983 came the real revolution in which the old rear-driven line was swept away altogether and a brand-new Corolla took its place.

The new car was very close in size to the one it replaced, in that there was barely an inch (2.5cm) of difference in any major dimension and the engine was the same size: 1.3-litres. There the resemblance stopped. Toyota even broke one of the principal rules in most designers' books by launching the new car with a new engine. This single overhead camshaft unit was designed with three main aims: to save weight, to be as compact as possible so that it could be installed transversely without problems, and of course to be economical. The transverse installation was chosen simply because it was acknowledged as the best way to achieve maximum interior space within a car of given size. This conclusion was reached only after exhaustive study which included producing another small car, the Tercel, with a complete different front-wheel drive arrangement in which the engine sat in line above the transmission. Toyota also opted for the 'Fiat 127' transmission layout with the gearbox in line with the engine crankshaft. From the outset, the Corolla was offered with a choice of five-speed manual or three-speed automatic transmission.

Toyota also echoed recent European thinking by adopting MacPherson strut suspension for all four wheels of the car, and providing the rear wheels with lower locating links which moved on their rubber mounting bushes in such a way as to improve the car's stability and cornering behaviour. The Corolla was conventional in its use of front disk and rear drum brakes, rack and pinion steering and 12 inch wheels with radial ply tyres. Many of these features had become standards for the 1.3 litre family car class in both Europe and Japan.

The Corolla was given two body styles, a sleek 'fastback' three door shape with rear loading hatch, and a conventional two door saloon. Later on a third style was added to the range, another three-door body although shorter overall and with a far more upright rear-loading hatch. This body shape also became the basis for a much more powerful and faster version of the car, once again reflecting the European trend which gave rise to such models as the Ford Escort XR3i and the Volkswagen Golf GTi. Even though the front driven Corolla proved only a little lighter than its predecessor, it was certainly a good deal better aerodynamically. These worthwhile benefits in performance and economy were helped by the fact that the new engine produced rather more power and torque than the simple overhead-valve unit that it replaced.

The Toyota Corolla is a further example of the optimum use of current technology: the mechanical formula of transverse and engine transmission driving the front wheels is ideally suited to small family cars with engines of up to 1.3 litre capacity. The Toyota Corolla also illustrates that apparently unimaginative but strong companies have the ability to 'catch up' very quickly.

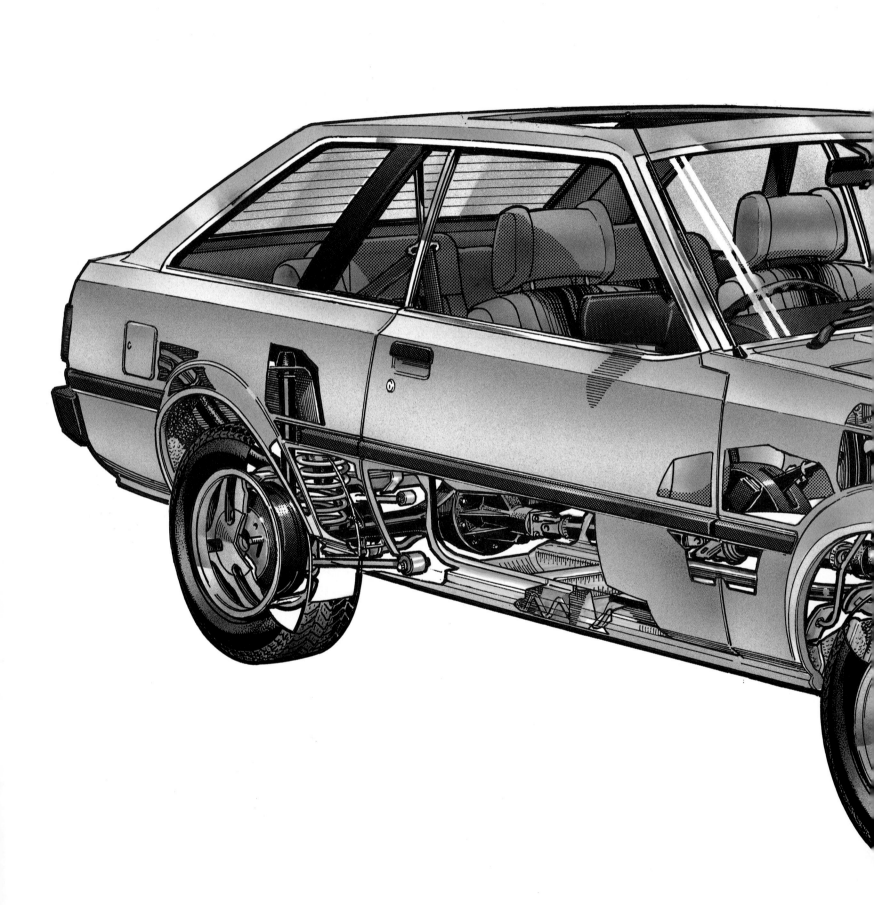

Toyota Corolla GT
Country of origin: Japan
Date: 1985
Engine: four-stroke in-line ohc four-cylinder;
electronic fuel injection; 119bhp at 6,600rpm
Bore and stroke: 81 × 77mm
Capacity: 1587cc
Transmission: front-wheel drive; five-speed
manual gearbox
Chassis: integral
Suspension: front, independent with
MacPherson struts, coil springs, anti-roll bar;
rear, independent with MacPherson struts, coil
springs, anti-roll bar
Steering: rack and pinion
Brakes: discs, front and rear
Dimensions: wheelbase 95.7in (243cm)
        track (front) 56.8in (143.5cm)
        track (rear) 55.7in (141.5cm)
Maximum speed: 118mph (190kmh)

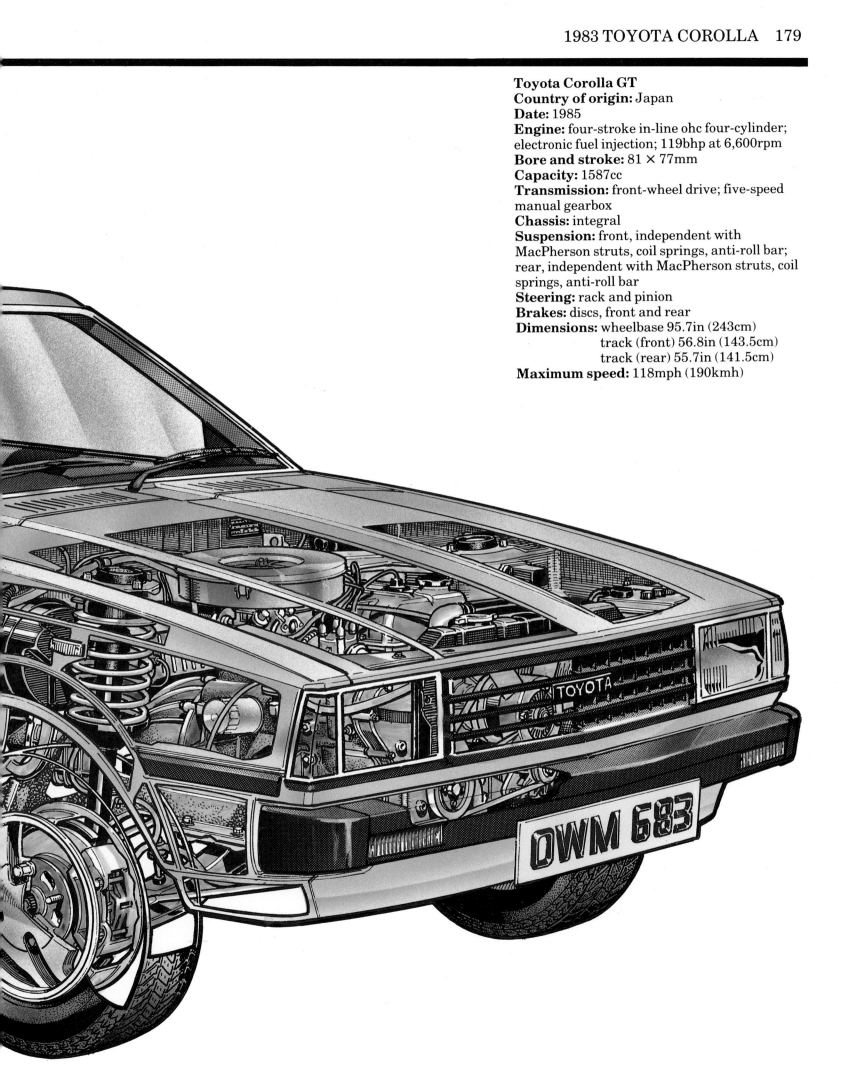

1983 AUDI 200

After its takeover by Volkswagen, the Audi company rapidly became the 'prestige' arm of the new combine and was encouraged to move its products up-market. In doing so it remained broadly faithful to the layout which had helped it to recover and which had helped Volkswagen itself to overcome the shock from the collapse of the Beetle market. In other words, Audi continued to build cars in which in-line engines overhung ahead of the front axle drove the front wheels through a transaxle arrangement.

This system had the advantage of simplicity while making it easy to provide a roomy cabin, a good direct gearchange linkage, and an easy adaptation to four-wheel drive. However when Audi worked to produce more powerful cars like the Quattro, this system caused problems Generally, a more powerful engine must of necessity be heavier, and this is not a good thing for the balance and handling of a car if the engine is installed as far forward as it will go. Audi's first answer to this problem was to stretch the four-cylinder unit not to six cylinders but rather to five, accepting the problems of balance inherent in the design and

compensating for the weight of something even longer and heavier. The five-cylinder engine was first used in the new Audi 100 of 1976. This car made worthwhile inroads into the lower end of the BMW and Mercedes market in Germany and elsewhere, but it was clear that something more powerful would be needed if Audi's upward expansion was to continue.

Since in Audi's view the engine could not be made any bigger or heavier without resorting to a completely different mechanical layout, the alternative method of turbocharging was adopted. We have already seen in the case of the Saab 90 – and indeed of the Audi Quattro itself – how this system of extracting energy from the exhaust can be used to force fuel/air mixture into the cylinders and bring about a substantial increase in power and torque output. From Audi's point of view it was an ideal way to obtain more power without upsetting the balance of the 100, and so the first Audi 200 was created simply by fitting a turbocharged version of the fuel-injected five-cylinder engine, still of 2.1-litre capacity but producing 170 instead of 136bhp, with a similar improvement in torque

This was sufficient to provide the Audi 200T with the performance to challenge the bigger BMW and Mercedes models.

In 1983 a completely new Audi 100/200 series was announced. Again, the 200 was in effect a turbocharged version of the 100 and the cars retained the same 2.1-litre five-cylinder engine with its single overhead camshaft.

The new cars retained the mechanical layout of the models they replaced, driving the front wheels through either a five-speed manual or three-speed automatic gearbox. They used MacPherson strut front suspension, with the now familiar Volkswagen-Audi 'torsion beam' trailing H-bar arrangement at the rear. However, larger 15-inch (38cm) wheels were fitted to match the higher performance of the 200 and they were fitted with low-profile 195/60 series radial ply tyres. Disc brakes were fitted to all four wheels – those at the front being ventilated – and anti-lock braking was offered as an important safety option. The 200 was equipped with power-assisted rack and pinion steering.

While the 200 offered superb performance and generally good behaviour, it also showed that in adverse conditions, it was close to the maximum power that could be handled through a car's front wheels alone. There were circumstances in which the wheels could lose traction much too easily if a lot of power was applied.

Audi therefore took a bold step into the future by offering a version of the car with the same four-wheel drive system as the Quattro. In this form the 200 naturally enjoys excellent traction and very good handling, making it possible to exploit the power output of the turbocharged engine even in poor road conditions.

The Audi 200 therefore holds two valuable lessons. The first is that there appears to be a limit on the amount of power which can usefully be fed through a car's front wheels – though the limit is high enough to suggest that smaller family cars are a long way short of it. Its second value is to show that the four-wheel drive principle, pioneered by the Jensen FF and taken up with success by the Quattro, is rapidly applicable at least to normal saloon cars of sufficiently high price and performance, and that it points one of the most likely ways to future development.

Further development of the turbocharging system had included the fitting of an intercooler (a heat exchanger which cools the mixture entering the engine after it has been heated by passing through the compressor). This raised the power available to 182bhp.

The other principal feature of the new Audi series was a body designed to have exceptionally low aerodynamic drag, with cleaner lines than had been seen on any previous production saloon car. This very low drag, when combined with the higher output, meant that the new Audi 200T was capable of over 140 mph and became one of the fastest saloons available.

Audi 200 Quattro
Country of origin: Germany
Date: 1984
Engine: four-stroke in-line ohc five-cylinder; Bosch
K-Jetronic fuel injection; 182bhp at 5,700rpm
Bore and stroke: 79.5 × 86.4mm
Capacity: 2144cc
Transmission: four-wheel drive; five-speed manual
gearbox
Chassis: integral
Suspension: front, independent with MacPherson
struts, coil springs, anti-roll bar; rear, independent
with wishbones, transverse upper link, coil springs
Steering: rack and pinion
Brakes: discs, front and rear
Dimensions: wheelbase 105.8in (268.7cm)
                track (front) 57.8in (146.8cm)
                track (rear) 57.8in (146.8cm)
Maximum speed: 139mph (224kmh)

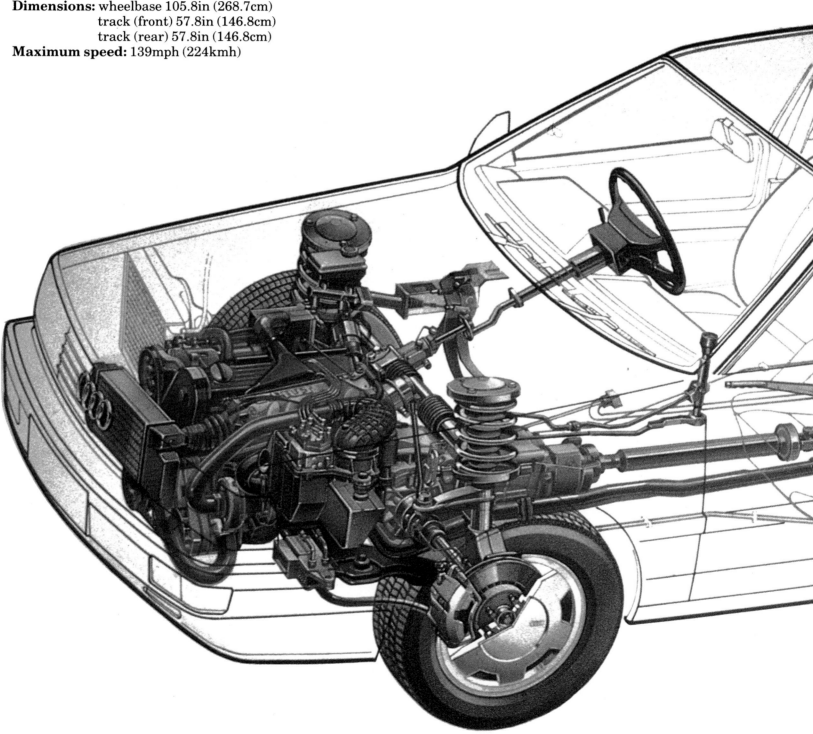

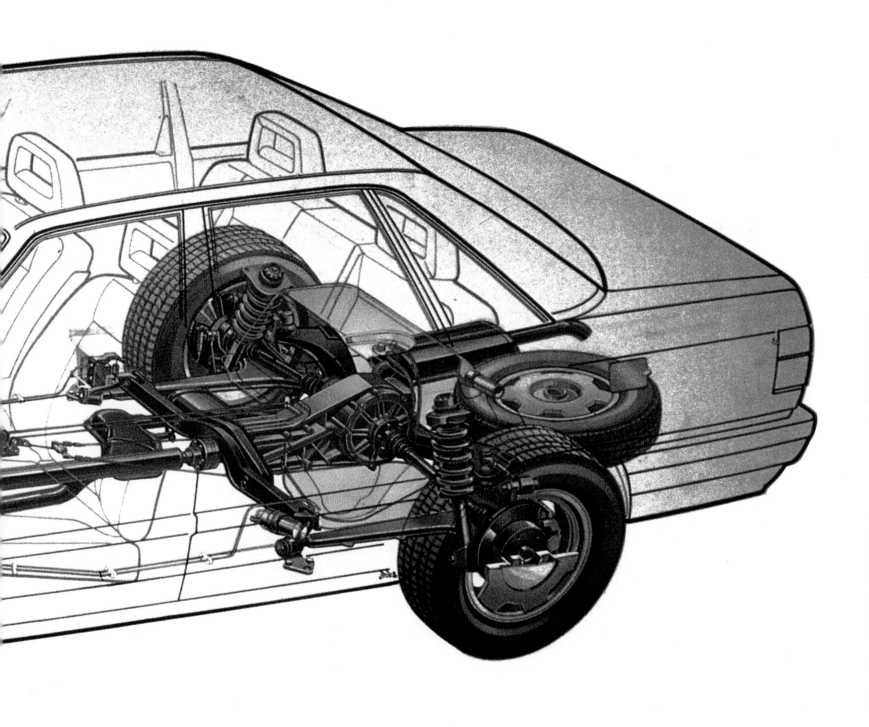

1984 ROVER 200

The significance of the Rover 200 lies less in the car itself as in what it stands for. On the face of it, this is a medium-sized front-driven car typical of many modern European or Japanese models in its class. Yet there is one important difference, which is that the Rover 200 in another guise is also the Honda Ballade. In other words, the Rover 200 is the strongest expression we have yet seen of the willingness of car manufacturers to work together at solving common problems.

The relationship between Austin-Rover and Honda is already of long standing. One previous Austin-Rover model, the Triumph Acclaim, was effectively a 'badge-engineered' Honda but the Rover 200 takes the principle a stage further.

The collaboration between the two companies solved different problems for each of them. Austin-Rover's need in the early 1980s was for a small but 'prestige' model to please customers who wanted something different from a smartened-up Austin Maestro and could not afford the much bigger and more expensive Rover 2300; the problem was that the company lacked the funds or staff to carry through such a development on top of all the other programmes then in progress. Honda's main interest was to find a way of investing in the British and European markets when its most obvious route – the export of cars from Japan – was precluded because of limitations on Japanese exports as a whole. The obvious solution was for Austin-Rover to assemble an adapted version of a mid-

range Honda car; hence the close resemblance between the Honda Ballade and the Rover 200.

Honda has long been a technical leader as far as the Japanese motor industry is concerned and the current Ballade has some interesting features. It is front-driven because Honda accepted the logic of front-wheel drive long before most other Japanese companies. It has built nothing but front-driven cars for many years but recently, has added some *four*-wheel drive versions to its range. Honda engine designs in the last twenty years have been especially noteworthy, and the Ballade/Rover 213 unit is no exception with its use of three valves per cylinder: two small inlet valves and

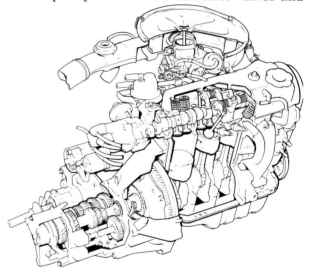

one larger exhaust valve make for easier gas flow than could be achieved with just two valves. All the valves are operated by rocker arms from a single overhead camshaft.

However, the Rover 200 does not use only the Honda engine – and this is the respect in which it differs from its predecessor, the Triumph Acclaim. While the Rover 213 is equipped with the 1.3-litre Honda engine, the Rover 216 is powered by the 1.6-litre Austin-Rover S-series unit. In other words, part of the agreement which gave rise to the Rover 200 was that apart from assembling what is virtually a rebadged Honda Ballade, Austin-Rover would also adapt the design to accept its own bigger engine. This enables the car to be offered over a fairly wide range of models of 70, 85 and 103bhp respectively, the highest output being that of the 1.6-litre engine when equipped with electronically controlled fuel injection.

The picture becomes even more involved when one looks at the Rover 200 transmission arrangements. While the 1.3-litre Honda engine naturally enough retains its own gearbox (or optional three-speed transmission) the 1.6-litre Austin-Rover engine drives the front wheels through a *different* type of Honda five-speed manual gearbox. And in this case, the optional automatic is not from Honda at all, but is a four-speed unit from the German ZF company!

In other respects the Rover 200 differs little from the Honda upon which it is based. One area of interest is the suspension. Honda has a long

history of making cars with MacPherson struts for all four wheels but the Ballade/Rover differs from earlier models in two ways. The front suspension still uses MacPherson struts but instead of taking their usual form with coil springs wrapped round the damper struts themselves, the springs are an ingenious combination of torsion bars and tubes which are both compact and effective. At the rear, the car falls more nearly into line with many of its class rivals by mounting its wheels at each end of a very light, carefully located 'dead' axle.

However, the significance of the Rover 200 lies less in the kind of car it is, as in what it stands for. Two companies, one British and the other Japanese, have worked together to their mutual advantage to produce it. This is a tendency which is bound to grow as other car manufacturers in different countries find common ground. The idea is by no means new since, as we have already seen, European companies like the Peugeot/Renault/Volvo group have had common interests for years and more recently there have been collaborative ventures between the main Italian car manufacturers (Alfa Romeo, Fiat, Lancia) and Saab to develop a new family of prestige saloons.

In many ways the Rover 200 has been important for Austin-Rover in the British and European markets although it was not of itself a significant car for all its clever details. Instead it points most clearly the likely way in which the world's motor industry will develop.

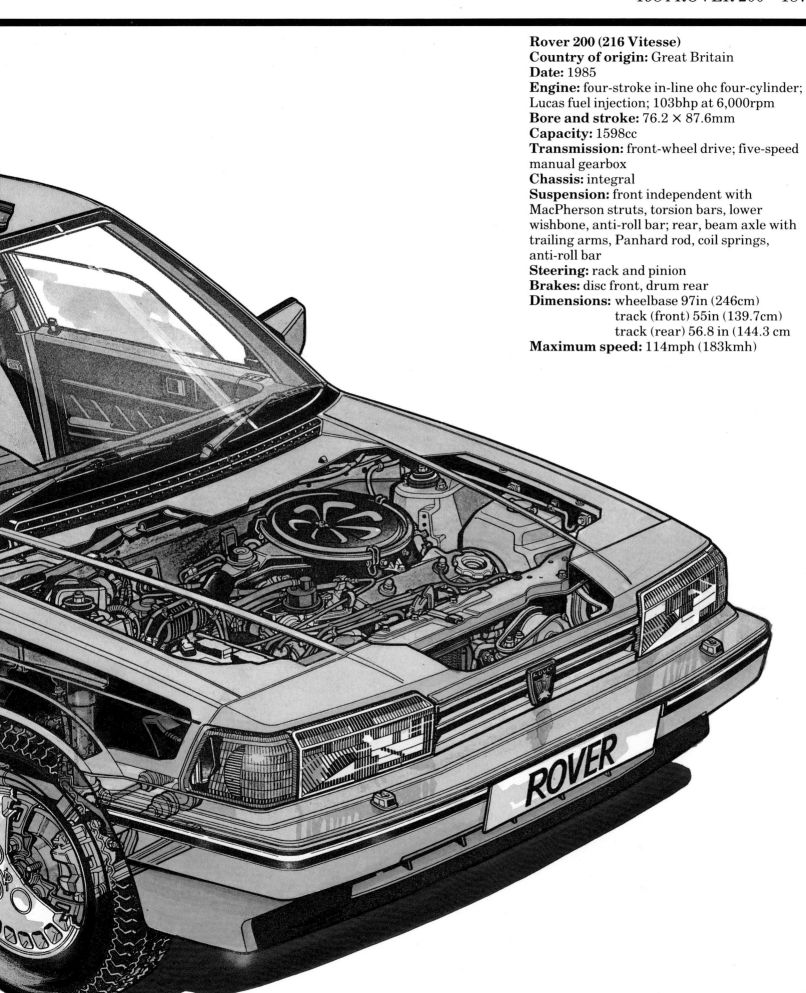

Rover 200 (216 Vitesse)
Country of origin: Great Britain
Date: 1985
Engine: four-stroke in-line ohc four-cylinder;
Lucas fuel injection; 103bhp at 6,000rpm
Bore and stroke: 76.2 × 87.6mm
Capacity: 1598cc
Transmission: front-wheel drive; five-speed
manual gearbox
Chassis: integral
Suspension: front independent with
MacPherson struts, torsion bars, lower
wishbone, anti-roll bar; rear, beam axle with
trailing arms, Panhard rod, coil springs,
anti-roll bar
Steering: rack and pinion
Brakes: disc front, drum rear
Dimensions: wheelbase 97in (246cm)
          track (front) 55in (139.7cm)
          track (rear) 56.8 in (144.3 cm)
Maximum speed: 114mph (183kmh)

1983 PONTIAC FIERO

One of the advantages enjoyed by the world's largest car manufacturers is that they can occasionally afford to spend a tiny part of their overall budgets running experiments which would absorb the entire energy of a small, specialised company. Such experiments are rare but they can be justified if they promise to teach valuable lessons for the future. That was General Motors' justification for proceeding with the Pontiac Fiero, arguably the most exciting and advanced car ever to enter volume production in the USA.

The Fiero was really two experiments in one – though in most ways the car was hardly an experiment any more, having proved more than sufficiently successful to have made its point. The first important thing about the Fiero is that it is a small streamlined, mid-engined two-seater. The second is that its outer body shell is made of plastic.

The team which designed the Fiero in the early 1980s argued that two things had happened to the American car market. It had become so affluent that second or even third cars in a family were commonplace; and there had arisen a 'social conscience' which wanted that second or third car to be small and efficient – as long as it was also attractive and advanced in its design. Thus, the team argued, the time was ripe for a sleek two-seater which would echo all that was admired in European GT cars.

This might not in itself have been a strong enough argument had there not been a second debate in progress within General Motors. This debate concerned the type of material that might in future be used for car bodies, to replace rust-prone steel. The obvious answer was plastic – but what kind of plastic? It is worth bearing in mind that General Motors had enormous experience of traditional GRP, the material used for its Corvette sports car (and, as we have seen, for the Lotus Elan and the Reliant GTE and Robin). However, GM was seeking a plastic that could be used in a highly automated, high-volume factory and that ruled out GRP.

For the Pontiac designers, this advantage – together with the modern, high-tech image of the layout – was more important than the disadvantages. The Fiero was intended as a pure two-seater, after all. Thus a four-cylinder engine (and later, a V6 power unit also) was installed transversely just aft of the seats, driving the rear wheels through exactly the same type of transmission that Pontiac already employed in its extensive range of front-driven cars. The front suspension used double wishbones and MacPherson struts were installed at the rear to allow for the necessary drive shaft movement. Steering was rack and pinion and disc brakes were fitted all round.

By most American standards the Fiero was small, with a wheelbase of only 93 inches (236cm), an overall length of little more than 13 feet (396cm) and a width of 5 feet 8 inches (172cm). But it was big enough to avoid appearing under threat in heavyweight American traffic and its 2.5-litre ohv engine gave the sort of lazy power to which American drivers were more accustomed. In the circumstances it mattered little that the Fiero turned out to be rather heavy and that some enthusiasts called its performance sluggish (until that optional V6 was offered). The important thing was that the specially-built factory proved capable of turning out the planned 100,000 Fieros per year, a much higher

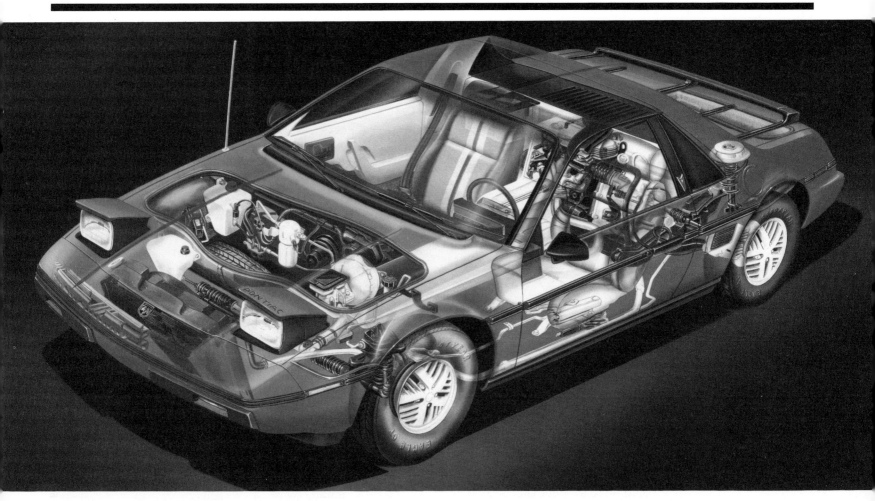

production rate than had ever been achieved before with a plastic-bodied car, and that at least that many American buyers existed for whom the appeal of an attractive, rustproof two-seater was considerable. As yet, it is too early to say whether the lessons of the Fiero will help to reshape the American car market or hasten the day when steel bodies give way to plastic. But if either of those things happens, the Fiero must be acknowledged as a highly influential as well as an interesting design.

One of the most promising alternatives was polyurethane – a very tough plastic already used in large quantities to make the 'soft' nose and tail sections of many American cars. Polyurethane has the advantage that the two chemicals of which is it made are liquids that can be squirtied into a mould from which, a few seconds later, a solid polyurethane part can be extracted. In other words, the process can be carried out almost entirely automatically, quickly and safely. The two questions which still worried the GM planners were first, whether polyurethane panels could be made stiff enough to form a complete set of 'clothes' for a car and second, whether all the other problems associated with a completely new form of body production could be overcome. Thus the Fiero was eventually born out of the proposal that GM should not only test the market for an advanced two-seater car, but that its body should be made of polyurethane to see if the material really fulfilled its promise.

The Fiero was laid out as a mid-engined car with all its main mechanical components located within a steel 'skeleton' not unlike that seen nearly twenty years earlier in the Rover 2000. In this case though, the outer body panels were to be of plastic. Polyurethane was not the only plastic used, as it turned out, since the Pontiac designers reckoned it was not stiff enough for large horizontal panels like the bonnet, roof and boot. Instead these were made out of another plastic composite called sheet moulding compound (SMC); polyurethane was used for the nose and tail sections, the front and rear wings and the door panels.

The Fiero was interesting in its mechanical layout too. It is the only 'mid-engined' car to appear in our list and it is important to appreciate what the term means and why some designers favour the layout. In a mid-engined car, the engine is installed behind the seats but in front of the rear wheels which it drives. As a layout it has several disadvantages. Putting the engine so close to the seats invites a cabin noise problem; the engine is inevitably difficult to get at for servicing; it is almost impossible to give the car four proper seats and there is no chance of providing good luggage space. Nevertheless, the mid-engined layout has one great advantage: because the engine is close to the centre of the car, much less effort is needed to turn the vehicle than if the engine (and transmission) is near one end. This makes the car much lighter and quicker to respond to the steering – which is why all modern racing cars are mid-engined.

PORSCHE 944 TURBO

Some Porsche devotees were horrified when the first front-engined rear-drive model to carry the famous badge appeared in the early 1970s – many were aware that it had been conceived to carry a VW badge – but it proved to be the forerunner of a line of Porsches with their engines water cooled and mounted ahead of the cockpits. The 924 was not outstandingly successful; simplicity, however good the execution and despite the performance that came with turbocharging in the 924 Turbo of 1979, just did not associate too happily with Porsche prices. The 928, a V-8-engined GT car, was also front-engined but in a different category. Then in 1985 a four-cylinder model that did fit the Porsche image was introduced: the 944 Turbo.

This was the first of Porsche's front-engined family to match up to the high-performance 911s, as a sporting car with a maximum speed over 150mph. This was achieved with the all-alloy 2479cc four-cylinder engine rated at 220bhp – its compression ratio was lower than in the normally-aspirated unit, so that it would comfortably accept the forced induction from the intercooled KKK turbocharger. A sophisticated

Bosch Motronic 'black box' took care of engine management, for example adjusting fuel feed and ignition timing to give optimum efficiency as it monitored boost pressure, throttle position, inlet manifold temperature and so on. To maintain power output in markets where strict emission controls normally led to enfeebled engines, turbo boost pressure could be appropriately increased and the black box re-programmed.

The 944 body was refined in detail for the Turbo, for example to improve directional stability with the addition of a rear spoiler that reduced lift, and to give an impressive overall drag factor of 0.33. The driver's visibility was excellent (and that could by no means be taken for granted in high-performance cars of the 1980s!), handling precise and balanced, ride reassuringly firm, power steering exemplary in its performance, coupled with a high degree of comfort for two (if not those in the seats behind them). Porsche had achieved all that might have been hoped for in the 944 Turbo's distant 924 predecessor.

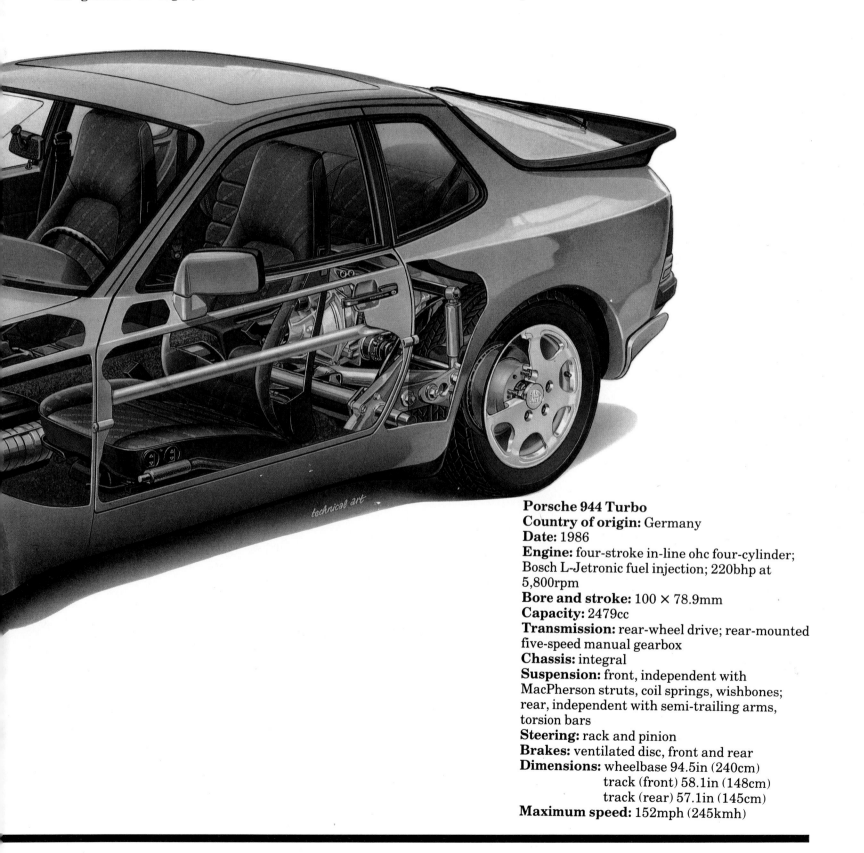

technical art

Porsche 944 Turbo
Country of origin: Germany
Date: 1986
Engine: four-stroke in-line ohc four-cylinder; Bosch L-Jetronic fuel injection; 220bhp at 5,800rpm
Bore and stroke: 100 × 78.9mm
Capacity: 2479cc
Transmission: rear-wheel drive; rear-mounted five-speed manual gearbox
Chassis: integral
Suspension: front, independent with MacPherson struts, coil springs, wishbones; rear, independent with semi-trailing arms, torsion bars
Steering: rack and pinion
Brakes: ventilated disc, front and rear
Dimensions: wheelbase 94.5in (240cm)
　　　　　　　track (front) 58.1in (148cm)
　　　　　　　track (rear) 57.1in (145cm)
Maximum speed: 152mph (245kmh)

INDEX